COMING
FROM
CUMBERLAND

By

LINDA K. DECAMP

Coming From Cumberland
"A Memoir"
By
Linda K. DeCamp

FIRST EDITION
Hard Cover ISBN 978-0-578-33492-9
E-Book ISBN 978-0-578-35501-6

Library of Congress Control Number: LCCN 2021924283

Cover design by Karen Major

Coming from Cumberland

Author's Disclaimer:

The book you are about to read is a memoir. It reflects the author's recollection of views and experiences. The story is based on real life events as I've perceived them.

My intent is for the book to document details of my life and times for future generations. I have considered some social changes that have taken place over time, in relation to currently accepted cultural norms. Some narrative includes dialogue that has been recreated. Some events are out of sequence or have been compressed. Some names, characters, places and incidents in the story have been changed for reasons of privacy. Some relevant information has been drawn from a variety of published materials.

I've done my best to make it truthful, but memories can be like pieces of a puzzle that don't always align with precision and they often have their own story to tell. No liability for harm will be accepted by the author or publisher for loss, damage or for any errors or omissions of content. Aside from all of that, when I have been blessed with such colorful relatives, why would I want to make things up?

Linda DeCamp holds a Bachelor of Science degree in Business Management from Park University, Parkville, Mo.

She has 64 years of work life beginning at age 13, as a waitress in a tea room, retiring at age 77 from Florida Real Estate. She has a rich tapestry of experiences from 22 varied and interesting jobs in those years. She is a passionate storyteller who loves creative writing and is anxious to bring her memories to life. Her hobbies are writing, reading, traveling, genealogy, sewing and card crafts.

She has two adult children who have produced six wonderful grandchildren. She lives in Punta Gorda, Florida – along with her husband of 60 years. COMING FROM CUMBERLAND, a memoir of DeCamp's life and the journey of her ancestors, is her debut book.

DEDICATED TO:
Doug and my 'tribe':
Greg, Julie, Lauren, Nick and Holly,
Shelley, Danielle, Dillon and Savannah.
*~ **AND TO HONOR:***
All of the ancestors who came before me,

Especially for my mom,
Barbara Ann Resor-McMillen-Saum
July 5,1918 - March 10, 2003
"God Rest Her Soul"

Contents

MCMILLEN FAMILY HISTORY:

Our McMillen descendants came from County Down, North Ireland with my great-great-great-great grandfather, James McMillen immigrating to the USA (b.in Ireland in 1735 and d. 1821) in Turkey Foot, Somerset County, Pa.

His son, William Green McMillen, is my great-great-great grand-father (b. 1770 and d. 1819) in Turkey Foot, Somerset County, Pa.

His son, William W. McMillen, is my great-great grandfather (b. 1794 in Pa. and d. 1880) in Elida, Allen Co., Ohio.

His son, James Jackson McMillen, is my great grandfather (b. 1827 in PA, and d. 1897) in Van Wert, Van Wert Co. Ohio.

His son, Albert Tildon McMillen, is my grandfather (b. 1870 in Van Wert, Ohio and d. 1923) in Albuquerque, New Mexico.

His son, Gordon Alonzo McMillen, is my father (b. 1915 in Warsaw, Kosciusko Co., Indiana and d. 2002) and lived in Bluffton, Wells Co. Indiana.

NOTE: Due to the early deaths of his parents in 1922 & 1923, Gordon was raised by his maternal grandparents, Charles Kirk and Lillian (Jones) Kirk, living at 654 North Walnut Street in Van Wert, OH.

Resor Family History:

My mother's maiden name is Resor. Our Resor descendants were third generation immigrants arriving in the USA from Berne, Switzerland, with Aldi Resor (b.1847 in Switzerland and d.1928) in Van Wert Co. Ohio. His son, William Henry Resor, is my grandfather (b.1878 in Van Wert, Ohio and d. 1945 in Van Wert, Ohio.) He married Mina Blank-Lane-Resor-Fogt in 1917 and divorced in 1932 in Van Wert, Ohio. Their daughter, Barbara Ann Resor -McMillen-Saum, is my mother (b. 1918 in Van Wert, Ohio and d. in 2003) at Columbus, Franklin Co., Ohio. She married Gordon A. McMillen June 12,1936 at Van Wert, Ohio and divorced in 1965 in Van Wert, Ohio. Gordon Alonzo McMillen and Barbara Ann Resor were the parents of five children:

Gordon Kent McMillen b. Dec. 13, 1941 in Van Wert County Hospital, Van Wert, Ohio.
Linda Kathleen McMillen b. May 7, 1943 at home in Big Lick, Cumberland, County, Tennessee.
William Stephen McMillen (twin) b. November 24, 1945 at hospital in Crossville, Tennessee and d. Feb.1, 2020 in Franklin Co., Columbus, Ohio.
Barbara Sue McMillen (twin) b. November 24, 1945 at the hospital in Crossville, Tennessee.
Frances Ann McMillen b. October 8, 1950 at hospital in Van Wert, Ohio.
   *Additional Genealogy information and details are available on Ancestry.com/ DECAMP_Family_File-1A

A Short History Of Cumberland Co. Tennessee

Cumberland County, TN. was formed in 1856. The county was nearly evenly split between those supporting the Union and those supporting the Confederacy. Crossville, TN. has an elevation of 2000 feet and allows an average summer temperature of 74 degrees. Cumberland County includes Grassy Cove, a National Natural Landmark featuring geological wonders and farmland. Crab Orchard which is the country's oldest community and home of the world-famous Crab Orchard Stone. Pleasant Hill, settled since 1819, is the site of the Pioneer Hall Museum. The county seat is Crossville, has a 95-year-old court house and a 1920s train depot. During the 1930s, as part of the New Deal, the federal government's Subsistence Homesteads Division established the Cumberland Homesteads outside of Crossville. The program provided land and houses for 250 impoverished families. Cumberland Mountain State Park was built as part of this project. The homesteads are designed as a National Historic district and featuring Homesteads Tower and Museum and the Crabtree House. The county was named for the Cumberland Plateau, with a total area of 685 square miles, being the fourth-largest county in Tennessee by area. The county is located atop the Cumberland Plateau. The southernmost of the Cumberland Mountains, known locally as the Crab Orchard Mountains, rise in the northeastern part of the county. Rivers were cut by treating glaciers after the last Ice Age formed tributaries that carry the spring run-off from the surrounding mountains, winding their way down to the Tennessee River, which is over 50 miles away.

A Short History Of Van Wert County, Ohio

Van Wert County was created by the Ohio General Assembly on April 1, 1820, from old Indian lands. However, there is no record of the white man having permanently lived here at that time. Van Wert County was a dense forest and parts of it were covered by the Great Black Swamp. The lands in western Ohio were obtained from the Indians by the Treaty of 1818. The village of Wilshire served as the first county seat of Van Wert County until 1835 when the Co. commissioners moved the county seat from Wilshire to the village of Van Wert. The town of Van Wert was incorporated in 1848. Following the Civil War and with the development of the railroads, the County's destiny is linked with timber and the resulting products. At one time there were 15 staves' factories (bands for wooden barrels) in Van Wert County. When it became apparent that the timber supply would eventually be exhausted, the lands were cleared, and attention turned to tilling the soil. In addition to the crops, the County became known for the fine draft horses and dairy herds raised here. Today the County is known for both agricultural and manufacturing goods. The 406 square miles of land in Van Wert County are now more than a quarter million acres in farm land divided into 12 townships. The county and the city of Van Wert were named to honor Isaac Van Wart, the capturer of a British spy. Due to an error on the part of those preparing the act of Congress recognizing his contributions to the American victory, the name appeared mistakenly as Van Wert and the new spelling stuck.

PROLOGUE – How It All Began

Barbara's Story:

When Barbara is a child growing up in Van Wert, she lives with her family of two older half-sisters and her parents. She lives nearby her grandparents. Sometimes, during the depression, they even live WITH her grandparents. When Bobbie, as she is often called, is three years old something happens that changes her life.

Her mother tells her eight- and ten-year-old sisters, to watch her while she is playing in the yard. But no one is paying attention when she gets too near the trash and her dress catches on fire. She runs from the trash fire that causes severe burns covering a large part of her face, arms and body. This accident and the resulting burns become a source of shame for her mother; shame for leaving her baby daughter unprotected near a fire.

Bobbie is so severely burned that she is hospitalized for about three months. Being so young she is terrorized by being left there with strangers in a strange bed in a strange place. The separation anxiety is very hard for a three-year-old, but they are not allowed to stay with her and she is too seriously burned to come home. Even though she clings to her parents at every visit, they have to leave her at the hospital screaming and crying for long periods of time.

Bobbie survives the burns but never recovers from the trauma. Her arm forms a wing by skin grafting her arm to her body. In a few years she has a major surgery to separate her arm from her side so she can wear clothes. When she begins school, her mother starts sewing dresses with long sleeves for her to hide her arms so people can't see her burn scars. As she grows, she knows all about the scars inside these long-sleeved dresses but she thinks no one outside of her family knows about them. Her mother is telling her *never* to expose her arms for people to see the scars. This dark secret that she holds inside makes her feel unacceptable to the outside world. She is learning to *hide* those scars, but she isn't learning how to *live* with them. Her mother's shame becomes her secret and the scars are her shame,

I

as well. She continues wearing the long-sleeved clothing winter and summer until her mother dies.

Mom is 46 years old in 1964 when she occasionally begins exposing a small part of her arms with only slightly shorter sleeves. But there is more: five years after her accident her younger brother is killed in an accident at home. This accident involves her father driving over his son with a tractor. Having been through one child maimed and the other one killed ultimately costs the parents their marriage. She blames him for Billy's death and he blames her for Barbara's burns. He drinks and she rages. Herr parents are divorced when she is a young teen and her mother never allows her to see her father again.

Mommy loves to tell me how she met Daddy. She is walking down Jefferson Street in Van Wert, along with some school girl-friends, when he comes up behind her and she notices immediately that he is, *"Oh, so handsome!"* She is a very naïve young girl and just fourteen years old. As the baby in their family, her experiences are very limited. She is young and cute, wearing a bob haircut. When he flirts with her, she is *"so excited by his attention."* When she meets Gordon, she probably thinks she knows him and she falls in love with him immediately. At fourteen, there are few people for her to love, so falling in love at her age is exciting.

Her mother and sisters immediately begin to question her, asking, *"What gives?"* Her heart-broken mother never 'sugar coats' her dislike for him from the beginning and she never gives it up! Bobbie doesn't see what she is getting into with him, and there is nothing in her history that will prepare her for all that he has been through.

As it turns out, she is the perfect partner for Gordon. With her past, it is no wonder she does stupid things for love. Mommy is so anxious to get away from her momma's excessive shame and control, that she says *"yes"* when Daddy proposes and they plan to move to Tennessee. She winds up setting herself on a very strange course, partly to defy her mother. He wants her to come to Tennessee right away. Her love of him is as soft as a new baby.

Barbara is just 17 years old in 1936 when she graduates from Van Wert High School. On June 12th, just days after she graduates high school, Mommy and Daddy are getting married. My grandma, Mina Blank-Resor, tells her, *"You are too young, and he is not the right one!"* Bobbie doesn't listen to her mother's advice, but she should have! She only wishes her mother and husband would "*just get along*!" But Gordon and Mina never do. The ongoing animosity, between her husband and her mother, presents Barbara with a lot of stress over the years. She loves them both and feels '*caught in the middle.*' I never do understand as a child that she is too young to be married, but, of course, she is! She won't be eighteen until her *next* birthday July 5th.

After the June wedding she says '*Good-bye*' to her family and off they go. She is a young woman, brilliant and energetic, but also anxious and complying. In the beginning, she is married and happy to leave home with him, or so I imagine, as I place her wedding pictures back into the shoebox that holds her story!

I have read that it is unusual in those days, to be moving out of state. It is a fact that in the 1930's and 1940's only 50% of people ever move more than 50 miles from the place where they are born. Because this move is so unusual, her mother says, *his place is too far, you are too young and unprepared for who he is!*" Grandma is right about that!

Barbara comes from a proper family. Grandma knows what China pattern to buy and she has sterling silver tableware. She keeps a nice home. But sadly, Mom's life does not turn out the same. She has never been '*house proud,*' even when she lives at home with her mother.

Even though she loves him immediately, he has a personality problem that will not allow him to have empathy or love for anyone, other than himself. Before long his heartless control of her is iron clad. Mommy tells me that her own mother won't allow her to make any decisions of her own. She says," *I had no idea that his control would be even worse!*"

Gordon's Story:

Gordon, also, has an unfortunate childhood, maybe even more so than hers. Born in Warsaw, Indiana in 1915, he soon moves after his birth to New Mexico with his parents until 1922. Daddy is the fourth child of Albert T. McMillen. Albert's oldest son, Leo is twenty-three and away at Law school. Carl is twenty and Harriet is fourteen, both living in the Midwest with an aunt. Gordon seldom sees any of these siblings in his adult life. He is the first child of Dorothy Kirk. Both were married previously, but she had no children. He is only seven years old in 1922 when his mother dies from the Spanish Flu. Soon after that, his father sends him, and his baby brother, Eugene, to Van Wert, Ohio. They are travelling via train with a caregiver. She is taking them to live in Ohio with his maternal grandparents, Charles and Lillian Kirk.

His father, Albert T. McMillen, dies of Bright's Disease the following year in New Mexico. Baby brother, Eugene, is adopted immediately by distant McMillen relatives. Young Gordon never sees his father or Eugene again. He lives in Van Wert, Ohio, with his grandparents after that. I hear that Lillian loves and coddles her only grandson as she raises him. In second grade he gets $1.00 for his grades. With that dollar he buys an alligator and he named him, "*Algo.*" The roaring 20's didn't roar quite

so loud in the small towns and rural areas, one fifth of the US population being poor farmers and immigrants.

Gordon attends Van Wert City schools while living with his grandparents. He develops many interests during his youth such as hunting, taxidermy, and many other manual crafts. He learns taxidermy from a book at the Brunback Library. At Van Wert High School he takes classes in Manual Training, electrical, wood working and machine shop. These classes help him in many jobs and hobbies in his future life.

Gordon is fourteen in August 1929 when his grandmother, Lillian, dies of breast cancer. His grades plummet immediately! After Lillian dies, he becomes a troubled teen; his own puberty goes unnoticed – almost to himself. Gordon is a defiant teen with a sense of entitlement while living with his grandfather, Charles J. Kirk. He becomes a street fighter during his adolescent years. The grandfather isn't patient with him like his grandmother had been. I don't know much about my paternal great grandparents because they all die long before I am born. What I do know comes from the stories my daddy tells me about them. He says that the grandfather is very strict and an unusually mean-tempered bully, without any sense of humor. That sounds like how I will describe Gordon!

When Gordon is telling the story, he says precisely that "*he is the meanest son-of-a-bitch in the north end of town!*" His stories tell us that as *a tough and mean S.O.B*, he *takes down* 'most everyone around! But I see it this way: he is a small guy at 5'7", with curly red hair and green eyes. He has a harsh surly mouth and a demanding personality. Being a bully, I can only assume that quite a few of them "*cleaned his clock!*" On January 1, 1934, when Gordon's last remaining relative, Charles J. Kirk, dies of a heart attack, he is left totally alone in the world at the age of seventeen. Gordon is appointed a guardian by the courts, but he refuses to move from his grandparents' house, where he grew up. He delivers a milk route each day before school. He is an artful dodger–surviving by drinking the milk from the delivery truck. As a youth his grandmother has given him a .22 caliber rifle for varmint hunting. He lives by his quick wit, sound knowledge and a strong back as his means of survival for a few years.

Family history is such a romantic place to explore the things that keep sliding around in my head. Gordon and Barbara date throughout high school and he drives her to school in his Velie Automobile.

"Velie is a brass era American automobile brand produced by the Velie Motors Corporation in Moline, Illinois from 1908 to 1928. The company is founded by and named for Willard Velie, a maternal grandson of John Deere." Wikipedia:

Barbara climbs in beside him; Gordon gives it some choke as she struggles over the sharp hump to sit near him. Gordon is a proud red-headed man with Irish roots. He's always looking for attention. He says, *"Give me a look, will you?"* Even as a teen, he can't stand the agony of sharing any of the aura of *'himself'* with her. He praises her, makes her feel loved at first, but in time his 'mask' begins to drop and he devalues her. He is 21 years old when he emigrates from Van Wert to Tennessee in 1936. He does not plan to return.

My story begins in the early 1930s– when the world is caught up with the Great Depression. Our Tennessee house is being built by my daddy, Gordon A. McMillen. He is a scrappy frontiersman crafting the house with his own hard-working hands. He works with a high school friend, Harold Hogue, who is also from Van Wert, Ohio.

Neither of them has ever built any structure, but both of them think they are pretty good with a hammer and saw. They believe they can do anything if they set their minds to it. In the Crab Orchard area of Tennessee, narrow, two-lane roads, still unpaved in most places, wind through shimmering alfalfa fields, gently rolling hills, and over small stone bridges and switch back through deep draws of old-growth woods that may only see direct sunlight for an hour or two each day. These roads transit through colorfully named areas such as Big Lick, Crab Orchard, Pleasant Hill and the Homesteads. He starts building the house in the spring of 1935.

He builds a massive crab orchard and sandstone fireplace chimney on the front of a small one and a half-story square house located on one hundred acres of land, near the Homesteads. They are camping out in the barest frame of a house that is only partially finished in the spring of 1936. When Daddy and *'Hogie'* go back to Van Wert, *'Hogie'* stays there. My mommy and daddy are planning an exciting Tennessee adventure! She graduates high school and they marry that June.

In 1932, wheelchair bound by polio, Franklin D. Roosevelt is elected President of the United States. At the time the White House is not wheel chair friendly, with ramps and elevators being added after he arrives. He takes office in 1933 and promises America a "New Deal."

A part of this "Deal' is the federal government buying about 10,000 acres in Cumberland County, Tennessee, and turning it into what becomes known as a "subsistence homestead." Between 1934 and 1938, two hundred-fifty homesteads are built just south of Crossville, Tennessee. The original purpose of the project is to provide work for men who are out of work and homes for their families. It might be appropriate to tag Cumberland County a 'New Deal County' because of all the federal money that is poured into the area in the 1930s and 1940s. The Homesteads project is heavily government funded and short-lived. They even start a business—a factory where residents prepare and can vegetables and fruits to be sold elsewhere. Mom's first job in Tennessee is canning beans. But that business can't make ends meet and doesn't last long. After World War II, these federal government homestead projects are shut down. The homesteaders aren't able to survive here. The project is heavily criticized for being a big government-failed experiment in Socialism.

Gordon and Barbara arrive to live nearby, but not in, the Homestead area of Crossville in Cumberland County, Tennessee. The house is still far from finished, leaving them a lot of work to do there. They are happy there together, but living off the grid is hard.

Mountaineers in the 1930s are often weaving and doing needlework that can be sold. Any artistic expressions are usually in mountain music, banjo, fiddle or dulcimers for dancing and storytelling. Lively folk music sets the pace for ballads or "hoe downs" and square dancing on Saturday evenings. Radios begin to appear in remote areas of the plateau in the 1930s. Even the poorest mountaineers can scrape together enough money to buy one. Radios are on from morning to night providing church sermons by fundamental evangelists, soap operas, news and music. Area houses are wired for electricity after the TVA and the Rural Electrification Administration brings in electricity in 1938. This is the golden age of Radio. Radio music from the 1930s is replaced later by the live country music on the Grand Ole Opry Radio Show every Saturday evening in the 1940s.

Their only radio is in the car. They never do get a radio in our house, because we are too far off the grid to have electricity. Over time they build some fences, plant a garden and acquire some farm animals. Mom goes about working in the garden in the summer, and into fall, she picks vegetables, digs potatoes and cans and pickles food for winter. They live off the land, like pioneers. They make some local connections by joining the Big Lick Presbyterian church and meeting local area mountain people who are the back bone of this area. Because my daddy has thick curly, wiry carrot-red hair, most of these undeniably southern people around Crossville call him "*Red*."

The pasture, joining our homeplace to the beauty of the distant mountains, holds a horse and cow. Daddy's horse is for riding and the cow is for milk and butter. The goats are for keeping the grass munched short near the house, while a few chickens in the chicken house provide eggs and meat.

Mommy tells me of a time, before I am born, when Daddy wants to shoot an apple out of her mouth with his 22-gauge rifle! She says, "*He asks me to stand behind a tree with just the apple peeking out, and do you believe, I allow him to do it.?*" As the story goes, he hits the apple and she goes unharmed. When she tells me this story, the most amazing thing to me is that she agreed to do it! Barbara does whatever he asks, but Grandma does not like this type of thing!

Their times are more stressful when her mother visits about once every year. Mina and Gordon both have dominant controlling personalities vying for control of Barbara. Grandma is the real thing; you always know where you stand with her and she can hold her own with him. She tangles with him about his lackluster interest in a home and the needs of a family. With her jaw set in anger she is critical of their remote lifestyle. She comes down hard on them both, but more often her disgust is with Gordon!

Coming from Cumberland

A Memoir

Growing up in a particular neighborhood, growing up in a working-class family, not having much money, all of those things fire you and give you an edge, but can also give you anger."

- Gary Oldman - English actor

CHAPTER ONE

Culture Shock in Ohio

I still have a clear picture of that initial morning when I first awaken in Van Wert, Ohio. A culture shock '*hits me head on*' in April of 1949. My story begins that morning. I'm five years old, but going on six, skinny and pale, standing slightly over three feet tall when we emigrate to Ohio. We've been traveling in the car for over 14 hours, arriving after midnight. Tangled blond curls frame my face and my tiny nose is pressed against the hazy window pane, when my brother whispers, "*Let's go!*"

We shake the three-year-old twins and we stay together creeping outside to take a closer look at where we have come to live. We stand huddled together, studying the houses all around us. Van Wert, a town of concrete sidewalks, contains older two-story homes surrounded with lawns and flower beds. Most of these are more than fifty years old with wide front porches with porch swings in place.

I am '*pie-eyed*' because I have never seen a tree-lined brick street with manicured green lawns. Wringing my hands, I worry about who might live behind those doors. I am very glad that no one is outside yet. Rows of clapboard wooden houses also bring sights I have never seen! In the early morning light this old neighborhood street glows like the America that only Norman Rockwell could have imagined. I notice the brick chimneys, the Victorian scrolled artwork, the chipped wooden sills and window panes on these old houses. Most have bathrooms inside, but a few have outhouses, just like we had in Tennessee. Most of these neighbors have lived in these houses for many years, but they are all strangers to me! All of this is hard for

1

me to reconcile because I don't know much about people in general. All in all, nothing here looks even similar to anything I have seen in Tennessee.

I startle and jump back when Daddy opens the front door. He gestures with his cigarette for us to *"Get back in here!"* His voice speaks of us doing something wrong! Clueless, we quickly move back inside. He clears a pile of blankets and sheets from the couch where we have slept. He gestures for all four of us to sit down. I sniff cigarette smoke as he moves close to my face and I loathe the smell. He tells us, *"You don't ever stand in the front terrace staring around at the neighbors!"* Though we have no understanding of any rule like this, he says, *"Never do that again!"* My guess is that we must have looked like hicks as we stood there. Something similar to a Beverly Hillbillies *'look alike'* family.

I have experienced no ordinary life! I say this because I am born at home in the back country of Tennessee in the early 1940s. In the first years of my life, I have never seen people beyond the occasional trips into the local town for supplies. I have never been in any town or city, but I believe the dresses that Mommy sews for me, made from flour sacks, could make me look *'wrong'* here. Luckily, we don't have a Southern brogue in our language because our parents are from Ohio and, therefore, we have seldom encountered the southern dialect.

Mommy is 31 years old when we move from Tennessee to Ohio. Many times, she has wished they could head back to Van Wert. She is excited because this trip is going back home to family and friends, but leaving my home on the Cumberland Plateau is a real shock for me. It seems like there are moments when people change. These moments are not isolated and not separate, and not removed from the rest of life, just a part of our lives that change us. I have lived in an unordinary way, in an unordinary place, in an unordinary time. I was born into a sometimes difficult and challenging family.

* * *

Join me, as I describe my journey!

* * *

We travel here by car with some strangers named Ross and Frances. Daddy knows them, but I haven't ever seen them. My daddy and brother are flying to Ohio in Daddy's Porterfield Airplane while these

2

strangers drive Mom and me up north with the three-year old twins. Everything we own is stuffed into some cardboard boxes.

Our travels go like these trips usually do–it all begins as soon as we get into their car. Stevie pulls my hair and I punch him. Our mother is sitting quietly looking out the window, maybe even sleeping. Soon the twins are huddled tight–his head

heavy against hers. I am getting car sick, as are the twins. We have to stop for Susita to throw up.

Next, I say, *"I'm going to puke!"* With no one listening, I manage to pull through with great effort. Susita is whining because she has food stuck in her hair. She pushes into me and I move to the floor and draw a line.

"No feet over this line," I say, but feet are still touching me. She is crying harder now; feeling motion sickness again, her face is all red and snotty. She lifts her shirt to wipe her nose. She calls out, but no one answers. Stevie wiggles and I want him to stop. I tell him to move over and I still feel him twisting. I feel his knee in my back.

Someone says *"Shut up and go back to sleep."* Shut up is a *bad word* that we aren't allowed to say. This time I say nothing, because I don't want to get us into trouble. Finally, I feel the car stopping; we can get out for just a minute. I feel cool air hitting my face. I am so happy for the fresh air, because I have motion sickness. Before long we are all back in the car and threading our way north through the narrow mountain roads with switch backs and curves. We travel mountain roads, making hairpin turns around every corner passing through a few small villages.

U.S. Route 127 connects middle Tennessee through the villages of Dunlap, Pikeville, Crossville, and Jamestown. This area is rich in Appalachian culture and scenic beauty. As we drive down this road there are hundreds of handmade quilts offered for sale to passing travelers. They hang on clotheslines in the front yards all along the road. It is this blaze of bright colors that stands firm in my memory. I remember the weathered houses and barns and the quilts are the part of middle Tennessee culture. Small towns, tourist cabins in rolling hills and fertile valleys dot the mountains of the upper Cumberland Plateau. We travel this rural road meandering through the mountains and valleys with sharp switchbacks and winding mountain roads as we emigrate to Ohio from Tennessee in 1949. The drive to Ohio takes us around 14 hours from early morning to late at night. But this travel experience is far different. We are seeing, feeling, and even smelling the differences in each town, sampling regional food, occasionally stopping for gas and chatting with locals, getting lost on back-road detours, and stumbling across tourist attractions not on any map. We continue for hours through the high mountains and lower hills of Tennessee and Kentucky. We finally roll into Ohio and we begin seeing flat land and open spaces. Fields of wheat are blowing in the wind. In Ohio there are rows of corn as far as I can see. We have been scrunched in, pushing and shoving as we are lying all over each other in the back of the stranger's car for hours. So, *"Where are we now?"* I ask them, probably more times than they want to hear. When we finally arrive at our new home it is late at night. We are dropped off at Daddy's grandparents' house in Van Wert, Ohio. We arrive all rumpled and tired and we are really just happy to be out of the car. The strangers head for Detroit. After that night, I don't ever see them again.

The old house on North Walnut Street is where Daddy grew up. As her only heir, Daddy inherits this house and some money when his Grandma Lillian succumbs to breast cancer back in 1929. While we are living in Tennessee, he rents the house out for $20.00 per month. That $20.00 is all of the income my family has in the early years. The place is empty and tatty; a tired-looking old house needing more than paint. The upstairs walls are slanted. The 'little room' as we call it, is very small located under the eaves. Not much has changed here in the past 15 years.

Meanwhile, as we have traveled, we have moved between two very different worlds! In Tennessee I felt happy and secure, but this new place is like a punch in the stomach. There are about 15,000 people living here in 1949, so it isn't entirely a small town. The change causes a lot of tension for me as I fight to adjust. The distance between a primitive back country place like Cumberland County, in Big Lick, Tennessee and a town like Van Wert, Ohio, is like going to another universe that is light years away. I don't know much about *'how to be'* around people. I am too shy to go outside very often. I want to make the adjustment but this is a place that is completely foreign to me. We begin exploring and I know right away that I do not know how to live in this *'new Ohio world.'*

As I continue looking around I see even more old cast-off furniture, including some full-sized iron beds with flat blue pinstriped cotton mattresses and a little table, acting as a night stand. Much of this stuff is left behind by the past renter. Maybe some has even belonged to his grandparents, who lived here before the tenants. Regardless, I do not recall us bringing anything from Tennessee in the car.

~

My daddy is never empathetic, and kids often make him crazy. But he is not angry all of the time. He can even be playful and fun at times. He likes to nickname people and things in his own funny words. Our black cat is named *"Ke-ke"* because when a child says, "Kitty-Kitty" the words came out as, "Ke-ke." Daddy thinks it will be fun to name our cat *Kek-in-tine"* and that becomes his forever name. I am nicknamed, *"Kat-queen"* and *"The bird"* and sometimes I am even *"The ole' bird."* My older brother is nicknamed, *"The Bug," "Bug boy"* or *"the ole bug."* We did call my sister, *"Sue baby"* until my daddy nicknames her, *"Susita, the Cat"* and her twin, Stevie is, *"The Monkey."* When their last child is born, he calls her *"Wagtail" or "Wagtail Dog."* He calls Mommy, *"The Eat Time Dog,"* because cooking is her job. With all these nicknames we just decided to name him *"OUGSTER-T!"* Just "Oug" for short!

~

Many people eat in their dining rooms on Sunday afternoon, often having dinner guests after Church, but we never do! In our dining room, where we never do sit down to eat, there is a distressed buffet and a slightly tilted Duncan Fife table with a few unmatched chairs. The table is piled high with papers, books and various stuff in many layers. In the living room there are a few more dust-covered, cross-flapped boxes, two older brass floor lamps, and a blue damask print sofa that soon 'sniffs' a lot like the Sir Walter Raleigh tobacco in Daddy's pipe.

I spend the first summer looking in the cross- flapped boxes, one brimming with old Trade-A-Plane magazines. I keep digging through other boxes and pictures, hoping to find some faded images from the past.

~

I am a very backward child and afraid of folks. I'm not burdened with a lot of rules and restrictions, other than rules that I impose on myself. That first summer in Ohio is very tense for me. We are told to just use common sense, but I am growing up *'lost'* in Van Wert. I become conscious that everyone scares me. In Tennessee, not many

strangers were coming back into *'them woods where we are a-livin!'*
My siblings and I play together, not venturing out much to meet
anyone in the neighborhood. In this neighborhood there are kids in
almost every house, but we are comfortable sticking together, a lot
like we have done in Tennessee. Despite my freedoms, I grow up
controlled by my own fears.

When we move into the house there is no running water in the
kitchen and the only appliance is a wood stove. There is a cistern and
pump for getting water into the kitchen sink. A hard pumping action
brings a trickle of cold water up from the inground cistern below.
Still, how wonderful to have water in the house – no more carrying
water from an outside well. Yet, overall, this place is only marginally
better than the house in Tennessee.

There are single, white-painted cupboards on either side of the
sink containing only a few mismatched dishes. The linoleum in front
of the kitchen sink is wore down to the wood floor below, caused
by a lifetime of washing dishes. The lower cabinet holds a black cast
iron skillet and two sauce pans. The refrigerator is an ice box. We
buy blocks of ice from the *'ice man'* who comes around in a truck or
we drive across town to the *'Ice House.'* Also, in the kitchen is a small
wooden kitchen table painted white with some wooden split-seat
chairs. On the cinder block ledges of the basement are some more
boxes, most full of canning jars, mayonnaise and pickle jars all dirty
without lids and spider webs inside. There are even more canning jars
with blue and green bubbled glass on the back porch.

On the back porch we use a 1920s model grey Maytag ringer
washer with a 4-legged free standing rinse tub alongside. This is a
step up from the washboard and tub from before. There is no running
water on the porch, and the porch floor is very noticeably slanted
with several holes in the rotted wood allowing an open view of the
ground below.

Each week Mommy fills the washer and rinse tub by pumping
water from the cistern, followed by heating the water on the wood
stove and carrying the hot water to the washing machine on the back
porch. She runs the agitator about 10 minutes, then she pushes the
clothes through the wringer to rinse, then back through the ringer.

For my blouses and dresses, she uses Argo Starch powder, stirring it into boiling water with a wooden spoon. She carries the wet
clothes to a hanging clothesline rope stretching between the buckeye

tree on the south end and the box elder tree behind the garage on the north end for the clothes to dry. After she hangs the starched clothes to dry stiff-as-a-board, she finishes hanging the rest of the laundry. She is humming to herself as she comes into the kitchen as she does a few chores. Gathering the now dry laundry from outside, she sprinkles water onto the dry clothes with a Coke bottle and a sprinkler with holes in the top. She sprinkles and rolls up the clothes and stashes them into a basket for ironing later in the day. Sometimes she puts the damp clothes in the refrigerator if she is going to iron later on. Ironing can be a day's work, in addition to wash day. I remember one day the clothesline rope breaks and the clothes drop in the mud! She cries because she has to start all over!

She doesn't have an automatic steam iron; no one does. The iron slab of metal weighs about 10 pounds and has to be heated on the stove top. Heat and weight are the magic components for getting the wrinkles out of the old cotton fabric. A heap of shirts, skirts, pants, handkerchiefs and pillowcases are piled high in the basket, waiting to be ironed. Nothing is worn without ironing and nothing is naturally wrinkle- free.

Mommy always heats water on the stove for baths in a wash tub on the kitchen floor. It is the custom in most families to bathe the youngsters first, and to add a little warm water for each kid. But at our house, sadly, we have a much different approach; our dad goes first, kids next and Mommy last!

In the bath room we have a single lavatory that hangs alone on the wall. A thin towel hangs on a nail alongside. She puts an old wooden buffet in the bathroom as storage for a few other thread-bare towels. We don't have enough towels to go around, so we share and reuse the towels until wash day.

Around the corner from our bathroom is a bedroom, where all manner of things must have gone wrong; the plaster and lath have disintegrated. The plaster is crumbling and the wallpaper is coming apart at the seams. The board floors are covered with plaster dust that falls out and always needs swept and mopped.

In his 'take this or nothing' way, Oug sells Mom on buying some wallpaper 'close outs.' Without fixing the bulges in the wall, Mom and I attempt to replace the wallpaper. She will get the top sheet pasted and situated, then she drops the strip down to me. I stand under the ladder and I carefully brush the lower part into place. We hang

7

wallpaper on each of the four walls in unrelated colors and prints in that downstairs bedroom and also in the dining room. This is not a pretty sight!

The upstairs has two small bedrooms and a hall room. All of these upstairs rooms are cramped with boxes under and around the beds. Due to lack of dresser drawers, we store clothes in boxes and fiber drum containers. Sometimes our clothes are lying in piles on the already dusty floors. All of this looks a bit like the stockroom at the Salvation Army Store.

Our old wooden front porch floor is buckled and warped from years of weather with very little paint. I plop down in my favorite nest, the porch swing. I hang around there, twirling and flipping around to make the swing smack against the house. Other times I spin around and around in the yard, until I fall down. Generally, I am just not sure what I can or should be doing, but I do love spinning and twirling.

Daddy thinks that our mother does not feel free in the world because her mother keeps her tethered close after the accident. Mina often says things like *aren't safe, be careful, don't go too far* or *don't take risks.* Our dad thinks it is good for us to do whatever we want, to explore, to take risks, to look and examine and to get dirty because we learn how to run freely in the world. His idea is that we will learn a lot by our interests, risks and mistakes! This is an ongoing difference in their parenting.

We DO run freely! We roam daily and nothing ever settles here, not even the dirt. There are some up sides to it and there is also a big downside. There are neighbors all around our house. We can go anywhere and do anything. Untethered and unrestrained, we know no limits. We never could have imagined that our freedom to roam wouldn't suit these Ohio neighbors. The neighbor next door has no children. We soon become a nightmare for them, causing them more problems than any of the others in the neighborhood. Sometimes we creep over to 'spy' by looking in their doors or windows. 'The Bug' and Stevie have a daily game of sitting along the fence connected to their back yard, firing walnuts over there, erupting in laughter and calling her names, like *'Haggai'*. That's a name from the bible, I know! But they mean she is a HAG! They even make up a song about her.

We think she is a wacko who hates people like us! We hear that she has a shotgun ...and if we were to walk across her lawn – BE-

WARE! 'Bug boy' and Stevie aren't afraid of her, but I am! They heckle and torment her endlessly. She hates us all, but who wouldn't?

"There's a southern accent where I come from
The young'uns call it country; the Yankees call it dumb.
I got my own way of talking, but everything gets done
With a southern accent Where I come from."

Tom Petty

CHAPTER TWO

Memories of Tennessee

I don't remember ALL about life in Tennessee, I am just under six years old and under 3 feet tall that cool spring day when I leave there. I will tell you all that I can remember, as well as some that I have been told about later. I am born at home, there are no doctors or nurses to assist. Our home is in the back country of Tennessee in the early 1940s near an area called *'the Homesteads,'* which is near Crossville, but we live in the nearby community of Big Lick, Tennessee. Every year on my birthday, Mommy tells me again this story about that day. Her story is this: *"We plan for you to be born in a hospital, but that night when my labor begins, our old car will not start! The car problem isn't a part of the plan. We panic!"*

She explains that late in the afternoon on Thursday, May 6th, my daddy begins walking about six miles from the clinic in Big Lick, where my attending nurse, Anna Mary Bradley, works. While he is walking, Mom's labor progresses and she is FIERCELY into the delivery. She is going it alone at home. Before the pains come, she puts water on the stove to boil. Even though she knows what is coming, she isn't prepared for the force of the pain.

She puts my 18-month-old brother into his crib and she lies down on the bed beside him. She is in heavy labor, and Daddy isn't back yet! My brother is agitated, shaking his crib and crying along with her. She thinks, *What am I going to do? I can't stand this much suffering!* She cries out, *"I can't do this by myself."* She is so weak and flat on her back and scared because there is no medication to dull her

10

pain. She clenches her fists and grits her teeth, but no help arrives. Hours and hours pass and darkness falls. At about 3:30 a.m., she gives birth to me at home alone! When I am finally born, I begin crying, too. After this is all over, my daddy finally comes back with the nurse; she ties the umbilical cord and she records my birth on May 7, 1943.

My dad is a proud Irish-American. I am the second child born into this Irish family. Because of that heritage, they give me an Irish name, Linda Kathleen McMillen. They call me by the middle name, which later becomes a nickname and the whole *'middle name calling'* thing is a nuisance for all of my life.

My problems begin that night because of how the birth happens, I get a little messed up and I come out ugly; my face is smushed up with a crooked little mouth that causes her some concern. Her very first thoughts are, *She is so ugly that I will just have to stay home with her!* Mommy is preparing to raise me with thoughtful guidance. Yet, she plans to isolate me like a child who *"only a parent can love."* By the next day Mommy is doing better and my color slowly improves. As it turns out, she loves me and my crooked face straightens out, after some time. No matter that I still have the crooked mouth! No matter that one of my ears is *"LIKE A SAIL!"* as my daddy points out. She says I am all right, just like I am. As I get older, I think about all of this; I guess that if she stays with him after that night, she is surely planning to stay with him for the long haul!

When I am small, he lets me call him Daddy, but he really likes *"Red"* better. His hair looks orange to me! His given name is Gordon Alonzo McMillen but he has a lot of different names in his life. I don't know of anyone who calls him Gordon. My sister calls him *POPS;* my mother calls him *"Mick,"* derived from his last name. Since he has a pet alligator, I call it an *'oug-da-gaiter'* from that name. I call him "OUG" and it continues from there! He NEVER will let anyone call him *'Grandpa,'* no matter how long he lives and no matter how many children and grandchildren he has. I suppose he gets it from his own antagonist, Grandpa Charles Kirk.

~

My mother's hands make up my young life. She churns butter, bakes bread in a wood stove and corn bread in a skillet, and she kneads dough and cuts biscuits with a can lid. When I don't feel well, her hands check my head for a fever as I lounge on her lap, making her body my couch.

~

In 1943 when the Roosevelts are in the White House, Eleanor spurs 20 million home gardens by planting a *'victory garden'* on the White House grounds. She challenges Americans to *"enjoy fresh food, fresh air and a fatter wallet by growing your own vegetables."* In these post-depression years, our garden is one of them. We have enough good dirt to sustain a big garden in back near the field where the horse and cow live. Almost all of our food is grown in our garden. We grow green *'snap'* beans, brown speckled beans, okra, cabbage, peas, carrots, potatoes and tomatoes to eat fresh or for canning. The seeds in our garden are planted and hoed by my mother's hands. All summer the seedlings grow and produce food by late summer into fall. Everyday life is hard for everyone in 1940s Tennessee; not even remotely similar to the way people live today. Mommy puts in years of hard work. She is always busy feeding her young'uns, the animals and tending her garden all summer. We live almost self-sufficiently on our own land.

We have enough grass around the house to feed the goats and a few chickens. We get meat from our chickens. Our animals live in the pasture. With hunting and occasional fishing, Oug can keep us fed. Mom milks the cow and churns the butter. I see Mommy getting the milk out of the cow and I try to help but I never do learn how to make that part work! We don't have a refrigerator, so we just milk the cow when we need more. We get all of the raw sweet milk we want to drink. Grandma doesn't want us to drink the raw milk. She thinks we will get tuberculosis, because it isn't pasteurized. Daddy says that isn't so and we keep drinking the raw milk right from the cow. No one gets tuberculosis! Sometimes I help Mommy by shaking the jar of milk. When I shake about half an hour the top part of the milk magically turns into butter! We skim the butter off the top and put some salt into it and press it into a butter bag.

We have a few chickens that my brother and I claim as our own. We don't really own them. They will all be dinner, sooner or later. Mom tells us to *"go fill the egg basket'* as the cackling hens gather around my legs. My brother finds that *'my'* chicken is trying to roost in a spot that *'his'* chicken wants. They are gathering and rustling as they squabble at each other about the roost. Pitching a fit, Bug Boy climbs up on the top of the chicken coop, with a garden hoe in his hand. He is trying to chase my chicken away. I am standing below, looking up, when he loses control of the handle and drops the hoe blade down onto my forehead! Daddy always knows what to do, so he sews me up with a sewing needle and thread. Then he puts a little iodine on the wound. The bleeding stops and I am as good as new... except for the scar! That hoe leaves a deep gash and I still have the scar to prove it!

~

In our early years, as previously mentioned, our house is near the center of the state, and up on the Cumberland Plateau in Cumberland County, Tennessee. We live near *"The Cumberland Homesteads,"* an area that is built in the 1930s Roosevelt's New Deal. The Homestead project is a depression Era effort to promote home ownership. The project includes building stone cottages and farms for over 256 *"Homesteaders."* The project is visited by Mrs. Eleanor Roosevelt, and is designated as a natural historical homage to the hard work of all those involved. We live in the homesteads area, and in a homestead style house, but my dad owns 100 acres of land bought for $500.00 in 1935, and paid for with his inheritance. There are 20 acres in pasture land, and 20 acres in *'new ground,'* where the trees are cut near the house. The balance is in uncut woodland toward the front of the house. A creek runs out from those woods. There is a road that only leads to local neighbors' houses. We know a few other local country folks around the area of Pleasant Hill and Big Lick. No neighbors are near enough to walk to for a visit. These families are where we go to visit and occasionally for Sunday dinner after Church.

~

I do not realize it at the time but I will remember this house we live in like it was yesterday. The sandstone outcroppings that breach the maple and evergreen woods supply the *'field stone'* that provides the distinctive exteriors of many of the local homestead houses. In 1943 our Tennessee house has no water or electricity. The first floor is a kitchen with a wood cook stove, a living room and 2 bedrooms. Hand pumps are commonly used in remote areas to supply water from underground wells. Mommy cooks on the wood stove and she fetches water from a well using a hand pump in the yard. Her laundry is done in a wash tub with water that she heats on the wood stove. She washes clothes on a washboard in a tub. That same tub is also our bathtub, along with a bar of Ivory Soap. We have unfinished wide wood plank floors. Our furniture is a table with chairs, a few homemade beds and two stuffed chairs in the living room by the fireplace.

We have an outhouse for a toilet. We use a chamber pot at night and the outhouse privy by day. When evening comes a full moon pours through the window until the morning sun comes in on my face. I sleep in a homemade bed, in the same room as my brother. Our beds are made of unfinished 2" by 4" lumber with holes drilled in the sides to thread rope across the frame with some cardboard placed over ropes to make a mattress. As we sleep, our clothes hang nearby on some nails on the wall.

The outside of the house is made from rough-hewn wood. The inside walls are unfinished logs with open spaces. I can look right through cracks and I see the outside light. There is never any finished inside walls or doors on the rooms. It is a square house with a field stone fireplace on the front with a split shingle roof. It is partially surrounded with a split rail fence that I am sure Daddy must have built. My parents, Gordon and Barbara, work together here for thirteen years, but the house is never finished.

These woods are lush, green and beguiling. My brother and I walk down trails padded with years of pine needles alongside wood ferns and moss on the trees. We putter around in fresh water, spring-fed creeks and swamps. We play in this *living and breathing* world of creeks and trees, every day.

We light the fireplace with wooden matches in the late afternoon. We heat the house with a wood stove and the river stone open fireplace. Our fireplace warms the room and the flames illuminate the space with flickering light. A good-sized log is in the fireplace with white edges as flames dance on the hearth. The house *'sniffs'* like a burnt wood smell. The burning logs are cut from the woods surrounding our house. Daddy and Mommy take turns fetching logs from the woods for the fire each evening. Even when we cut some trees down, there is still a big tall forest left.

There are glass lamps in the living room with their wicks dipping into a kerosene bowl. The little flames waver to show us a dim light when the darkness comes. Mommy and Daddy read every evening by the light from the oil lamps. The books they read come from the Calvary Presbyterian Church's *"Little Free Library."* They take turns reading aloud to each other, in our cozy living room. I remember hearing them read Ernest Hemingway's *"For Whom the Bell Tolls"*, and Tolstoy's *"War and Peace."*

Daddy is reading while Mommy sits in her chair, writing letters to her family by the light of a kerosene lamp. Postage stamps for letters are 3 cents then. Mommy is making an embroidery picture of the United States, as a gift for her mother. Sometimes she lets me help. I stitch just a little bit, but I make only a few stitches. She also makes rugs out of rags for the front of their chairs. I like to sit with her, snuggling in her chair as she puts her *'sugar arms'* on me, rocking me, and I think she likes that, too. I fall asleep on her lap. Mommy's voice is also real soft and sweet like a sugar cookie. When she sits down to read or embroider or make a rug, I like to scoot in beside her for a *snuggle.* I never do have her *all to myself,* because there are always other kids, some older, some younger. But her love goes a long way for all of us!

~

Our mail box is a mile away, up through the woods on the main road. We never have two pennies to rub together and nothing that we can sell. A bright spot in our month is the day the $20.00 rent payment arrives from Ohio. There is no mail that our family looks any more forward to than that rent check for the house that Oug still owns in Van Wert, Ohio. Crossville is the nearest town, just seven miles away, but we're so cut off in the woods,
it might as well be farther. It is a special day when we take the check to town to buy needed supplies.

We have no utilities or mortgage so we don't have many expenses. We've been eating squirrels, rabbits and cornmeal during the winter months when the canned goods are gone. We do without a lot of things, but we can't do much without cornmeal. With cornmeal we can make cornbread, mush and breading to fry fish, rabbits and squirrels. There are about two blocks of small stores in the downtown. People in town live in clusters of houses. I have heard that some even have curtains at their kitchen windows and water from their wells is piped inside their houses.

During the war there are things you can't buy unless you have stamps in the ration book. Some of these government rationed items are shoes, sugar, meat, coffee and automobiles, tires and gasoline. We might have to stand in line to buy a few basic consumer goods during the war, because some things are not readily available. Daddy pays cash for everything, but we also need WWII war time *'ration coupons'* for some food and gasoline.

Once we hit town, we cash the check and walk across the street to the grocery for corn meal, lard, flour and sugar, while Daddy drives to the service station for gasoline. The next stop is the feed store for bags of animal feed for the horse, cow and chickens. Sometimes we need something at the hardware store. With the ration coupons we can sometimes get salt pork, dried beans, potatoes, coffee and corn syrup. This diet is bad for mountain people's teeth and often other diseases caused by an improper diet. Daddy's teeth are all pulled and replaced with dentures by his early thirties.

When we buy flour or chicken feed, I like to pick out the bags because they have prints of pastel flowers. Mommy sews feed sacks into dresses for me with her treadle sewing machine as well as making some other things. In goes the feed sack, and as she peddles, out comes dishtowels, pillow cases, aprons, and my dresses.

~

We don't usually pay much notice to the summer heat. The wind is blowing through the open windows and the house is getting hot. I wake up to the smells of home canning. In the late summer, when the growing season is over, canning begins. I want to help, but Mommy tells us to stay out of the kitchen today, because canning is hot and dangerous. This is a time when we know to ask no questions and to do as we are told! Pans of water are boiling; and pressure cookers are steaming on the wood stove. Ball jars are being sterilized on the stove along with the 2-piece lids. The sterilized jars are upside down on a white feed sack that covers the top of the table. Daddy is overseeing it all. As she works the sweat runs down her face until she can't recognize herself in the mirror. She knows how to cold pack the tomatoes, peas, beans and okra by boiling in a pressure cooker. She doesn't need his help! The colander is full of tomatoes for the next cold pack batch.

Both of my parents are working constantly around the house and yard, working the land, growing food, hunting squirrels and rabbits to put meat on the table and baking corn bread, etc. But life is especially busy in the fall harvest season, as they prepare food. When fall air brings in chilly air, she has to get ready for the coming winter.

Crossville, TN 1940's

Downtown Crossville, Tn. 1940's - Wikipedia

The only water we have in our home comes from the well that is outside in the yard. Every day Mommy pumps the water and carries it to a tub in the house. In front of the hot black cast iron stove is a round tub she fills with warm soapy water. I sit in the tub for my weekly bath. She uses the same tub, some Lifebuoy soap and sometimes the same water, for bathing kids and for washing clothes. She has a rope clothesline outside. I see her hanging my socks and she holds the clothespins in her mouth between each piece. When she finishes the clothes, she begins chopping wood and stacks it for the wood kitchen stove and fireplace. She is small and not strong physically, but she is brave and determined. She calmly tells me to go back inside and she will be there in a minute.

Growing up with little supervision, 'The Bug' and I go out with our eyes focusing on all of the stuff in the woods that excites us! We don't have or need much to play with as small children. We play among the chipmunks in the peace of the woods near our house. We are looking for worms, bugs and any small animal life. We climb on rocks and trap lizards in our shoe box snare, down by the creek. In spring and summer, my brother, the Old Bug, and I go without shoes many days. Slap, slap, slap, we play barefoot in the mud puddles. We like the feel of soft dirt under our feet while the sun is warming our shoulders. We play barefooted until our feet grow thick and tough.

Tennessee has four seasons, spectacular colors in the fall, mild winters and warm spring and summers.

We follow the shallow creek to the branch nearest our house where we find salamanders and crayfish under rocks. We jump from rock to rock to cross the creek. We make mud houses and rock walls for the salamanders that we find. We make sling shots with sticks and we chew pine needles that taste like spicy gum.

In the woods in the autumn, the red, yellow and orange leaves swirl and flutter in the air until they finally cover the ground. We run through the deep leaves in the woods, kicking up the newly fallen leaves. We raise our arms in excitement as we laugh and play. Life is easy and simple here. Playing in that wooded place, at that special childhood time, creates a happy feeling of wonderment that lives in my mind today. Winters are mild here, with very occasional snow. A light smattering of snow falls on the thick brown leaves in the woods, looking like sugar sprinkled on dry bran flakes.

We are taught early to leave the rattlesnakes alone! We learn the sound that a rattlesnake's coiled tail makes when Daddy brings a 'rattle' into the house. This is cut from a real snake just for us to learn the sound. A few times we discover snakes in the yard and the 'new ground' beside the house. When we see a snake, we call Mom and she comes out and she cuts the snake into bits with an ax. When she is done, we go back to our play, as if nothing has happened. I won't say we are neglected but my mother never worries about what we are doing because she carries a heavy work load.

Mom puts more logs into the big black kitchen wood stove for cooking cornbread in her cast iron skillet. We eat cornbread with soup beans most every evening for supper. We seldom have any pork during the war. We have cornbread so often that I don't want it again, but there is nothing else to eat! I get cornbread, even if I don't want it! One night I crumble it into little pieces and drop it on the floor for our cat. My daddy does not like for me to throw food on the floor. He looks mad and I am in trouble! I know he doesn't like it, because he sends me to bed before the dark even comes! My tummy rumbles hungry. I know I should have eaten the cornbread. I close my eyes and clamp my ears so I won't hear him yelling anymore! I cry and cry so long I feel tired and I just sniff. My crying face gets all red and snotty. I call, but no one is coming. He just scares me with a small child's fear. He mostly gets mad with kids, so I stay quiet and fall asleep. My brother can make my daddy mad, too. We don't know how to stop making him mad. We forget and he thinks that we are just bad! I push my brother and he pushes me back. I don't push again or tell on him. We don't want to get in trouble. I think Daddy doesn't like kids much because being loud is bad! Mommy makes him angry, too, but, she knows better than we do how to keep him happy. She learns to keep quiet when he is mad, but I'm not good at that!

* * *

~A HOMESTEAD HOUSE IN TENESSEE~
https://en.wikipedia.org/wiki/Cumberland_Homesteads)

The house where we live from June,1936 to June, 1949 is near Big Lick, Tennessee. This makes it off the beaten path, about 9 miles south of the County Seat, Crossville, Tennessee. Cumberland County is in the eastern part of Tennessee between Nashville and Knoxville. Nashville is 120 miles west and Knoxville is 75 miles east. The altitude here is 1771 feet elevation.

The area we call home is a part of the western edge of the Smokey Mountains, and our home town rests atop the Cumberland Plateau. The highest peak is one thousand, seven hundred and sixty-five feet above sea level; the flat apex of the plateau is ringed by mountains which help keep Cumberland County a little cooler than the surrounding "flat-lands" in the summer, albeit about 10 degrees colder during winter.

NOTE: Our actual house burns down years after we left the area, but there are about 100 of the homestead homes still standing today. All are very similar homes. The Homesteads area is now designated in the register of National Historical places.

* * *

At first the rent check is enough and Daddy doesn't need to go out to work until we get more kids. My daddy does not have a job that anyone can put a name on until early1944. During the darkest days of World War II, the secret city of Oak Ridge, Tennessee is 'born' near where we live. Some 3000 area residents are given a few weeks to move and vacate some 1,000 home properties after Oak Ridge is chosen as the site for the Manhattan Project. Some 59,000 acres of beautiful hilly farm fields, and pretty homes are being replaced by a muddy government construction project. The Federal Government, under Franklin Roosevelt, chose this remote area of Tennessee due to the availability of labor in this poor and remote Appalachian area. Local hill folks are swarming Oak Ridge to apply for these great government jobs. Not many of the applicants have cars due to the war time unavailability of gasoline and rubber for tires. Most applicants are unemployed people needing a good paying job, including my daddy. Additionally, this project is located here because of its proximity to the new TVA dam at Norris, Tennessee for electrical power. This is the largest government scientific and technological effort of its time.

My dad is just 29 years of age, married with two small children, when he drives about fifty miles to Oak Ridge to look for a government job. He applies and he is hired immediately when I am just 18 months old. Mom is back in Crossville area living with her two young children in their partially built home in the back country without inside utilities. She writes love letters to him as she battles her own rollercoaster of emotions — from missing her husband dearly to feeling angry because she is pregnant with twins and living so isolated in the home where they planned to build their life together.

He occasionally rides a bus back to Crossville on a weekend, but he usually works 7 days a week. He has a 'dorm rack' in Oak Ridge, where he rides a bus back and forth each day to "West Town area." Here the men have beds in the dormitories at the bottom of the hill.

The dorm room costs $10.00 for a month and bus tickets from the dorms to the project costs $5.00 per month.

The bus from the dorms is like a cattle car. Workers ride in that car with seats on each side. They ride it to the entrance, but they have to stop at the gate where some guards get on board for a real shake down checking employees' badges, lunch pails, etc. Then they will go on to "*the fenced portal*," where they get off of the bus to enter work. As they get off of the bus, they are checked again before going inside. At the entrance narrow muddy walkways allow the workers to enter the building.

The secret city has guards at check points at every entrance, to secure the secret operations. The town is open and busy 24 hours a day, but very few people know it is there. The "*Secret City*" soon grows to 75,000 people. The increased size and population make it the fifth largest city in Tennessee, yet it is not on any map It is amazing how quickly the new city is built. Within two years, the town of Oak Ridge, with its inhabitants, is developing into a city to make this project happen. Brilliant scientists and local people are hired within the years between 1942 and 1944 to process Uranium-235. This is the primary ingredient used to build the first atomic bomb. (**https:// home.nps.gov/mapr/oak-ridge.htm**)

From January to August 1945, Gordon spends less than a year on the Manhattan Project. Unknown to him, at the time, this job is the key to the government building the atomic bomb. Oak Ridge is home to a major element of the Manhattan Project, ushering in the Nuclear Age. At the time of the second world war, this atom splitting process has never been conducted on such a large scale.

The very first thing they tell him is that all employees are supposed to "*leave everything that happens there*." When he is trained, he is given only information regarding what he is to do. He is told this is "*vital government work*" for "*the War.*" He isn't allowed to know what kind of government work they are doing.

But even though he is not allowed to know much at the time, some departments are monitoring dials and watching meters for a calutron, a mass spectrometer that separates uranium isotopes. The enriched uranium is used to make the first atomic bomb. He is soldering widgets and others are adjusting knobs, but no one knows what is being done. (**https://en.wikipedia.org/wiki/Calutron_Girls**)

There are about 22,000 workers on different rotating shifts. They work 3 shifts: 7:00 to 3:00 and 3:00 to 11:00 and 11:00 to 7:00 rotating all the time. When they are asked how many are available to work extra hours, most everybody is available on most of the shifts.

Signs are everywhere to let workers know to keep their mouths shut and they mean it! Employees are told of the consequences, and the fines. If they are caught doing something wrong, they will be automatically discharged, so if they want to stay, they had better listen. The security mantra is *"If the enemy beats us, God have mercy on us"*!

On April 12, 1945: After years of conflict in Europe and the Pacific, America is stunned by news of President Franklin D. Roosevelt's death. Roosevelt has been president for 12 years, one month and eight days when he dies. After that, term limits are set for presidents.

In an instant, Vice President Harry Truman is president. He has been kept out of war planning; he knows nothing of the top-secret Manhattan Project to develop the world's first atomic bomb. Truman quickly assumes command of a nation at war on multiple continents—and is confronted with one of the most consequential decisions in history. His journey begins as an inexperienced President confronted with a decision that he knows will change the world forever. Truman soon goes from learning of the bomb's existence, to wrestling with the devastating carnage that results in the order to use as America's first weapon of mass destruction. There are turbulent days, weeks, and months to follow, leading up to August 6, 1945 when Truman gives the order to drop the bomb on Hiroshima. **(https://en.wikipedia.org/wiki/Presidency_of_Harry_S._Truman)**

Most of the people who work on the Manhattan Project never know its true purpose, until August 6, 1945, when a voice shouts out into the night from the second floor of an Oak Ridge dormitory, "*Uranium! Uranium! Uranium!*" a word that no one in Oak Ridge has dared to utter until that day. President Harry S Truman is announcing to the world that the U.S. has dropped a uranium bomb, on the Japanese city of Hiroshima. For everyone who works at Oak Ridge the secrets of their work are out and they quickly know what they have been working on in Oak Ridge. The work is considered to contribute to the successful conclusion of WWII.

Soon after that a lot of these people, including Gordon, get laid off. Gordon is a pacifist who wants nothing to do with a war. Later he says, "I *wouldn't have taken the job if I had known.*" The Manhattan project has the impact of an unequaled series of events in the 1940s that forever changes our world.

(https://en.wikipedia.org/wiki/Manhattan_Project)

After the Government job at Oak Ridge is over, my daddy establishes an electrical wiring company. He is a self-taught electrician. He and his friend, Alton Swaford, became partners in the "*Service Construction and Maintenance Company of Crossville, Tn.*" They start an electrical business for wiring houses after WWII. Once he establishes this company, sometimes he finds work, and more often he does not. He finally gets a break when the Rural Electrification Administration brings electricity to the area where we live. After his work at Oak Ridge, they made a fair living for several years hooking in each house when the power lines come down the road and they bring electricity to the houses, but this is only on the main roads.

* * *

~ CALVARY PRESBYTERIAN CHURCH ~

Church is the center of life for local families in the 1940's. We attend the Calvary Presbyterian Church in Big Lick. My parents are friends with the minister, Rev. Smathers. We are members of his congregation, and along with about 75 other local residents, we attend church there. Mr. Eugene Smathers is the son of a Kentucky tenant farmer and a graduate of Louisville Presbyterian Seminary. He attributes his success to his concept of evangelism, which is; *"I've got to be with people and show the love of God through our love for them."* Under the leadership of the Reverend Eugene Smithers the church community builds the church building almost exclusively by using volunteer labor. The church is built in the heart of the depression. The building takes 140 days to construct with a budget of $3,000. According to Reverend Smathers, *"When the last stone is in place, we still have forty cents."*

The building still stands, as an enduring tribute to the community of Big Lick, TN. It is a building which reflects both the beauty of its surroundings as well as the strength of faith and character of the people who make it possible. *"The church has a long history of community development in the poor back country of Tennessee during the depression and beyond, including sponsoring the rural health clinic, The Calvary Church Homestead Project, The Little Free Library and the Annual Big Lick Homecoming. Those who come to Big Lick and Calvary Presbyterian Church find the open door with a warm welcome."*
(https://biglickpc.wixsite.com/calvary)

I am excited to read a May 26, 1967, Time Magazine article, where Rev. Smathers is nationally recognized for his *"work in difficult places of the world among the forgotten."* The article says he became prominent nationally for his work in the Presbyterian Church, *"as a pioneer in social work, developing health clinics and organizing farm cooperatives in the 1940s in the remote poverty-ridden area, deep in the Cumberland Mountains, around Big Lick, Tn."*

Life is never easy here for anyone, but Mommy has to work harder than most Mommies!" She is warm and snuggly and when she sits down, I like to sit with her and I think she likes that, too. I am on her lap; we're snuggling when I notice she is soft and fluffy on the tummy part. I am about 2 ½ years old when she tells me she is *"getting some twins"* to take my place on her lap!

My first distinct memory is of visiting the hospital in November of 1945 when the twins are born. Daddy brings me and my brother to the hospital to look at these two new babies. But my only memory of this visit is of a dog that is outside the door. I am afraid of dogs! We go inside to visit Mommy. She tells me the babies just came out *'one after the other.'* I think she says the boy baby left 15 minutes early, to wait outside for his baby sister. These babies are really small, with tiny hands and feet. They are all pink and bald. Mommy talks to them in a voice as soft as melted butter, but I don't know why she does, because they can't talk. I just wonder what all of the fuss is about!

My world changes overnight when they come home. I am her *'big girl'* now! I am quickly moved off of her lap and I go from being the baby of the family to being *"Mommy's helper!"* Mommy usually needs help with holding two babies' bottles. I can feed one baby while she feeds the other one. I am bringing her cloth diapers and lotsa other stuff! Before long they learn to crawl around and get into things in the house. When they get into something and they are caught, they crawl away, each in a different direction. I have to pick up their baby things, even if I don't cause the mess. I have to put things away that I don't even get out! Soon that changes into big girl jobs like bringing diapers. Sometimes I am washing bottoms, and picking up the diapers. I know that when she tells me in the *'I mean it'* voice she needs some help, because she has two new babies and I tell her that, *"I'm coming!"* With Daddy not having much interest in babies, I find that she mostly needs my help with all four of us pre-school aged kids.

She especially has her hands full when we all had the measles at the same time. Daddy demands to be waited on, too. He's smugly saying, *"That's Barbara's job."* She endures everything, often quietly saying *"Praise God for small things!"*

The worst part for me is when I have to take care of babies, when all I want to do is to play in the woods with my brother. We are inseparable companions. As soon as the twins can walk, we have to bring them along! They really bother us when we play, but we still have to bring them along.

The families I can remember are the Alton Swaford family because he is Daddy's partner in the Electric Business, and an elderly woman named Mrs. Ray who is Alton Swaford's mother. The Strunk Family are our nearest neighbors, they live just a mile away. There is no one within easy walking distance of our house. Not many strangers come back into *'them woods'* where we live! For some reason my daddy is also the only car driver in our family, there is only one car and it is *his* car. He drives his car about a mile on dirt-rutted paths through the woods to get from the main road back to our house. I am allowed to walk anywhere within a mile of the house, even though I am 'little.'

When I am nearly five, I take the twins for a walk. The twins are young toddlers around 2 or maybe 3 years old. They are almost not babies, but they are toddlers. As we thread our way down a one-mile-long sandy path through the woods to the Strunk's house, we see chipmunks and squirrels playing in the sand. The woods and trees bring a feeling of enchantment to me and I am completely unaware of the passing time. The night is beginning to fill with mysterious sounds. Soon shafts of moonlight dapple through the trees. As we walk along the sandy path, I tell them that the sand on our path is *"brown woogie,"* which means *'brown sugar'* in big people's language. I even get them to take a taste! The twins have a sandy drool on their chins when we come to the neighbor's front door. The Strunks are shocked to see three small children standing at their door at dusk.

Thinking out loud, they said, *"Y'all must be the McMillen's kids from over yonder!"* The concerned family walks us all back home to return us to our parents! As we walk back it is getting dark and I can see stars in the sky. The dusk can't go unnoticed as the sound of crickets fills the air. I don't want to get in trouble but I don't really think there will be a problem. My parents like for me to take care of the babies. Daddy says, *"I'll be 'Dag-gonned!"* Mommy chimes in with, *"We haven't even noticed they were gone!"*

~

My daddy has a horse that he rides around the house in the yard. I am afraid to go near, because the horse runs fast. I get so afraid because one time when he is riding, the horse runs so close to me that I feel like he is running over the top of me. My daddy isn't watching out for me! I am scared because the horse is too big to see me, when I am standing near his fast legs! So now when the horse is outside of the pasture, I scoot inside the house.

~

I love Grandma, but at the same time, I am afraid of her fierce tone. I don't know how to '*be*' with her. I can't get things right. She sure does believe in Christmas though! She is our '*one last hope*' for getting anything for Christmas. Every year she mails something to us in Tennessee. It is often something she makes. She knows how to make good things for Christmas like rag dolls and sock monkeys that she makes out of brown work socks!

She made a rag doll for me! My dolly has yarn hair, an embroidered face and she is soft from her stuffing. I immediately love that doll. Dolls are supposed to have common names, like Sally or Betty, but I name her '*Digsty.*' I know my dolly loves me, too. When she looks lonely, I can tell her with my eyes, *"I am here!"* Digsty stays close with me when I sleep.

Towards evening, I jump into my homemade bunk bed. My brother is already sleeping above. I tuck myself in, lying on my back and hugging my dolly. The windows are propped open by sticks. It's dark outside and I can see stars out the window. A day breeze lightly blows the dingy muslin curtains in my sleeping room. The night breeze ruffles the curtains, sucking them in and blowing them out again through the open windows. Soon my eyes begin getting heavy as I listen to the sound of my brother's nose with his air coming in and out as he sleeps. By morning the air gets quiet and the wind is almost not breathing at all. In the mornings we put some baking powder on the palm of our hands or dip our wet fingers into the soda box to clean our baby teeth. I'm pretty sure everyone does it that way! (Today it will be called toothpaste.) We both have chicken pox in that room. We stay in bed all day when we are sick. We bang a pan with a spoon when we need something and Mom comes running!

27

~

During the 1930s, the firm of Porterfield Aircraft Corporation, located in Kansas City, built only 250 planes of a Model 35 light aircraft - a tandem two-seater built of traditional steel tube fuselage with a wooden wing - all, of course, covered in fabric. The exceedingly slim fuselage is nicknamed, *"Slim Bird"* by pilots and enthusiasts. Aimed at the lower-cost sport flying market, a variety of engines with 55HP to 90HP are available options.**(http://porterfieldplane.ning.com/)**

Sometime when I am between 3 and 5 years old, my daddy buys an old porter field airplane. The coverings are in bad shape. He removes a side wall of the upstairs of our house, and carries it up a ladder in pieces, to rehab in our unfinished upstairs. Mommy sews a new outer shell for the airplane using her treadle sewing machine and some white muslin fabric. She cuts the edge trim with her pinking shears. Down in the yard, I can hear Mommy's soft voice and sometimes I hear his mad voice as they work upstairs. His stories can be told in all kinds of lengths. As a child I remember how hard it is to listen to him talk on and on about airplane pieces and parts. I can mostly hear daddy talking nonstop up there as they work. I wonder how he has so much to say! However, Mommy listens carefully to what he's saying, no matter how long he goes on or how often she's heard him say it before.

One day he comes home with a propeller for his airplane, only to discover it is the wrong size. No man wants to admit he is mistaken and it is unnatural for my daddy to admit a mistake. His mouth wrinkles up and he leans against the wall, lighting a home-rolled cigarette, and he says, *"Hell's Bells, how did that happen?"* He tells her, *"This propellor is as worthless as tits on a boar!"* He is bold and innovative and looking for a solution. He finds someone to buy the propeller but he sells it too cheap! Now, he doesn't have enough money to buy the one he needs. It is unusual to hear him so discouraged. With the wonder of a child, I am inclined to consider him infallible, though he often isn't. I can't remember him ever sparing us much affection or attention.

This is particularly unusual because he usually maintains control of his projects and seldom makes mistakes. Mommy softens this by trying to take a part of the blame herself. She is fierce in her family and in her marriage to a bossy, contentious and self-centered husband. If she doesn't, he isn't happy. He has the narcissistic personality, and all his acts of self-love are both subtle and exact.

Living with a narcissist can be exhilarating; it is always onerous and often harrowing. Mommy is powerless against him in most every angry and controlling situations. It is easier for her to let him blame her, than to work with his rage. She accepts this traditional women's lifestyle that her mother and all of my grandmothers before her have accepted. Being submissive is the only acceptable route for any woman in the 1940s marriage, family and home. In those days her ignorance of alternatives is a closed door. She never wonders "*What if?*" or "*What else?*" She wants a marriage and children and nothing more. If anything else is available to her she doesn't know of it. Even though every couple is set up this way, we seem to have a worse time than most families, because his heart is as cold as steel in January. He has projects of his own and she works on his projects, too.

Upstairs they are busy building the airplane. Going up to see the airplane is like a '*dream place*' to me. I am mostly kept downstairs watching and playing with the baby twins, because she needs for me to do that. I have wanted to see up there for a long time and finally, she brings me up the ladder that leans on the back side of the house. I am still remembering the day that she let me watch them build the airplane. Mommy tells me to be quiet, because his work is easier when no kids are around. Now that there are four of us, we know that, "*Every blasted one of us makes him mad!*"

Daddy keeps working on his airplane daily. He is seldom ever interested in anything else. Mommy is cutting and sewing and I see Daddy stretch the fabric around the fuselage of the plane. He keeps painting it over and over with lacquer until the many coats draw it in tight and strong. They work on the plane in our upstairs for quite a while. I'm not sure how long that is in kid years. He finally spray-paints it cobalt blue and bright yellow; he attaches the official FAA numbers and he takes it out of the upstairs in pieces.

He is the only pilot, and not professionally trained, but I go on flights with him! Grandma says, "*Do not ever get in that airplane because he doesn't know what he is doing and he will kill you all!*" I know he knows how to fly a small plane, so I am not worried. I listen, knowing that after Grandma storms off, he will disregard it all. Beneath her control and anger at Oug, I sense that Grandma cares about us kids, but all of her controlling causes trouble.

~Me at three~

~

Bug Boy is starting school at the Laniary School (historical now) located in Grassy Cove, TN, which is five miles from the homesteads. There is a school bus about one mile away, but unfortunately, he doesn't get there regularly enough and he has to withdraw or repeat the first grade.

Fall is working around to winter. I am three when Christmas-1946 comes to Tennessee. We're not people who make too much of Christmas. It's a day like any other for me, but a neighbor says to me, "*What is Santa going to get ya?*" I jump back behind Mommy and whisper to her, "*Why is Santa going to GET me*"? Since I don't know who Santa is, I sure don't want him to '*get me.*' This '*No Santa*' concept is an intentional part of our upbringing. My parents do not allow any Santa myths! Because they have never told me anything about a Santa Claus, they know I won't ask for anything. Daddy never wants us to know any of the good things about Santa Claus. He says, "*I don't want to tell you something that is not true, because you might think I lied to you!*" He goes on to say, "*Other parents are deceiving their poor children with these lies!*" He warns me, "*Don't tell anyone else that truth!*" We quietly keep his secret! But, after I learns a little more about the Santa story, I am a little more suspicious of the reasons he gave to me. Now, I think that he doesn't want to introduce

30

Santa, because if we don't know they don't have to buy any stuff for us. He doesn't like Christmas, not even a little bit. He doesn't want anything about Christmas going on at our house, and that is his real reason!

When we are older, we see what other families are doing at Christmas. Mommy sneaks and buys a few extra things like small gifts for kids or special food for Christmas dinner. Daddy gets real grouchy mad, like the *'Grinch'* in Dr. Seuss's books because he has no Christmas joy inside of him. Mommy believes in the *'Santa life'* if Daddy will allow any of that in our house, but he doesn't! I would love to have known about Santa Claus and be allowed to believe in him, but I never have that chance!

~

Every summer Grandma comes to visit us in Tennessee. She is coming on a Greyhound Bus to Crossville; which is still about nine miles from our house. Mommy doesn't know how to drive but she sure is excited as Daddy drives into town and picks her mother up at the bus station. Daddy is *NOT* excited to see her come! Grandma has strong opinions about how things should be done. Soon enough they will be *'at each other.'* Daddy can top her in cuss words, but Grandma can yell louder. She wants to see him gone! Mommy tells her mother, *"There's nothing I can do now, he's, my husband!"* and she adds, *"I just wish you two could get along!"*

"For God's sake, all I'm saying is you could do better!" She adds, *"I'm not telling you how to live your life or telling you what to do!"* But, of course, she is!

They never do get along, and Grandma is really bothered by any dirtiness. *"Child, whatever is on your face?"* She licks her thumb and rubs my smudged face to give me a spit bath. I hate that! Her attention to cleanliness might be her way of avoiding what people are thinking about people like us. All the while she is lecturing my mom, saying, *"The way you're living is a disgrace."* Grandma is brushing away cobwebs with a broom, covered with an old shirt, yowling all the while, that she doesn't know where Barbara gets some of her habits because she has been raised in a spotless home! She usually stays at our house for about 2 weeks, cooking, canning, and cleaning our house. Moreover, she says, *"You must commence to keeping a clean and spotless house and bathing these children more often"* She sets out many changes that she thinks will get Mommy back *on track.*

She strips us naked and scrubs our skin until the rings of dirt on our necks are completely gone and she digs her fingernails into our heads to get our hair cleaner than it has ever been before. These things might sound right, but, oh my! She upsets our household, every time she visits!

I love the doll she made for me–but I love her to death! Her cloth face is dirty and her yarn hair is as worn as the *"Velveteen Rabbit"* but I still love her. I never do notice when she changes. Digsty is dirty and barefoot, like me! On one of her visits, Grandma gets her hands on my *'Digsty'* doll. She throws her right into the fireplace!

Grandma says, *"Digsty is too dirty for you to love anymore!"* I still want her; she is my only friend. I tell her it doesn't *'matter any 'bout the dirt!'* How sad my face is when I find my dolly burning in the fireplace flames. (Today, if I shut my eyes tight, I can still see my favorite dolly, burning in that Fireplace!) When Grandma's visit is over, we take her back to the bus and she heads home. As soon as *"venomous Mina"* leaves, we get back to living like we have lived the rest of the year. Daddy uses his temper as a weapon that he can wield; he can be soft or hard, but always controlling. My dad is always able to get my mom back onto his own idea of *'on track'* so he can quickly take charge and regain CONTROL. He says, *"There was a time when a woman wouldn't have gotten into a man's marriage that way."* A marriage can be hard under the best of circumstances, but having a third person interfere makes it all the more difficult. Daddy loves to control my mother and Grandma also enjoys controlling her daughter! The two of them pull my mother *'every which way'* until she just gets just too tired to fight either of them.

My parents aren't active politically beyond voting for president every 4 years. There is no mention of feminism in our house, either. News comes in snippets on the car radio. Sometimes they sit outside in the car just to hear music. National news trickles in slowly here. My earliest memories of national politics are when Truman wins over Dewey. It is Tuesday, November 2, 1948. I am 5 years old when my dad hears on the car radio that Incumbent President Harry S Truman, the Democratic nominee, defeats Republican Governor Thomas E. Dewey.

"Quite an upset," he says. Truman's victory is considered to be one of the greatest election upsets in American history. My parents are both Democrats and I just remember them excitedly discussing

the election. I curiously just want to know what they are talking about, but try as they might, there aren't any words that I can understand, regarding the election that has just happened!

World War II finally brings an end to the Great Depression. People are willing to pay more in taxes and buy war bonds to support the war effort. Federal spending helps the factories. There is greater demand for farm products, as American farmers shoulder the load of feeding the world. By 1948 most of the electric power lines are run through the rural area main roads and surrounding houses are wired. My daddy says his business, "Service Construction and Maintenance Business of Crossville, Tennessee, *"is going to hell in a hand basket."* Mom loves her life in Tennessee, but she is homesick, and she misses her family in Ohio.

The McMillen family lives here from June, 1936, to April, 1949. I remember that the entire frontage at our home is an untapped wilderness at the end of a long mud road. The mountains rule the rear view and green hills run softly to flatten into pasture land behind our house. My thoughts can't seem to place exactly where the house sits in the woods, because I am small, but I have this vision of the Cumberland Mountains that we can see each day; far back in the distance, beyond our pasture. I have a clear memory of the vision of a perfect view of the Cumberland Mountains as I looks over our pasture in the back.

~OUR VIEW OF CUMBERLAND PLATEAU~

~

When we pack up and sell everything out, I can't quite understand what is happening, but it is clear that something is going on.

After spending the early years in Tennessee, the magic is splintering all around me, but I still don't realize yet that I won't be coming back! They have lost the will to stay on the remote land and they decide reluctantly that we are ready to live someplace else.

We sell out and move back to Van Wert, Ohio, in April, 1949. The Rev. Eugene Smathers buys our house for a needy family in the Church. He pays us just $400.00 for the house and the land and we leave the Cumberland Plateau forever. After fourteen years of hard work – how very little we have!

~

I am five years old, but I'm 'going on' six in April, 1949, when my family moves from Tennessee to Van Wert, Ohio. U.S. Route 27 ascends into the Cumberland Plateau as a two-lane road to pass through downtown Crossville. Leaving Crossville, and narrowing to two lanes, the route continues north through more farmland. It then crosses into the next county through some mountain switchbacks and winds its way through this rural area for several miles to intersect with another county road. This area straddles the line between East Tennessee and Middle Tennessee.

As my story demonstrates, I lived in the Southern charm of Appalachia for the first six years of my life. Life on the Cumberland Plateau is usually smooth and easy for kids like me! I remember how freely we roamed; we go out unrestrained and happy most every day. The quaint hilltop area is remote and not well-traveled, but it is one of the most gorgeous sights in the state of Tennessee. I have limited learning and no outside social interactions here. During the second great war and after, my mountain roots are deeply imbedded in this area. These experiences didn't prepare me for the outside world.

The Crab Orchard Mountains are still one of the most rural areas of all Appalachia today, even though the area is now connected by a two-lane highway. The elevated location brings delightful views and warm weather all year.

As I make my way into adulthood and out into the world, I move beyond the comfortable familiarity and the southern upbringing where my life began. I don't return to the homesteads again until I am grown up. With this growth there is a widened cultural disconnect between the outside world and the carefree moments that I treasure from so long ago. I return to this area when I am in my twenties with my husband and our two kids. Even then I am just passing through!

On that trip my husband tells our kids that I once knew Daniel Boone and that I have one leg shorter than the other from running around these hills. Also, he tells them that he "*has to be careful so I won't run back into the hills and she will never come back!*" But truthfully, I never knew Daniel Boone, my legs are the same length and I don't plan to run back into the hills. But I still think I was born in the best of times when life was slower and easier.

Though I was so young when I left, I still have fond memories of Cumberland County, Tennessee. Now it is possible that I recall this place, with more fondness than it deserves. Yet I still hold these childhood memories and my *hillbilly roots* near and dear in my heart.

"Growing up in Ohio and just being kind of an average guy from flyover country – My dad was a factory guy – I try to put things on a screen that reflect reality."

- Roger Ailes

Chapter Three

School in Ohio

I have not been in Ohio more than a few months when, for the first time ever, I have to begin going to school. I am so afraid! I have never been inside any school. We need 3 fat red pencils with heavy thick lead for first grade, a yellow golden rod tablet that is wide ruled, and a small package of Crayola Crayons with 2 rows of colors. There are stores around here where we can get everything that we need and they are near enough that we can walk there. This is exciting! Mommy takes me down on Main Street in Van Wert to Murphy's Five and Dime store. We get just what I need for school and nothing more. I want to look in there longer, but she drags me right '*outta*' there!

Mommy sometimes makes my dresses cut from old clothes that have been given to us. She tears some rags into strips to curl our hair. She wraps our hair around the strips. We wear the rags to bed to make our hair curled in long spirals.

She saves all the buttons from any old clothes in a button jar full of used buttons. She can alter a blouse or recut something to create a skirt. I have a few changes of clothes for school that Mommy sews for me. I have a church dress from Grandma and a few hand-me-down play clothes from older cousins. We aren't allowed to play in our school clothes, and we don't wear play clothes to school. Right after school we have to change into play clothes.

~

We have a school-enforced but modest and respectful dress code. Girls always have to wear dresses for school and boys wear cotton pants with camp shirts. Jeans are for work and play but no one wears jeans to school. My dresses are usually a red school girl plaid with a fitted bodice with white Peter Pan collar, puffy short sleeves and a gathered skirt. With my dresses I wear knee socks and brown oxfords. I wear my hair in braids throughout my childhood. School clothing has to be spotless and neat and dresses cannot be above the knee. After the school year if we have outgrown pants, we cut them into shorts for the summer. Girls don't usually wear shorts or pants but I like to wear the Bug's jeans. They are too long, or maybe I am too short and I walk off the bottom of the pant legs into rags until Oug orders me to stay out of them because I am ruining them. He tells me, *"Girls have got no reason to be wearing britches!"*

Daddy has many qualities that I admire, but patience is not one of them. As I remember in Tennessee, my parents are always together, both working on projects, and she never seems to resist. She plays a big part in his life and his interests. My daddy still doesn't have steady jobs since we moved to Ohio. Today he sits with a pencil and note paper, adding up some numbers. Shoes, school books, doctors. Where will he get enough money? He tells me he's worried and that *"Money doesn't grow on trees!"*

Even before I start school, I put on my Buster Brown oxford shoes only to find them too small. I'd only had'em for 6 months – I don't want to tell Daddy that I've outgrown my shoes again, but I have to! Inhaling his cigarette, he says, *"Ye gods, Kid! There are people in hell wanting ice water!"* He wails on, *"Where will I get money to buy you shoes?"* Well, don't ya' know, the very next day my cousin gives me her old outgrown shoes!

The fall of 1949 Mommy walks with me to Horace Mann School for the first and last time. She puts me in Miss Ruby Rigging's first grade class. Some kids are in their second school year because they have been in kindergarten the year before, but not me; I was living in Tennessee last year. Kindergarten could have been fun. It's the first year of academic study and I missed it! That level of under exposure is sure to hold me back. The first years of school can matter for a lifetime. As you can imagine, I have no preparation for what is ahead for me! School is the scariest and most intimidating thing that I have experienced, so far! I generally have no idea what to do because I enter school with no socialization, no stimulation or enrichment from home. I don't know colors, counting or alphabet.

I can hear the teacher saying my name, but I don't say anything. What can I say anyhow? Mommy puts her hand on my back and pushes me forward from her leg as she turns to leave. I move on in but I am shy and afraid. My face scrunches up and I cry. My hands stay behind my back and I look down at the floor. The first day, I come into the class room where there are windows along two sides and chalkboards on the remaining two walls. I notice a 48-star American flag in the room. I have never seen an American Flag before! We are assigned to a desk. I learn that I can't just plop down anywhere!

There are alphabet letters, both capital and small, above the chalk board. Until first grade I have never heard about the 26 letters of the alphabet! I push through the first layers of fear only to learn that school life is never going to be easy until I begin memorizing all those 26 letters. I don't know what any of those letters mean, and now they have to be in a special order! There is a big wooden paddle called '*The Board of Education*' and that scares me! Miss Riggins is an imposing sight and my tears certainly disappoint her. She drops her head into her hands. I know she is feeling mean toward me because I am crying. As the year goes on, I notice that my teacher is often mean with a sharp tongue. She is mean even without my crying face so I quit crying after the first day.

~I sure did, this is me! ~

On the second school day and all the days that follow, Mommy quits coming. I hope to walk the three blocks to school with 'Bug Boy', but he makes some new friends, and before long I have to go by myself. The Bug isn't a 'fraidy-cat' like me! He tells me, "*I can't stand by twiddling my thumbs waiting for you!*"

I keep trying! As the year goes on, courageously I keep learning at school, but I am afraid everywhere I go. Miss Riggins gives me some white paper that has two blue solid lines and one dotted blue line. I begin trying to fit my whole long name in that small space. It is double hard for me to wrap my small fingers around those fat red pencils with fat lead. My parents want me to be called Kathleen and not nicknamed. I have a long name. LINDA KATHLEEN MCMILLEN is a long and hard name for me to learn. I cannot make the letters small, but I learn to print and spell my whole, first, middle and last name. After I learn the alphabet letters, I begin to like the reading and spelling classes a little more than before. I am not understanding much about the numbers or adding and subtracting and even counting yet.

After learning the alphabet and writing our names, we start to read *Dick and Jane* primers. My lips move while I follow along each page, marking each word with my finger, but I am dangerously close to tears. Students could recognize the word "house" or "down" more easily than they could sound it out, since this era is before the introduction of phonics.

In the 1950s, almost 80 percent of primary grade classrooms use *Dick and Jane* readers as the predominant readers in public schools. The books are created because reading consultants believe that the "whole word" method is the ideal way to teach reading. They are among the educators who became enamored of what is known as the "whole word" or "look-say" method of reading. This method teaches children to look at each word as a whole unit. These educators feel millions of American schoolchildren learn to read more easily using the *Dick and Jane* readers. The books take their name from the series lead characters who, with a dog named Spot and a kitten named Puff, inhabit a nostalgic, innocent American landscape of white picket fences and neighborliness.

These *Dick and Jane* stories are etched into the minds of the Baby Boomer generation and their immediate predecessors so firmly that the repetitive phrase, "See Spot run! Run, Spot, run!", is today remembered by millions as the very first sentences they could read on their own. It has been estimated that four-fifths of the nation's schools were using *Dick and Jane* readers, ranking the books with the venerable *McGuffey Readers* of the nineteenth century as a tool of universal literacy. The *Dick and Jane* readers emphasized non-phonic sight reading and repetitive, limited vocabulary, a formula that became a parody of itself by the time their approach is jettisoned in the tumultuous 1960s, to be replaced by phonics and books with more diverse characters and situations.

https://www/encyclodepia.com/media/encyclopedia-alma-nacs-transcripts-and-maps/dick-and-jane-readers

Look, Jane, look.
See Baby.
Oh, oh, oh.
Funny, funny Baby.

~ My First Grade Reader in 1949 ~

We start every school day standing with a hand over our hearts, to show respect, as we face the flag to pledge allegiance to our American Flag. Miss Riggins leads us in the pledge and she takes a daily attendance. America is founded and established in Christian principles. *Our God* holds a place of honor in all public-school classrooms. We sing Christian songs and we learn Christian values. Parents and communities trust our teachers to provide an education, without any political indoctrination. Discipline is the key to learning and achievement. In 1950s, parents and teachers agree it's very important for students to be attentive, quiet and disciplined. When students talk or don't listen during class, our teacher tells them to lay their hands palms down on their desk and, chop, chop, chop, she hits them with a ruler across the tops of their hands. I stay careful so this won't happen to me! My legs feel like '*pudding*' and my tummy is sick when she is doing this!

A classmate of mine is accompanied to school every day by her mother. When her mother tries to leave, she cries. That goes on for the full school year and the crying makes Miss Riggins frustrated. One day she gets out a teacher-sized board paddle and she paddle her for crying. Teachers were allowed to do that. I learn to be happy that

Mommy makes me come alone. Another first-grade student wets her pants in class. I am sitting in my desk watching the spreading puddle under her desk as it rolls down the oiled board floors in my direction. This leaves me worrying, again! Will this happen to me? This is one of the moments where confidence is created or destroyed. Day by day and little by little, Miss Riggins erodes any self-esteem that I might have had. I hesitate to leave the house each morning before leaving for school. Finally, I leave the house alone, just walking normally. I startle when I see someone passing in the other direction. My curiosity makes me walk backwards, as long as I can, just to watch them pass. I try breaking this habit, but I can't miss a moment of them, even after we pass. I am still turning around as I walk; my eyes follow others who are passing on the sidewalk. I try so hard, but something about me just doesn't fit! It is a very long time before I quit '*looking backward*' at people. I can't imagine what causes me to be so timid.

First Ward School, Van Wert, Ohio.

~'The old brick Horace Mann School~
- built in 1893.'

I am amazed by the heavy white ceramic water fountains and toilets, tall single pane glass windows, the clunking steam radiators and the smell of oil polish on the wood floors. There are wooden desks anchored on runners of wood to immobilize the desks. Grades 1 through 3 in each corner are on the first floor with cloak rooms between. Grades 4 through 6 are in each corner on the second floor, with the final corner being a small school library. The school has no cafeteria, so we walk to and from school twice a day, going home for lunch. This means that we are taking off and putting on our outer-wear several times each day. Mommy usually makes us soup or sandwiches of either toasted cheese or sugar and butter mixed together on Wonder bread. 'The Bug' can eat peanut butter sandwiches for weeks without ever noticing. I don't like peanut butter, so I have bread and butter sandwiches or lettuce and mayonnaise and I call these lettuce sandwiches.

The days of summer are fading and the air is chillier. On warm fall days we have recess outside on the playground. We go outside by the metal fire escape stairs to play on the swings and merry-go-around. Those are our only pieces of playground equipment. Otherwise, the girls play jump rope and hopscotch. I don't know how to play any of these games.

One day I find a new friend. Carol has just moved to the neighborhood. She joins me at the teeter totter. When a girl on the other end drops off, she grabs the board and holds it until my feet reach the ground. I like that she didn't let the other end hit the dirt. We quickly become fast friends. When the recess bell rings, I get in line to go to the playground as fast as I can, because I am afraid of Miss Riggins. Most of my classmates fear her, too.

Several days each week we have art class. We are expected to color inside the purple lines of the mimeograph papers that she assigns. Our art is never freehand. I like art class because I can work without talking to anyone. The pictures are easy teddy bears and other fun, easy stuff like that. Crayons are new to me and I love using my crayons. The mimeograph paper that is used in classes has an unforgettable smell of the pale blue ink that is intoxicating!

On the days we don't have Art we have Music. We learn to sing simple songs like *"Row, Row, Row Your Boat" and "Twinkle, Twinkle Little Star.'* After a few months and a lot of coaching, I get a little more social and recess becomes my favorite part of being in first grade at Horace Mann School. We play easy games like *"Farmer in the Dell, Ring Around the Rosie, Red Rover and London Bridges* at recess. We play on the swings and climb on the monkey bars. I learn to jump a rope. After a few months when Thanksgiving is near, we learn to sing *"Over the river and through the woods".* At Christmas we sing secular music like *"Jolly Ole Saint Nick," "Up on The Housetop,"* and *"Rudolph the Red Nosed Reindeer"* and *"Jingle Bells"* as well as religious hymns like *"Silent Night"* and *"Away In A Manger."* We also have school Christmas Nativity pageants at school and in church with spoken scripture and solos.

There are cloak rooms outside the class rooms with evenly spaced hooks for our wraps to hang, neatly side by side, with our galoshes which are supposed to be set below each coat. We spend quite a lot of time the first year, just learning the exhausting and tedious job of putting on and taking off our outer wraps and buckling our boots. The cloak room turns into a jumbled heap of garments. Kids, like me, are often wandering around looking for a misplaced boot or a lost mitten so Mom helps me by pinning my mittens to my coat sleeve where I can find them and slip my hands right inside.

We go through the winters with bitter cold and ice everywhere. The weather in Ohio can't have been cold and grey every single day for years, but that's how I remember it! Fall and winter in Ohio is dreary and often windy with slush and ice. Most of us have running noses from mid-fall to late spring. If we do not have boots, we tie or tape bread wrappers over our shoes to protect the shoe leather and to keep our feet dry while we play in the snow. We spend many school days in sopping wet socks that stretch out longer than our feet. We have hacking coughs, and some wheezing and sneezing. In the mornings, our breath makes white clouds above our lips. We have a lot of home remedies such as gargling salt for sore throat, breathing steam to clear a cold and, of course, eating chicken soup and drinking plenty of liquids.

~

In Spring, flowers bob around in the wind and birds are chirping. As the month of April rolls to an end, we begin gathering flowers to put in May baskets to hang on the doors of friends, neighbors and loved ones on May 1st. I love doing this around the neighborhood and running to hide before I am seen. May Day is a spring rebirth celebration as an assurance that we've survived the winter. On May 1st at school, we are dancing around a May Pole, a galvanized pole garnished with flowers and ribbons to symbolize a tree. The tree represents masculine energy, and the ribbons and floral garlands that adorn it represents feminine energy. On the last day of school, we have Field Day. We spend the entire day outside enjoying competitive games at school, like 3-legged races, sack races and playing ball. Field Day is the perfect signal that the end of the school year is near and we look forward to an exciting and well-deserved break from the classroom.

Chapter Four

Growing Up on Walnut Street

My new neighborhood friends are Nancy and Carol – most of the time, three is a crowd. They are both school mates, but my really best friend is Carol. Carol does everything perfectly, she is a 'good-grade, book-reading, strait-laced kind of girl.'

I don't know much about how things are or how they should be done. I imagine that the '*goings on*' at our house are going on about the same in the rest of the world. Families in the 1950s had a whole lot less of everything. My daddy is betwixt and between jobs when he takes a job working at his brother-in-law's Gulf Oil station. Even though Daddy has no steady work; I think he is just going through hard times. That time gets even worse when he is seriously burned in an explosion at my uncle Ted Pheneger's gas station, Ted's Gulf Service.

Golf Oil remains a major global oil company until 1901 until March 15, 1985.

Ted's Gulf Service

620 East Main Street
Van Wert, Ohio

BOILER BLAST INJURES 2 TODAY
EXPLOSION, FIRE DAMAGES

Gordon McMillen, 34, Employee,
Hospitalized for Severe Burns.

Two persons were injured, one severely, and heavy property damage resulted in an explosion and fire shortly before 10a.m. today at Ted's Gulf Service Station at the southwest corner of Main and Race Streets, operated by Ted B. Pheneger.

In Van Wert County Hospital is Gordon McMillen, 34, of 654 North Walnut Street. Station attendant McMillen, according to the attending physician, has mostly first and some third-degree scald burns over about one-third of his body, a puncture laceration in the small of his back and a laceration to the palm of his left hand. His condition is considered satisfactory. Owner Phenegar is suffering from shock but is not hospitalized.

An investigation as to the cause of the explosion of the boiler of the coal heating system is under way by Fire Chief Paul Conn. No estimate of the damage to the building has been set.

Pheneger told firemen that he had walked from the office into the lubrication room when the blast occurred. McMillen was seated beside the heating unit and was waxing an automobile owned by Jacob Owens.

Steam from the boiler was so dense that he was unable to find McMillen, who was stunned and lying on the floor, Pheneger stated. The steel door of the stove was hurled across the room and hot coals that fell onto the floor probably ignited the grease and oil. The blaze was quickly extinguished without much interior damage.

The terrific blast wrecked the west wall of the building which is constructed of brick and tile. The wall is cracked in large sections and although badly bulged, it did not collapse. Oddly enough, the south wall, next to the boiler, is seemingly undamaged.

McMillen, who was hit by steam and scalding water, is believed to have been struck by parts hurled from the heating system, which is wrecked. He is taken to the hospital by Pheneger. The service station is owned by Calvin Neeley of Lima. *(Van Wert Times Bulletin – March 8, 1950)*

~VAN WERT COUNTY HOSPITAL IN 1950~

Daddy hears the blast but he has no time to react. His heart is hammering as he is knocked down by the explosion. He immediately falls unconscious on the floor. As it turns out the steam boiler hot water heat system has an over pressure valve that failed.

He has 2nd and 3rd degree burns over 80% of his body. After the hospitalization he lies in the downstairs bedroom, unable to feed or take care of himself, his legs hanging in traction, mostly drinking soup. He is covered with gauze, like a mummy. We do have basic necessities and our family is trapped in electric bills with little money for food and for coal, in the cold spring months.

Pink slips for unpaid bills pile up for about three months, until he can work again. Even then, no relief is in sight because he doesn't have any job prospects. The post office is sure to deliver every bill to our post box, even in all kinds of weather.

Ted Pheneger is married to my mother's sister. Her other sister is married to a local attorney. Pheneger has no insurance to cover the hospital bills and my dad wants his attorney brother-in-law to sue their other brother-in-law, Ted, for medical damages coming from this accident. But the perplexed attorney doesn't want to involve himself between his two brothers-in-laws, so we take on this loss with no insurance and very little compensation.

~

We usually play in the streets but sometimes we play on the playground behind the school. One day I go to the school playground alone, when the school is closed. I am twisting the swing around and winding the chains on the swings. I let the chains loose to twirl. I am genuinely happy there alone; I want this moment to freeze for-ever, but minutes later that all changes. A family lives behind the

46

school with a lot of tough kids. One by one they come onto to the playground. They begin by asking what I am doing there. An older punk boy casually asks me, "*Just out of curiosity, do you have any other clothes?*" He asks because I wear the same few dresses to school. I don't know the answer–if I have any other clothes I don't know where they are. I don't know which cardboard box they might be in or even where to look for them. I think, *EEK!*, because I am afraid of big boys. He corners me in the entryway of the school, taunting me and not allowing me to leave. I am a child just a little over 3 feet tall with no money. I'm not very fierce either, so what could he want with me? I need a straight-thinkin' adult, but there is none. I tell him to '*go away*' but I could not have been more afraid of the devil himself! As soon as he leaves and this scare is over, I take a long breath and run home, '*like a little tornado,*' with my braids flying in the wind.

I have a better time in the second grade at school because Mrs. Jenkins is very nice and she has been helpful. At times school has even been interesting and I am not so afraid. I am finally catching up in reading and I'm doing the second-grade level work.

As scared as I am at school there is even scarier stuff happening at home. Mommy is pregnant and Daddy is mad! As Mom's stomach grows, I'm remembering the twins. The last thing I want to do is to help with more babies! I am just one month into second grade when my youngest sister is born in early October, 1950. We don't have and don't need a bassinette. Mommy brings her baby home and lays her on a pillow covered with a plastic dry cleaner's bag inside a dresser drawer in her bedroom. She sleeps there for a few months. Whenever she wakes up it is time for me to "play mommy" with her. When Mommy hands the baby to me, I stiffen at first, but I pick her up and pat her when she cries. I don't want to take care of a baby, but I never tell Mom that I don't want to, because she is tired and she needs my help. Before long I take over her care whenever I can. Being the oldest girl in the family is detrimental to '*the little mother's help*er' I become. Looking for a way to cut through, I try not to make things worse by asking for things. Actually, there's no reason to ask. We are regularly told, "*There're people in Hell wanting ice water!*" which is clearly a '*NO.*' What's the use of asking, when we won't get things anyhow?

Mommy has a surgical hysterectomy very soon after the baby is born. Because she cannot lift and care for her baby, her sister, Louise, cares for our baby at her house for a few months. My aunt decides she wants to keep our baby and she tells Mom, *"You already have too many kids and not much money to care for another baby!"* Yikes! Aunt Louise actually thinks Mom will let them keep our baby forever! They really do try, but she is still *'ours!'* On the way out, Mom asks her sister, *"What does all of this have to do with the price of eggs?"* The baby is following every movement between them with her eyes. She wiggles her tiny fists out of the blanket and Mom pulls her closer and puts her lips to her child's face.

They lavish so much attention and care on the baby that when Mom is well, she wants to stay with them! When we finally get our baby back, she doesn't remember us! Mom's feelings are hurt, but that soon changes and the infant is happy to be with us again. Mom feels *'dithery'* about all of this! This means she is nervous and unable to think straight. Mom loves kids, but she has not the energy nor the drive to succeed with five. This is a scary time for a seven-year-old because I take on Mommy's painful life without her invitation or her permission. Oh, how I hate feeling so scared!! As a little dreamer I recognize them as more normal.

I am just beginning to understand some of this and obviously I need a lot of help, but I take this very seriously. It is exhausting for me to feel distress this way when I am too young to do anything about it. I believe Mommy has too many problems and I think I am helping her to hold things together. This is what I came up with, as though it is some holy mission of mine. The weight of this falls on me, like a blow! Delusions like this need a firm hand to discourage them, and there isn't one around. I don't bother her with any of my problems. I can't describe this childhood stress beyond being *"so tired."* I dare to dream that my life will be different when I grow up.

In the 1950s the homeless and less fortunate are called 'Tramps' or 'Hobos.' They ride the country on trains, live in boxcars and travel in small towns via alleys. Tramps are nomads who travel far and near with hobo sacks. They migrate like geese to go North in the spring and go South in the fall. They must have a way of finding our house, and others who feed them, approaching from the back alley, unclean and in rumpled clothes. My mom, full of kindness, will always feed the tramps. She fries an egg sandwich and makes them a cup of tea that they will eat outside, on the back steps, but only if Oug isn't around. When finished they will walk off down the alley behind our house.

But this isn't the end of it at home, because if Oug finds out, they argue about the food money and her disobeying him. She is caught in the act and all hell breaks loose! Oug wheels into the kitchen when he finds out what she has done, and arguments follow. Holding a cigarette between his thumb and forefinger, the way he does when he wants to make a point, he makes it into a big whoop-de-do beginning with, "*I swear, don't that beat all?*

He is hollering now, "*Are you trying to tell me what you will do?*" He goes on, as cold as steel, "*I will decide who gets fed with MY money!*" He looks hard into her face - she has disobeyed and insulted him. "*I know you will!*" she meekly replies.

There isn't any sweetness left between my parents, but there aren't many fights either; just not much intimacy in their voices. He cuts under whatever she says. She never raises her voice or says cuss words. I am noticing a coldness or maybe even disgust with each other, but divorce has not been spoken in our house. In the 1950s, divorce is a four-letter word that will only be spoken in a whisper. Divorce seems like another world away and as sinful as "Rock and Roll!" It's something that other people do. Mommy believes, "*If you say it, even once, you let it in!*"

As a younger child I think of him as infallible, but I'm beginning to see him differently now. It seems that everything gets messed up and our lives get tougher after the move to Ohio! Another child coupled with his unemployment and the never-ending criticism of her family turns him into an angry man. His nerves are shot and the smallest thing sets him off, like a raging bull. Life is so hard right here that it bites right into Oug. All kinds of messes are going on in our family and Mom wonders how things went so wrong! In less than a calendar year; we have moved from Tennessee; he has faced months of unemployment, he has the accident, we have the new baby, Mom's surgery and we have no health insurance. The tragedy is that whatever life my parents are looking for in Ohio, they never find it!

* * *

The Social Security Act was enacted in 1935. The act, which was amended in 1939, established a number of programs designed to provide aid to various segments of the population. Unemployment compensation and AFDC (originally Aid to Dependent Children) are two of the programs that still exist today. www.welfareinfo.org/history

* * *

Though we could have qualified for some assistance, they choose not to accept any Government welfare because doing so is socially unacceptable in these years.

She won't allow herself to consider changing anything because she '*said some vows to him*' She plans to love, honor and obey that commitment.

There is no way she will change that now! Life in these years is quite traditional. Mom is a product of her times. A woman's role is primarily to support her husband and children in her home. Mothers spend most of the afternoon cooking dinner for the family and when the father gets home, they have dinner together as a family. She makes her life as a homemaker but she isn't very active with the house work part. Some kids in the neighborhood complain about the food their mothers cook at dinner or clamor for new clothes, but not us! We eat bread and butter topped with sugar for sandwiches and bread, mayo and lettuce sandwiches, glad for that.

This commitment she has doesn't seem to interest him much. Oug never does snuggle! He, seeking his own adventures, has his own set of outside interests. If a thing interests him, he will work on it all day. His enthusiasm for his projects is never faltering. As I understand it now, my daddy never did want to have any children; therefore, he often called us "*her children.*" I only wish they had learned where each other wanted to go before getting stuck together.

~

As a child of the 1950's, I have never been inside a restaurant. There are no fast-food restaurants or franchises around Van Wert. It's safe to say, if we don't like something Mom cooks for us, she will say, "*There is always peanut butter!*" Because I do not really like peanut butter, I learn to eat a lot of other things! We usually eat at home, everyone does. When we are all home together, we sit around a small kitchen table. We don't always have meat with every meal. If there is leftover food, no matter how small the amount, we put it into a plastic butter container and tuck it away for later. Before the night is over someone eats it; no food is ever wasted.

Sometimes we eat with Mom and other times everyone fends for themselves when she isn't very interested in cooking. She doesn't dress fancy or go out with any woman friends. She seems to make do with what is there and never asks for anything more.

~

In the summer of stilts on Walnut Street, every kid in the neighborhood has a pair of wooden stilts leaning against their porch wall. Our feet don't touch the ground all summer! We jump onto the stilts and walk to each other's porch to play. The stilts are made from 2x4's, with a wood step for our feet. We make them ourselves. The screen door slams, as I pick up my stilts and walk down to Carol's house. I stand in her yard and call out, "*What do you want to do? Stilts? Jacks? Sticks?*"

She doesn't care and wants me to decide. She walks outside, letting the screen door slam, as we all do. We only have to decide between playing jacks or sticks, or her personal favorite, which is naming movie stars by the movies they have starred in. I don't know anything about movie stars, so I choose jacks again! We walk with our stilts heading north down Walnut Street to see what Nancy is doing. She gets her stilts out and we all three walk back to Carol's house. On rainy days we play on the front porches.

My friend Carol's mother works on the night shift at a factory in Fort Wayne. We take care of Carol evenings while her mother works. Some Mommies, like Carol's mom, 'Ruthie Bell,' have jobs, but my mom wants to be home with her kids.

In the bedroom known as the 'little room,' the plaster is hanging down from the slanted ceiling overhead because of a house fire seventeen years before we came. The plaster overhead has been punched out for years. At night we can often hear the scratching noises of the tiny feet of mice that live in the walls and ceiling. One night we are sleeping in the little room when we hear mice in the walls. It sounds like twenty or more mice all running and clawing around between the lathe, which is exposed by the broken plaster. I know that there are even more mice living in our walls due to the dark and drizzly winter weather. I taunt her by telling her about the mice until she cries and wants to go home. She can't go home alone. She has to stay, but Mommy promises Carol that she will see what is in there and set some mouse traps. But we never do see '*hide nor hair*' of that.

~

My sisters and I share the upstairs hall room. I'm cramped in the same double bed with my younger sisters for all the years that we live together. But it doesn't stop there, two of us sleep in the same nightgown! Mommy's Aunt Helen Blank is a much larger woman than our mom. She sometimes brings bags of clothes for Mom to wear. In one of the bags, we find a HUGE flannel nightgown that is soon to be our favorite sleepwear. Snuggling and rolling together we both get into the same BIG nightgown. Our baby sister is zipped into a heavy fleece sleeper that covers her feet.

When Carol isn't there, my sister and I share the hall room. Two little girls are huddled in the dark and the baby is in a crib beside us. My sister and I sleep together in the same nightgown for several years. Every chance we get we bring the baby into our bed. She is never still! She sinks down into the pillow and looks up at us with her big blue eyes, or arches back toward the headboard as she squirms and fusses. She sucks her thumb while rubbing her nose with the blanket to fall asleep. We put her into the middle so she will not fall out.

From the git-go, we scare her with fairy tale stories and monsters like *big bears and camels.* These monsters live in the stairway and under the bed! Other times there is a scary face in the window! Anything to build a story that causes her to scramble back into the quilt in fear! Before we go to sleep, we all giggle and we tickle her and drift off to sleep. She rolls into the mattress on my side and I have to push her over. Warmth and togetherness!

~

As a kid I respect that my dad is a great hunter of varmints like rabbits and squirrels, but I despise hunting animals for food. 'The Bug' and I have to go along with him to help him 'scare' up the rabbits and pheasants. We spread out and walk fifteen to twenty feet apart in a field. As we step through the brush, he readies his gun for any varmints that we bring up. I hate the sound of the gun and I really hope that no animal will jump and run to be stopped by his bullet. He never minds eating things that I can't even watch him kill and skin. Pheasants, squirrels and rabbits are the main kinds of meat that we have for several years.

~

Oug and everyone else is reading Norman Vincent Peale's *"Power of Positive Thinking."* The simple message is to have faith in God and faith in yourself so you can change your life. This book is on the best-seller list for an incredible 186 weeks and is known to have changed many lives. He wants Mom to read it, but she isn't interested.

~

Daddy says that we all have to do a '*little of this and that*' to keep things going. Painting barns in the summer is one of those '*this and that*' things. Mommy and Daddy take 'The Ole Bug' along when they leave early in the morning. They're going to spray paint a barn in another town. He is 10 years old, so I think he doesn't mind going to work with Mommy and Daddy all day. But I notice that the Bug's face shows no sign of pleasure. Maybe he does mind, but he doesn't say it! He has to go along to get along–we all do! At the same time, I am eight years old and I am supposed to stay in the house all day and watch toddlers and babies. The twins are almost five and not yet school kids. "Wagtail' is only a one-year-old. I am '*like*' a babysitter, but not a real babysitter because I am eight years old. It's a beautiful day but I am not allowed to send them outside because Daddy says that neighbors can't know we are home with no Mommy and Daddy watching, so we have to stay inside all day.

I try to do this like Mom. I am pinning diapers, handling splinters and fixing food. I try holding some authority over the three younger children. I try keeping them quiet and out of my way. I can do this with clenched teeth and hard looks! These kids want me to fix break-fast; they still think I am a babysitter or a mom but I don't know how to cook! I try, because I am the only one watching them. I pour cold cereal and they are happy. I wipe their faces; it tickles and we all laugh. I tell them to get dressed but "Wagtail' doesn't know how, so I have to dress her. The twins are not babies, so I am not going to help them! They want me to help them and I get mad and my hands go into fists and I growl. Stevie is only five, but he knows I am big-ger and I can punch him if I want to, so he gets dressed. They won't listen to me so I scream at him once more and he scoots back in tears, I know he is scared. I say sorry, but I don't mean it. I'm mad, but not sorry.

Carol comes over and she wants to play, but she only wants to play with me, and not them. She never wants to play with babies and she never has to, because she is the only kid at her house. When her momma is gone, her grandma is always there watching. I am tired of babies! I don't want to play with them and I don't want to change baby diapers. Carol and I are pushing the porch swing back and forth with our toes. Before long she won't play with me because of the babies and I get even madder when she leaves to go to play at Nancy's house.

I get them all down for a nap and they look peaceful. The house is hot and I don't want to wake them so I lay on the floor with my eyes closed, but I can't sleep. I walk back into the living room and sit alone. I miss Mommy so much that it makes my tummy feel weird and I lose my fight against tears. I keep my tears secret, so the little kids won't see. When they wake up, I go onto the porch with them and put 'Wagtail' in to her Taylor Tot walker. A bright spot is when I can curl up on the swing with my beloved *Dick and Jane* early reader. I read to the twins as we play school and I am their pretend teacher. I wind up the chains of the porch swing until it creaks and it moves into a slow twirl. Before long, 'Susita' gets a splinter from the floor. She cries, so I lift her shirt to wipe her nose. I don't know how to get splinters out, so I can't help. I put a band aid on her and she is happy now.

Stevie says, *"I'm hungry"* and I am, too. They want macaroni with cheese but I don't know macaroni cooking and I don't know hamburgers either. What should I do? I call out in frustration for *"Mommy!"* but no one comes. I am getting mad because Mommy is taking too long. I make peanut butter and jelly on white bread. They eat that and smile. They make chomp, chomp sounds, because they think it's good, but I don't like peanut butter so I am still hungry.

After a while my heart starts rolling out of my chest and I can't put it back again. What can I do? I wait some more and I worry some more. I get so scared that I start to cry because it's dark outside. I turn on some lights. I am tired and sad and I cry even more. I think Mommy and Daddy should come home. Soon we are all crying! I don't want so much crying, so I wipe away their tears... and my own. Through wet lashes, I am still seeing out. I have a plan: I tell the kids that "nighttime is the same as day, but just not as bright" and with that we are all happy for a little while. We have a cozy snuggle and wait some more. But I'm a 'scaredy cat'! I worry because Mommy should be here by now! I know that we can't be home at dark time with no Mommy or Daddy. But I can't tell anyone that we are there at home alone, because Daddy said not to tell anyone!

When they come back, I say, "*You were gone too long, I'm scared and I'm tired! Why did you stay away so long?*" Mommy is covered with red barn paint and she looks not at all like herself, but she gives a hug and says she is so sorry. 'Bug Boy' is covered with paint, too, and he looks a lot more tired than me! Daddy has a temper and I can see the veins of his neck rising up and his eyebrows going down. He makes me feel dizzy like I want to grab onto something and hang on! I have done what he says I have to do; I have taken care of kids all day long, like he wants. I don't know what I do that makes him so mad. I tiptoe away, but not soon enough. He is staring straight at me saying, "Ye *gods, Kid, you are a part of this family, you have to help*"! My eyes are pointing at the floor now and I know he means I have to help even if I am eight and I don't know how! He looks down into my face with big eyes and his smoke-stained teeth. "*Haul your ass on up to bed!*" he shouts. His words pierce me like a thunderstorm. I think he knows that he is scaring me. Maybe that is what he wants!

~

I begin learning to ride a bike, when my dad says he will make one for me. Other neighbor kids have bikes that come already built! I am keenly aware of his hard-working hands, but I didn't know that he knows how to build bicycles! He is handy about fixing and making things, but "*Build a bicycle?*" I never think it will be possible. As soon as I learn to ride, my dad starts making my bike. We start out with an old 26" frame and a few rusty spare bike parts that he gets from the junkyard. The frame is a skeleton with no handlebars or chain or tires and with no seat. He soaks the parts in a lacquer thinner to destroy the rust and he strips off the old paint. I notice his short blunt fingernails have dirt and oil beneath each one, as he begins. He lets me choose the color from a few cans of paint he has around. I chose a bright yellow and a cobalt blue lacquer that is left over from his airplane fuselage. He sprays paint on the frame with several coats of the bright yellow and adds cobalt blue stripes. He proceeds to spray paint the bicycle upside down on our kitchen table. It's on the kitchen table for a few days while the paint dries. After that, he goes to the Western Auto store and gets 2 new tires with tubes and '*she*' is good as new.

Voila! I have a bike that weighs about fifty pounds like every bike in the neighborhood. I have only one speed with no gears. There are no chain guards, so I wear several rubber bands on my pant legs to keep my pants out of the chain. These heavy bikes are slow! I keep on trying, using fierce concentration as I pedal. He's shaking a cigarette out of the pack and pointing it toward me as he watches. He gives me a push and stands back to watch as I veer off with a scream and a crash. I pedal hard and fast to stay upright, but I haven't learned how to stop. I balance my feet on the pedals and with another push from behind, I am off again! He leans against the porch wall, watching with pride as I ride off again. He throws up his hands, says *"That's how you learn!"* as he goes back into the house. I ride off to points unknown.

I am 9 years old and have my own 'wheels' when the movie *"Jack and the Bean Stalk"* is released to theaters. I feel grown up riding my bike up to the Schines Movie Theatre to see my first movie. Sink's grocery is a small family-owned grocery store on the corner of Market and Third Street. The store is the size of a room in a house. They have meat, bread, milk, sugar, flour and candy. It's a safe bet that if we have a few pennies of our own, we will walk or bike there for penny candy. Later on, Daddy uses the same blue lacquer and yellow paint for the kitchen walls. Blue on the lower half, just below the yellow stripes. This looks exactly like the airplane and my bicycle!

~

We are the remnants of World War II. We are a generation playing like we are *'on the run'* with games of *'Nazi's'* and *'Japs'* and even occasional aliens from other planets. We spend summer days outside. We get an adrenaline rush by fighting common enemies. We imagine how we can survive them and how we will escape. We run through cornfields, or set booby traps and bunkers in the back yards on Walnut Street. We hide behind trees and punch each other to keep from giggling so we can scare off a passing *"imagined Jap"* friend. All of this is make-believe; very real to us! Our days are often spent climbing trees, digging underground houses, riding bikes, reading books, racing sleds downhill and playing Hide and Seek in the street.

About three years into living in Ohio, I am learning some things and flying by my seat many other times. I join the Brownie Scouts. After that, I become a Girl Scout when I 'fly up' from Brownies after finishing the 4th grade. Some of my favorite memories come from the years that I am a member of the Girl Scouts. Our leader, Mrs. Graydon Gribler, shows us how to do things the Girl Scout way. I will do anything to get another patch on my uniform. The troop meets every

week at the United Methodist Church. I am excited on October 3, 1953, because my name is in the Van Wert *Times Bulletin* article:
Girl Scouts Have Mothers As Guests
Girl Scout Troop Number 94 holds an
investiture service for new members, and
their mothers are guests.
Susan Greenawald, Grace Phenegar, *(my
cousin)*, Carol Ginzel, *(my best friend)*,
Kathleen McMillen, *(me)*, Kathleen Bricker,
Sharon Anderson, Donna Shomeok, Linda
Witten and Beverly Van Atta are the new
scouts.

The 1950's are different times; times where people are safe in their homes and neighborhoods. No one ever locks the door on North Walnut Street; in fact, we don't own a key for our door. Carol and I walk about 14 blocks in the dark on Wednesday nights for the scout meetings No one ever worries about us, because this is safe enough to do in those days. Girl Scout Day Camp is always fun and full of adventures at Houston's woods, South of Van Wert. We begin the week by making 'sit-upons,' which are seats for us to sit on the ground. They are made with two square pieces of oilcloth laced together with yarn and filled with newspaper. Once we get these made, we use them all week for sitting on while singing, learning knots, doing crafts and eating. I love being in the woods, walking down trails through swamps and pine flats and getting to know the other campers. We learn how to make safe cooking fires, roasting hotdogs and s'mores over a campfire. We play games like Tag and Kick Ball and we learn songs such as "*O' My Darlin', Clementine!*" and this song:
"*Do your ears hang low?*
Do they wobble to and frow?
Can you tie them in a knot?
Can you tie them in a bow?
Can you throw 'em o're your shoulder
Like a continental soldier?
Do your ears hang low?"
One morning I am coloring in my little clown-coloring book with a few crayons that I keep in the kitchen drawer, when the front screen door flies open and Oug comes in with some guy. No one ever

comes to visit us, so I stand staring at him, waiting to see who he is. *"Hey, Daddy, who is he?"* I ask. He ignores my question, so I ask again and again until he shushes me. Finally, I figure out that he is a guy that my dad has known since their high school days, about fifteen years ago. They both grew up on Walnut Street back when Oug was a kid, living in this house.

For some strange reason, I don't know why, they call each other the same name, "MOOSE FACE!" One moose face is my dad and the other guy is his high school buddy. I find out that he lives down the block with his mother. My daddy moves a pile of sheets and blankets from the old sofa for '*Moose Face'* to sit down. With one leg folded over the other, they both light up cigarettes and begin talking about their life and times since school. I sit down in a chair nearby. I'm not likely to budge because I want to listen to what they are going to talk about. They start with telling of some of the 'Tomfoolery' they were into at Van Wert High School.

Daddy has quite a flair for storytelling. He tells him, *"After high school I built a house in Tennessee."* Smiling, he says, *"Hell, we had a new house and some farm animals, we was a-livin' pretty good down there, fur durn near fifteen years!"* Moose Face is still living on Walnut St. in the house where he grew up, so he looks more than a little bit impressed. Oug kills a little time, then he laughs a little, like he remembers more. *"Had me some land, too,"* he adds. *"I owned 100 Acres!"* He cocks his head back savoring the moment!

"Goddamned shame we left there!" Oug follows up with, *"While in Tennessee, I also built myself an airplane!"* He makes a show of watching Moose Face for a reaction. *"I flew the plane back to Ohio. I'm keepin' it out to Wetzel now."* Daddy reels him in with an offer, *"Oh Hell, I'll take you up sometime!"* Moose Face can only add, *"Oh WOW!"*

I am anxiously waiting for more, when Oug cuts his eyes over to me and blares, *"Ye Gods, kid! Go and find something to do!"* I jump back and jut my jaw out, but I do as I'm told. I am forced to wander back to the kitchen table and color again, but I lie low and wear my crayon down to a nub just keeping an ear out for all of their stories. I listen really quiet, like I'm not even there.

Daddy is a storyteller of the first order but we scatter like buckshot when he begins a story. He can be resilient, full of energy, intelligent and talented in many different ways. He loves to read and learn about 'most everything. His main focus is historical information and 'thus and so' about how things 'used to be' in the past, or mechanical information about how stuff works. When he isn't telling us all of the amazing things he knows how to do, he is telling us about some things he is planning to do next. We call these "sermons." Out of necessity we move out as quietly as we possibly can, unseen.

Let me start by telling you that listening to him tell a story is 'like milking a cow with a bad teat'. When he gears up, he can't stop himself, even if he wants to, but he doesn't want to stop because he loves an audience, even with unwilling listeners. Whether we like to know or not, he tries to teach us things that might be good to know, but in so much detail that they do not hold our interest. He gives us a thousand details. I learn a few, but most of them I dismiss or never hear at all. My thoughts go willy-nilly to wondering how he can have that much to say about so many things! He is inhaling deeply, blowing smoke out of his nose, like a bull! I can sense an important piece of his story is coming.

He tells us things about 'this, that and the other.' By the time he finishes we aren't sure whether to cry in relief, or hide in fear that there might be more. When one of us is getting a sermon, the others will slip out the back door, gone, 'like water down the drain!' I press my lips tightly together, not speaking any words that will bring me into his focus! His underlying aim is to amaze all of us with all of this information! He tells us, "Never tell a lie, if the truth serves you better!" He's claiming this to be a life lesson he has learned from his grandma. I call that a foul!

Some neighbors gave us a complete set of Harvard Classic books and a two-shelf glass front bookcase. Mom praises us, while Oug brags up himself! His head is packed with all kinds of learning. He lectures us to read these books, 'cause "They are classics." He says, "You can't 'make up' an empty mind! Stock it with valuable information, your mind is your treasure." In my memory none of these books have ever been opened and read.

~

I am about eight or nine years old when Oug takes The Bug and me to the 5-span bridge at nearby Oak Wood, Ohio. He wants to teach us how to shoot a 22-caliber rifle and also to aim and fire his Hi-standard pistol while shooting beer bottles off a fence post. He wants me to plug a bullet into a bottle, can or light bulb as it floats in the river. I don't want to do it and I don't know how to hold it so I hold on with both hands. My throat tightens. I am afraid of the loud sounds and the gun banging against my shoulder so hard that the 'kick' almost knocks me down. I am just over 50 pounds and 4 feet tall. I don't care to learn anything about shooting guns. He keeps me going saying, *"What the HELL is wrong, kid?"* He is determined that I will learn. He says we will be here all day until we get this! I never do learn much about shooting his guns. Still today, I am twitchy around guns.

~

At the North end of Walnut Street is the Water Works Park. The reservoir is a public water supply for the town of Van Wert. The city street crews keep bins there. Hazardous wastes are stored in oil drums, bottles marked POISON. Big cement drain tiles are stored there. We like to roll around and hide inside the drain tiles. We do this regularly until a school mate is crushed to death between the tiles. After that we quit playing with the cement drain tiles, limiting ourselves to the sand bins and limestone gravel piles.

In the warm breezy spring Oug likes to make kites. There's nothing quite like flying a kite outdoors on a sunny, breezy day. What's even better is flying a homemade kite! The materials and tools for making these kites are very easy to find around our house, like wrapping paper from the butcher shop. Making a simple diamond kite is easy, but he likes to make box kites from balsa wood and tissue paper. We all learn how to build kites. It's motivating to see the end result floating about in the sky! We fly these homemade box kites each spring at the Water Works Park.

There is a fishing Derby at the park in the summer. We are excited because we usually can't get inside the high chain-link fence. My brother and I dig up some earthworms for fishing bait. But we don't have cane poles. Without a pole we go to the fishing derby anyhow. I stare at the water and I see about 100 minnows swimming there, just wishing we could fish. Before long we find out that the cane poles are being provided. There are prizes, but we don't win! Winters find us playing in snow and sledding on the hill at that same park.

~

In the deep cold of Ohio winters, the old coal furnace at our house isn't adequate to heat the whole house when the cold winds blow. On winter nights, we cover up in bed with huge stacks of old blankets and handmade quilts piled high. We burrow deep into the blankets. Even though we are cozy and warm in bed, getting up on the winter mornings is hard. We stay under the covers until Mom finally comes upstairs, stumbling through clothes, shoes and debris strewn on our bedroom floor, to try dragging us out of bed for school.

"*You have to get up now!*" she wails. Finally, I give up dawdling, sleepy and grouchy; I grumble and mope as I slowly make my way down the stairs. In the coldest days of the winter, we sleep on the floors downstairs and we live in three first floor rooms because these rooms are the only place we have heat. It's coming from the kitchen stove. I'm warm as toast when I hear Mom banging around in the kitchen. She is making oatmeal for breakfast.

We call rolled oats '*Oaties.*' I confess, I still do! Sometimes on cold mornings I will eat 'Oaties' while sitting on the floor with our bowls on the oven door. Other times I'm eating a bowl of cold cereal or I sit in my bed eating dry cereal. The single-pane thin glass windows have thick ice and frost that even forms on the inside of the panes. Not enough heat rises to melt the snow on the sparsely insulated roof and the frozen air creates great long icicles from above. We open our bedroom window and snap off for an icicle for an edible icy treat!

The kitchen pipes often freeze under the sink leaving us without any running water for several days. We have a wood cooking stove in the kitchen and a furnace in the basement that burns hard coal. The fire in the furnace goes out at night because we don't have a stoker. There is no insulation in the walls of our house. That old coal furnace has a hell of a time when the cold winds blow. Mommy will put some coal in the furnace before waking us. I wonder now, how many tons of coal she might have shoveled into the furnace! Even with that, I'm still shivering when she calls us for breakfast.

The living room register is above the furnace and is the warmest place in the house. I stand over that register with my knees pulled up to my chest and my nightgown is billowing over my feet and legs. This gives me a tent of warmth while I pull my dress over my head to finish getting dressed. Above the dining room ceiling is another register in the upstairs ceiling. This is made to bring heat into the bedrooms upstairs. The idea is for the heat to rise from the basement up to the second floor, but the upstairs is often so cold that drinking water will freeze to solid ice overnight in the glass at our bedside.

Things get even worse when the first thunder- storms of spring come and the storms evolve into a ceaseless rain. The warmer temperatures result in a snow melt that floods the basement. During the early spring the frozen land prevents melting snow or rainfall from dripping trees to seep into the sodden ground. The large amount of runoff in a short period of time causes our old basement to flood. As the hours pass, the dank water deepens as it seeps through the walls and window wells to completely fill the basement with water up to ground level. After that, the furnace is under water and can't be used at all and we have no heat. Is this what people call the 'good ole days?' How often does that happen? EVERY Spring!

In these pre-television years, we entertain ourselves with whatever is around. We girls play jacks and jump rope or pick-up sticks, while the boys play marbles games of 'Yanks Against Japs.' We make bows from tree branches for archery and sharpen sticks with pen knives, to make spears for games of hunting. This is an era of very casual lawn maintenance. Kids play on lawns and maintaining grass is not a high priority. In fact, crabgrass and dandelions are expected. I lie in the grass looking up at bits of blue sky. In summer, we dig huge cave holes in the back yard, covering them with boards and dirt and grass on top. We leave a small opening to go in and out. The girl's cave is larger around but not as deep as the smaller boy's cave. The caves are a cool place to hang out in the summer.

Most nights after supper the boys and I go on the 'junk route', this means we go up and down the alleys 'trash picking,' looking for the good stuff that people are throwing out or anything we can use in the tree houses or caves. We can find free things on the junk route like old rugs for mats in the caves. We look for broken furniture that we can fix and sell, bald tires we can use for a tree swing, bottles to return to the store for deposits, copper tubing we can sell for cash. The Ole' Bug finds a sewing machine that he refurbishes and sells to a neighbor. The quality of this junk, and the thrill of the hunt, gives us a breath-taking adrenalin rush; this is like garage sales today, except our treasures are free!

During the days we play games of soldiers, cowboys and Indians, making forts. Boys and girls both love softball. We make softball fields in a vacant lot of stubble with rubber floor mats for neighborhood games back in "the field". After dinner we go out on the front porch; this is the social center of the neighborhood. Kids all gather on front porches from one house to the next. We are happiest playing a neighborhood-wide game of Kick the Can in the streets or Hide and

Seek after dark. I'm '*it*' with my head against a tree, counting to 50 while they are hiding. I trot off in the dark to try finding everyone. The evening ends in "*All-y, All-y In Free.*" We play with dominoes and Lincoln Logs in the house. We have dominos but we never RE-ALLY play a game, we just stand them up on end for the crash!

After the stilts and the cave crazes, my brothers build a tree house in the buckeye tree in our yard. The sign says "*Boys Only*". I go up there twice, knowing that the second time I am risking being removed by force, which can be dangerous from the limbs of a tree. No problem! Carol and Nancy and I decide to take matters into our own hands and build a girl's tree house in the box elder tree, near our back door. We start with a wood pallet so we can 'spy' on the boys. We want to see everything that they have and to know all that they might do. We nail a rug onto our tree house pallet floor. I find a chair seat and back but without legs. We can use that in our tree house for a chair. Carol brings a vase. I planted a start of a Forsythia bush the year before and I am amazed when it actually grows into a huge bush. We cut some real flowers from my Forsythia bush for the vase. We spend more time fixing and changing our tree house than we spend '*living*' up there. We place a "*Keep Out*" sign for any friends who are our enemies on that day! Of course, we always have a "*No Boys Allowed*" sign. Our imaginations are endless. In our secret club-houses we play cards like "Old Maid" and "Authors "and "Checkers" and we love our tiny magnetic dogs. Playing school, church or house begins with, "*Let's say I am the mom and you are the kid!*" or "*Let's have lunch up here today!*"

Carol's grandma makes us sandwiches of fried bologna on Wonder Bread. Other times we read comic books up there or in the grass under a tree, titled "Jug Head and Veronica", "Alfred E Newman" or "Dagwood and Blondie."

~

My parents don't always flat-out fight; he loves to taunt her! Like fabric moving through a sewing machine, I can feel her dreams slipping away. Her killer despair is too often a deep unnerving silence that occupies our house. It weighs so heavy that I feel like I can't sit at home anymore.

She stands at the south window of the kitchen, with her back turned. She is running some water to wash our breakfast dishes. He is sitting at the table doing 'diddly squat,' thinking and flipping the top of his Zippo lighter open and closed. He finally lights his cigarette and has no more than finished his smoke when he flips ashes into his pant cuff and asks her, *"How about a cup of coffee, Barbara?"*

She always gives in to him! I don't understand, but who am I to sit in judgement of her? Things are changed in the world now, but it is a man's world back then. Daddies do as they please and Mommies do as they are told! Daddy is oppressive and has little respect for a woman's intellect. He decides how he wants things to be. She drops everything and without looking at him, she prepares a cup of instant coffee that she sits in front of him. She gets the milk out of the ice box without a word. He comes back with, *"Barbara, do you suppose you could fry a couple of eggs for me?"* Fixing to do it, she looks straight into his eyes with disgust.

He baits her, with a twinkle in his eye and tells me, *"A man could starve to death in this house!* She obediently gets out the cast iron skillet and slams it onto the stove top. She turns the gas flame up on high to fry his eggs and serves the eggs to him, without saying a word. Her silence is so profound that without a question, I know that she wants to dump the eggs on his head. She goes into the bathroom and closes the door, and he asks, *"What's wrong with her?"* As if he doesn't already know!

I run outside before it is too late, because I don't want to hear something that I can't unhear. He will never allow any woman to stand up for her rights. He has that idea down pat! I'm usually ill at ease around him! I make 'a thousand dreams' that I will grow up strong, unyielding and self-sufficient. I spend some time hoping my life will be different!

~

We are taught everything by the school of hard knocks! When school is out and we're home all day, we usually play outside, unless it's raining. Oug often says, *"Those who cannot hear, can sometimes feel!"* An example of this: In the late morning on a rainy summer day my siblings and I are all at home, and have a few friends playing Monopoly in the living room. Bug can usually win because he buys up everything he lands on; I only buy a few places because I hold onto my money. We know how to be quiet in the house – a habit we develop in trying not to irritate Oug. If he is sleeping, we creep around because he wants it that way. We play quietly, until we forget! Oug is sleeping upstairs as *'naked as a jay!'* We're interrupted by him coming downstairs like a 'wild man!' He comes down to the living room without a stitch of clothes on! He arrives lickety-split and, to our disbelief, offers to "*kick our hind-ends clear up between our shoulders!*" His '*willy*' is 'a-hanging' in his total nakedness when he swiftly kicks each of us in the butt, along with a couple of neighbor kids. Letting out a squawk, he yowls, "*HUSH UP, I am trying to sleep upstairs!*" With that he turns his bare butt and traipses back up the stairs leaving us, and our friends, stunned with amazement at what we have just seen! Oug is a flawed and complicated guy. I know a little about a lot of things before I am even a teen! I just don't know how to sum him up!

These are days before any credit cards, in fact, very few people in Van Wert, Ohio have checking accounts. People pay bills in cash and in person. Oug cashes his pay check at the bank and drives to the drug store to pay utility bills, then to the grocery store to pay for food we have put "on account" and on to the doctor or dentist office to pay any bills that we have there. We put cash under the milk jugs to pay the Globe Dairy milk delivery man.

~

It is unusual for me to have friends spend the night at our house, but Carol comes often, as she stays with us when her mother works at night. Her house is my house and vice versa. Our house is a mess and has been for several years. Yet, I have not really noticed that until I begin seeing neighbor's homes that seem more normal. I learn that my home life is not like the neighbor kids. I never have school friends in, and I usually don't let anyone outside of the immediate neighbor kids come in.

~

I first learned about a television in my weekly reader. I read that it is like a radio, except it lets you see the people who are singing and talking. By 1950, 4.4 million U.S. families have a TV in their home. The Golden Age of Television is marked by family-friendly shows like *I Love Lucy, Leave it to Beaver,* and westerns like *Gunsmoke.* After a while we actually see a real TV with a 7" black and white picture in a shop window. So exciting!

~

We either make or grow most things we need. In the summer we eat vegetables from the garden. In more recent times gardening has become more of a hobby, but in the 1950s the back-yard garden is a necessity and a center of everyday life. No salad is fresher than the one we pick minutes before a meal. I scavenge the often-untended garden for onions, lettuce and potatoes. Although in recent times gardening has become more of a hobby, I learn to plant, weed and care for a garden as a necessity. Summer gardens bring fall harvest, and late August starts the canning season. I learn to can food with Mom by the boiling water method, called cold packing. I can do canning and cold packing right along with Mom. The ingredients are prepared and loaded into jars with special lids that allow steam to escape. The jars heat to boil for about 30 minutes and as they cool, the food contracts and the lid creates an airtight seal that preserves the food for up to one year. Sweat is dripping from our faces; pots are boiling on the stove inside of everyone's house. We also make jams and jellies, using wax over the jelly to preserve the jelly for up to twelve months.

There is no torture for a child, like canning season! As children we stay outside, unless we have to help with the canning, like I do. The heat is nearly unbearable. All homes are HOT in the summer heat, no one has air conditioning. Daddy is usually around marshalling us, or ordering us to carry in food from the garden or to bring some hamburger from the grocery.

~

I am about eight and the twins are around five. We're all at home on a typical day. Oug is in his easy chair straightening out a cigarette from the ashtray to re-light it, while the butt is smoldering between his fingers. The hand that holds his cigarette has a permanently crooked finger.

Mom is napping under the Toledo Blade peach page, on the living room sofa. I am on the floor nearby folding clothes and stacking them into a somewhat disheveled pile. I place them on the floor of the stairwell for someone else to take upstairs. In order to avoid sorting, we dump everyone's socks together into a 'sock basket,' along with all of the other mismatched socks so that everyone can fend for themselves. As certain as sunrise, there are no matched sets in the basket and we will have to wear socks that either don't match or have holes.

The ole' Bug comes in making a few 'armpit farts' to annoy me. The twins are playing school under the dining room table; the baby is napping.

We have a stray, mixed breed, collie dog named Rusty. He is licking one paw and rubbing his eyes with it like a sleepy baby. He sweeps the floor with his tail. He gets up as if he remembers something, only to turn around and lie back down. Now Wagtail is sitting on the wooden back step teething on one of Rusty's dog biscuits. Later I smell dog breath and find doggie bone drools on her chin! Mommy is still napping and she doesn't notice!

Rusty is loose outside when we hear a screech of tires. Rusty howls, a terrible sound that we have never heard before. This pooch has been our family pet for about a year when this happens. Rushing to the door, we find that Rusty has been hit by a car. He hobbles into the yard with his hind leg broken. We kids gather around him. We want help or to bandage his leg, anything to help him walk again.

After a few minutes something happens that haunts me, even today! The *'ever sensitive'* Oug comes out to the front yard, just beyond the porch, carrying his hi-standard pistol. While we all look on, he takes aim and shoots our pet! A patch of blood is wetting his fur. I can't look!

I go to bed that night and with the blankets pulled over my head, I weep alone. Moments like this change who I am. This gives me ongoing nightmares for a while. We have several black cats like *El Gotto* and *Joby Daniels* but, Rusty is the only childhood dog we ever have.

~

I am eight years old when I wander up to Main Street with 'Wagtail' in the Taylor-tot, so that I can look around Murphy's Five and Dime store. I love to look at the games like Old Maid cards, Slinkys and yoyos, checking out barrettes and heart- shaped necklaces. There is a white leather diary with lock and key that I really want!

While I am uptown a storekeeper asks me, *"Does your mother know where you are?"* That stops me cold because my mother almost never knows where I am! Other times adults will ask me, *"Does your mother know you have the baby uptown?"* She usually does know if I take her with me and she's fine with it! We are allowed to do most anything. We McMillen kids continue gaining years, and presumably intelligence, without much direction. I think we are good children, mostly. We probably are a pain in the neck at times, I can imagine. My aunt once told me, "You are like *'Topsy'* from *The Story of Topsy from Uncle Tom's Cabin.* You just grew!" I suppose that's right!

~

"Your Cheatin' heart" by Hank Williams is playing inside on Carol's family's Philco table radio. We both love radio shows like *'Fibber*

McGee and Molly' and *'Burns and Allen.'* The Bug likes the Green
Hornet show. He saves a little money and he is up at Murphy's 5
and 10 Cent store buying a small pet alligator that starts out in a fish
tank. He names his alligator "*Albert Leonard*". He is the second alligator in the family. As a boy Oug had an alligator named, "*Algo*".

~

Carol and I traipse off together chatting about our favorite library
books. We are reading every day for the Brumback library summer
reading club. She loves the Bobbsey Twins series and Nancy Drew
books. My favorites are *Black Beauty* by Anna Sewell and *Heidi* by
Johanna Spyri. The Bobbsey twins' popular children's book series
is widely read in the 1950's and 1960's. The stories are about fic-
tional characters who are two sets of fraternal twins. The older pair
are named Bert and Nan, the younger, Freddie and Flossie. They are
featured in an extended series of children's books. Neighbor kids on
Walnut assume that because Bug and I are often together and might
look or act alike, that we are twins, even though we are 1½ years
apart in age. This is because we do have the younger set of fraternal
twins.

~

My dad likes to shoot his hi-standard hand gun inside the house.
When he wants to target practice, he will bring three bales of straw
into the kitchen and stack them against the back wall beside the refrigerator. He pins on a paper bullseye target.
   Glowing with determination and some anger he sets himself up
with bullets and he crouches inside the front door and shoots through
the dining room and kitchen where his bullets will land in the target.
He can't be stopped, even though Mom tries. It angers me to hear her
begging him not to shoot in the house. I am mostly annoyed because
her anxiety seems to encourage him to act out even worse. We are
all terrorized when he does this! We huddle together with Mom. She
holds all of us together. She is shaking and crying.

~

It is a warm summer afternoon in Ohio and my mother, my sisters and I are shelling peas in the shade of the walnut tree in our back
yard. The adults are sitting on a few chairs brought outside from the
kitchen. On this day my Grandma Mina Fogt, along with her husband
Asa, are visiting from Sidney, Ohio. They bring a live chicken for dinner. Until now, I have never seen a hen being killed.

Grandpa Asa wrings its neck with his bare hands. Then he throws it down on the back steps. With the down stroke of a bloody hatchet, he chops off the chicken's head. The headless chicken keeps flipping and flopping in the dirt, until it falls over dead. Grandpa dips it, feathers and all, into a pot of boiling water on the stove, followed by him ripping off the scalded feathers. He plucks out handfuls of bigger feathers and continues with a match to singe the smaller pin feathers until the skin is bumpy and shiny. When he finishes, he cuts off the feet and pulls out the guts. Grandma takes over and adds a handful of salt to boiling water and she begins cooking the bird. After all of this, my appetite is gone!

Before long Grandma Fogt comes out and announces that her now "Famous" boiled chicken with homemade noodles are ready and Grandpa Fogt carries in a watermelon for dessert. Soon after dinner, the women are cleaning up the kitchen while the men are sitting on the porch. The cleanup includes Mom, Grandma, Aunt Louise and Aunt Isobel and my girl cousins. This is where we can usually get an ear full of things that they will not otherwise tell us. We cousins plan to stay near because this is where we pick up on personal matters that are often for adult ears only! When the gathering comes to a close and the ladies finish with the clean-up work, they are sitting inside. I run upstairs to put my ear to the register in the ceiling above the dining room to hear what is being said among the women folks.

I feel lucky to have these memories of a few times when the backyard garden is the center of our family visits. That summer day as our aunts sit together downstairs, wearing sturdy shoes and nicely ironed cotton house dresses under their aprons, their well-meaning faces launch discussions about the hard questions of life. Women, in those times, usually deny who they are and what they have been through. The scars of their lives are held close and secret. Even though her sisters are curious where her marriage is taking her, my mother does not believe in exposing her inner most thoughts any more than she will expose the burns on her arm and body. It often seems like her family does not like "HIM." Mom's secrecy and denial are putting her into the greatest danger! She says, "*Small people discuss other people; average people discuss 'things,' but important people discuss ideas.*" With that said, she moves the conversation along and there are no more questions asked!

Oug leaves for a bow and arrow deer hunting weekend. He comes home with a story about the one that got away. My dad is so full of himself even when he is at home! Mom often cuts his hair, but this time, he goes to a barber for a REAL haircut. Then he puts on a tan sport coat and goes to a photography studio to get some portraits of himself. He is about thirty-seven years old when he tells Mom that he needs some pictures taken, *"because he is starting to fade!"* Her sisters can't hold back their hardy snickers when she tells them that one!

~

People around Van Wert mostly take vacation to visit relatives. Mom likes to go with the family to Sydney, Ohio to visit Mina. Sydney is about fifty miles away, but we don't often go there. Oug says, *"We've seen Mina, let's see something else!"* Otherwise, we often go to *"THE lake."* We have seen the same lake many times, too, but Oug doesn't mind seeing that again. We didn't have a cottage so we go camping at Crooked Lake Campground, near Angola, Indiana. Oug works nights at the Continental Can Company. We have a *"camping list'* so us kids get everything packed on Friday evening. We usually forget something! We usually take a pot of chili, bologna and bread. He comes home from work at midnight and away we go! Most campsites are sun without any shade. The best cite is on the point because it is in the shade, but you have to arrive early for that and once in a while we get the point space. The building with bathrooms and showers is usually clean and not too far away. The air mattresses that we use don't hold air. If Oug's air bed goes flat he takes ours and leaves us sleeping on the ground. We all sleep in the car if he will not set up the tent and he will go off somewhere, leaving us alone at the lake. If he drinks too much and we sleep all weekend in the car, he calls us the '*Arapahoe Nation."* We must be a tribe! For some reason Mom never likes to go! Who would want to miss this?

I'm raised at a time when child abuse is thought to make a kid tougher. It is not always our enemies who do us the greatest harm. Sometimes harm comes from the people who are supposed to love us. I am eight years old when he gives me a bottle of Schlitz Beer. Other dads don't give their kids beer, but Oug does. I have never been around lakes before and there isn't deep water around us in Tennessee. I don't know anything about swimming and I am afraid of the water.

Oug is drinking beer one afternoon, with a couple of guys. After he has a few drinks, he decides to teach me to swim by pouring beer on me and throwing me into deep water near the boat dock at Crooked Lake! As he throws me into the lake, he tells them that he is *"teaching her how to swim!"*

I sputter and choke in water too deep for me to walk. As I struggle, I take in water through my nose and mouth as I flop, hoping to grab a breath of air. I fight my way back to the shore jumping up for a breath, here and there, my chest heaving. While I flail my way back, my toes are oozing in mud, hair is over my face and I'm sputtering lake water. I can feel people around him staring at me. I see him on the dock, laughing with his friends. A cigarette, a near-permanent appendage, is hanging from his mouth. It bobbles there as he brags to his buddies that he has *"baptized me in beer."*

A sober man on the dock reaches down and lifts me up by both hands. When I am out of the water, he tells Oug this is a *'piss-poor'* thing to do. Oug reaches for another beer, telling his friends, *"A bird can't fly on one wing!"* He sips his next beer, lights a cigarette and tokes hard until he coughs and he throws me back in again! I only have time to rise to the surface for a breath of air before I go down again. He repeats this process several times, saying *"you're going to learn to swim"*! I am fearful over what Oug will do next. It angers me even more when he adds *"Don't get hurt either, 'cause I'm no damn nursemaid."* Meanwhile he is laughing with friends. I give him a dark look, full of blame. Though not fully aware of the tragedy of abuse, a dark idea of it begins to bloom inside of me. Reaching the dock that day seems like one of those quick miracles that separates life from death. I don't learn how to swim this way but I do learn a little more about survival. And I lost a lot of trust in him.

Later on, he says, *"Don't tell Mommy!"* I decide not to tell her about this, but when we get home, he can't resist *bragging* to her about baptizing me in beer! Hearing this, she quickly gets her dander up! When she frowns, two vertical lines slice between her brow and cut into her forehead. These lines appear and the feathers fly. She proceeds to *'tear him a new arse'*–figuratively speaking! When the feathers fly, I'm making myself scarce. There is no way I'm getting roped into a fight between these two! By this time, I know there is something *'not right'* with Oug but it takes a while longer before I begin to reckon that his *'problem'* is often about his obsession with alcohol. Women in the 1950s put up with an alcoholic husband because it's a part of a woman's lot.

~

My parents don't give allowances, even though most parents do. Daddy reminds us that if we want any money, EVERYONE has to help. Even though I notice that he never helps. He says he works outside the house, and doesn't do *"women's work."* No self-respecting man does back then! He is doing what he always has done. If we don't help, we don't get paid. Most of my siblings have a job of some sort, selling magazines, delivering papers. Sometimes Carol and I walk or ride our bikes along ditches in the country and pull pop bottles out of the dirt to cash them in at the grocery store for the 2-cent bottle deposit.

Grit is a 14-page weekly magazine, during much of the 20th century. It carries the subtitle "America's Greatest Family Newspaper." *Grit* is sold across the country by children and teenagers in small towns from the 1940s to the 1970s. www.wikipedia.org/wiki/Grit_(newspaper)

My first financial venture outside of the house is selling GRIT which is a small news booklet, but kids of any age can sell it door to door for a nickel and keep half and send in the other half. That's a pretty good gig for a kid like me!

When I am nine years old and in fourth grade, I find an ad for selling cards in the back of a comic book. I think I can do this so Mom lets me send an order. When my first box of Christmas cards comes in the mail, I run down the street stopping at every house. I take orders in the neighborhood and when my order arrives, I deliver and collect the money and I keep my ten percent profit.

Somewhere else in my Elementary School years, I go to stores downtown asking them for store sale flyers (a junk mail route) to distribute to houses. I get paid one cent for each flyer delivered. With this money I work one day and buy a piece of clothing at the Murphy's Five and Dime. I'm proud we learn to self-manage most things alone.

When we don't have outside work there are jobs at home to do for money. I notice that most of the chores we can get paid for are '*his jobs.*' Mom doesn't have any money of her own to pay us, so there goes Grandma's idea of getting us to help her. She has to do her own chores, because Oug will not let her make us work for FREE! After all, "*we aren't slaves,*" he tells her.

Oug decides how he wants the pay scale to be. His system is each chore has a price and Oug sets the wages. We can choose to do whatever we need to do to earn money. Eg: Washing dishes is 5 cents, and the family laundry pays 35 cents. Carrying ashes out of the basement for 15 cents is one of our least favorite chores! We are carrying out buckets of ashes and cinders from the furnace. We come up from the basement and carry the coal bucket across the dining room carpet to put the ashes onto the cinder stone driveway. All the while Oug is grumbling that he can't understand "*Why the hell does it take you so long!*" to finish a job. He calls it "*Letting the loose end drag*" when someone doesn't finish or follow through with the job at hand. Actually, I want to play, like any kid likes to play, but I like to earn money, too! Daddy tells us there is "*No free lunch.*"

~

The word 'love' fascinates me. I don't know what love is, we never speak the word love at our house. Because of that, I grow up wondering what the word love really means. I find that love isn't only about moonlight or fairy tales. Love is a decision, rather than a feeling. Love is real life and there are many ways to give and receive it. It turns out that everyone does it differently. Love is in our DNA, as unique as our fingerprints. Love comes in many forms, it shows up, not always in words but in the things that I do for other people. Love is in the food I cook, the clothes I wash and the things I sew. With what little we know about love in our family, I don't think I am deprived of love. I just feel strange speaking about it! Sometimes it may seem that I've done love wrong, because I can't always be who someone else needs me to be. My parents never say '*I Love You,*' because they weren't raised that way. It's a generational thing and they must have figured that we already know!

~

One day without warning, Oug comes home with a big Cadillac Eldorado automobile. We have only one car at our house and it unquestionably belongs to him. He drives a 1954 Cadillac Eldorado Convertible, yellow with tan leather seats. I will guess that if we are starving to death or needed meds, with no way to survive except for selling his car, we will all be in real trouble! We have no money for this car. Mom says, "*Mick, what is this?*"

He says, "*Well, Barbara, as you can see, it's a car!*" I look at him, feeling no sympathy! Solitude seems to be her best defense as she tries to ignore the problems around us. Their needs seem to be so great that they can't find time for us.

My parents do their share of fighting–mostly him picking on her. Seeing the insults becomes a part of our lives, it's how they speak to one another. He likes to agitate her at home.

He orders her, "*Barbara, why don't you bring me the newspaper and a cup of coffee?*" When he finishes his coffee and readies himself to go out someplace, she asks him. "*Will you be here for supper?*" I think that by now she might be used to him being "*out*" and she might know that he won't be with us at supper, but she doesn't seem to recognize his rejection. As I remember it now, sometimes he is with us for meals, but more often he is not. She endures his endless, shameless shenanigans but she can't please him.

~

Today domestic violence is any physical, sexual, verbal, or psychological abuse/violence to an intimate partner. The concept of domestic violence doesn't exist in the 1950s when doctors thought of wife beating "as therapeutic." An article in the issue of TIME dated 50 years ago - Sept. 25, 1964 - highlights a mind-boggling study that concludes couples stay in abusive relationships because their fighting can "balance out each other's mental quirks." **https://time.com/3426225/domestic-violence-therapy/**

Sometimes Mom stomps out the front door and down off the porch in a flash, even though she can't really make a dramatic exit because she has no place to go, no money, no driver's license or car! She can't pile all five of her kids into any car to leave Oug. She might even be horrified at the suggestion. I watch her grow smaller and smaller as she walks up Walnut Street toward town. In a little while Daddy gets in HIS car. He drives past her while flipping his cigarette out the window and marginalizes her even further, by avoiding even a glance of recognition as he drives past!

~

One day, I find them together and I ask, "*Are we poor?*" Barbara answered first. "*Yes, we are poor because we don't have nice furniture, an automatic washer, electric refrigerator, no phone and no TV and many of the things the neighbors are enjoying.*" Oug answers, "*No we are NOT poor, we have a Cadillac car, an Airplane, I eat steak often, I take weekend camping trips and therefore we have many of the finer things in life.* This conversation reveals his own perception. HE eats steak, goes out for drinks and smokes cigarettes, we don't! HE is rich in the things that are important to him and this has nothing to do with our family. So, HE'S rich, we aren't. When he has money, he doesn't spend it on us! This conversation is my first key to my understanding to who he is and what is going on around here!

All about his own interests, he is not a lazy man, but also is not a 'family man.' If something interested my dad, he will work on it all day, his enthusiasm for his own projects is never faltering. I am keenly aware of his dirt-stained hard-working hands and his blunt fingernails with black oil underneath each one. When not out on the town, his austere style is faded, rumpled work clothes.

~

Beside the reservoir is a settlement of small Quonset huts built by the government during the Second World War housing shortage. The people who live in the projects are tougher and more street wise than anyone living on Walnut Street. If they weren't, we sure thought they were! The boys and girls use cuss words and their parents let them because they cuss, too.

Sometimes I walk to school with a shy, quiet girl, named Sally from the project. I am not really afraid of her. Usually, she stops at my house when she comes past and we get along ok on the three blocks we walk together. Sometime around the third grade Sally and I get into a fight in the morning before school. We begin rolling, punching and jabbing on the ground. This becomes a flurry of fists and feet. Crowds of kids from Walnut Street and the park are gathering around us. We fly at each other, locked arms and we push and pull while a crowd forms around us. They are all cheering us on. This becomes a real push and shove match. Finally, we're both down and I finally pin her! I am so proud because I have never fought before and I win! I beat her and everyone knows it! The word on the street is, *"A kid from Walnut Street beat up a kid from the project!"* I have never been such a source of interest. I feel completely transformed that day. WOW! I think I am a good street fighter!

When I get home, I tear into the house looking for Mom. I find her on a chair in the kitchen. I never like to brag, but my pride shows as I tell her *"I beat up Sally!"* I expected her to be proud of me, but she is not proud at all! Her facial expression is that of a person who has been poked by a needle and is stoically enduring the pain!

"You mean YOU were fighting? Rolling on the ground fighting? What were you doing fighting? I am so disappointed in you! "I can't imagine you'd DO that!"

By the time she finishes with me, she isn't even a little bit proud and all of my proudness is gone, too! I want to be good at something! I never do fight again but I keep looking for that perfect something that I will be good at doing.

~

Summers are hot and no one has central cooling in their homes in the summer. The upstairs is unbearable, so we make blanket beds on the living room floor during the heat of the summer and we run table fans. We pile the blankets on the sofa every day for the next night.

Sometimes I sleep in my clothes. Still wearing the dirt from yesterday, I am ready to run out in the morning for play. Or, other times I like to wake up in the summer and play inside in my night clothes. Stevie decides that we girls should be dressed at least by noon. I burst out laughing when he says, "OK, it's noon!" He shoves me onto the porch and locks the deadbolt. There isn't much we can do at that point because we aren't dressed to go anywhere. At times he holds us outside for an hour. If Mom is there, she will let us back in.

~

Like migratory birds, every summer, the revival tent is set up at Waterworks Park for a week-long Evangelistic event. If attendance is low, enthusiasm is not. The service starts with more than a half-hour of exuberant worship. We call the gospel singers "Holy Rollers" as they clap and sing the lively gospel songs.

Nightly during revival week, the Bug and I lay quietly in the grass just outside the tent, to listen and watch. Sick, infirm and crippled people line up waiting for the overly exuberant preacher to 'lay a hand' on their heads to help God to perform a miracle that will surely cure them of all ailments. The Evangelistic preacher asks for people who want God to bless their finances to bring up another $20. Bug and I stay very quiet, so we won't have to pay.

~

When I am ten years old, I go to the Van Wert County Hospital to have a surgical tonsillectomy. The hospital is spotlessly clean and shiny. I like things orderly and quiet. Everything from the walls to the nurses' uniforms are white. It is so quiet there that I can hear the nurse's shoes squeaking as they walk down the hall. I hear people speaking in polite and calm voices. They bring me things to eat and drink and they change my sheets daily. I like people asking if I am hungry or if I need anything. They bring me meals three times a day, with Jell-O and ice cream. I am not used to this much attention. When I am at home, I am sharing a bed with 'Susita and 'Wagtail'. I like having my own room! I like being here! I'm happy to stay here forever.

A 1950's slogan among my parents' generation is "*Waste not, want not.*" We never waste anything and we save money any way we possibly can. I am sent to the grocery to buy cocoa. I see a package of cocoa with sugar added for the same price. I think, "*What a great deal!*" But as soon as I get back home, I find out that I am wrong about that!

I stiffen when Oug tells me that it is a 'piss poor' idea. He calls me a '*damn fool*' when I get home with the cocoa and I get a long '*sermon*' from him about the price of sugar (cheap) and the price of cocoa (expensive) and I have paid cocoa price for the sugar! This is a very big deal to him.

~

Several scenes from the days at Horace Mann School linger in my memory. Such as spelling bees in the class room and listening to the World Series as the Yankees played the Dodgers on the intercom in the gym, and fire drills where we file out onto the lawn. That is almost as exciting as going out to recess.

In the fourth-grade classmates begin calling me Kathy. At home I am strictly called Kathleen. With Mrs. Stose as my most favorite teacher, we begin studying band instruments. First, we begin with tonettes and learn the notes and how to blow a tune. We meet with the Jr. High band director and choose our instruments. I have no choice to make! My dad says I have to choose the clarinet because he already has one at home there is no need to buy something different. It is his clarinet, but he thinks we can share it, which is unusual because most of his things aren't shared with us. I think he shares the clarinet because he wants me to learn to play it in his style of Dixieland Jazz, and he doesn't care one bit about me being in the school band.

I love the velvet inside the case and I love feeling the soft cleaning cloth. Clarinets require a strong blow, which is not easy for me! We have to pucker and move our fingers at the same time and that is not easy either. I never catch on how to make a real note come out, and I want to do everything quickly. My bigger problem is I will not practice because I have to share reeds and spit with Oug. I can taste his spit and I loathe the smell of his smoke, beer and coffee. Since the clarinet smells bad, I decide to quit band.

Next, I take up piano lessons with Mrs. Boyd. She explains about keeping my wrists raised and I try to learn to read the notes to make the music. I play many months of 'imperfect' scales, with my small stumbling fingers. I really am trying to learn. My mother can play and she never had any lessons, because she plays by ear. I think I will begin playing by 'ear' sometime, but I never do.....

Within a year the piano is boring and stupid and I quit that, too. All of my musical opportunities are lost. I decide I'd rather play outside. Oug turns and walks away from me, giving me the back of his shirt! He's disgusted with me, as he tunes in the recorded music of Guy Lombardo and his royal Canadians.

~

When I am eleven, I get a nice red and black plaid winter coat from my cousin. It is a beautiful coat. I can't wait to wear it. On the first snowfall, I proudly wear it to school.

On my way home I stop to make a snow angel. Don't ya' know: just then Oug drives past! He sees me lying in the new fallen snow in my 'newest' hand-me-down coat. By the time I get home, his temper is flaring! His eyes narrow to China man slits and as 'quick as a snake' he opens a bible to Matthew 7:6 and he reads me the following verse:

"*Give not that which is holy unto the dogs, neither cast ye your pearls before swine, lest they trample them under their feet, and turn again and rend you.*" As he reads, I study his face and wonder..."
HOW DID HE EVER FIND THAT VERSE IN THE BIBLE? This must have been a verse he learned from his grandma, Lillian Kirk. I feel sure that he has never ever looked inside any bible since I knew him. People praising the Lord make him uncomfortable. For no reason at all, I want to laugh myself cock eyed, but I struggle keeping a straight face. If he wasn't so mad, I might have bust out laughing about all of this! But I know better than to engage his flaring temper.

It is a warm Saturday night in August, 1954. Oug smells like Aqua Velva after-shave as we stand on the porch. He is bragging to me on how well he lives; he uses his Camel cigarette to point toward his Cadillac convertible sitting in the driveway. Our parents are on the way downtown in Van Wert to the Moose Lodge for the Saturday night dance. She is wearing a dress she has sewn herself, and some worn down wedge shoes. He is smoking a cigarette and, as always, he is dressed up in tan gabardine dress pants, his kelly-green sport coat with a silk ascot tie. He is looking like he '*has just beat the house in Las Vegas*'!

She sits quietly at a table, thinking her own thoughts while he enjoys himself. Like a man of Irish heritage, Oug drinks daily. He is holding a long-neck Schlitz beer and chatting it up with a buddy. Oug lowers his voice as he speaks, as though talking in confidence. He looks around as if someone might be listening. Mom is out of earshot as he proceeds. He talks out of the side of his mouth while telling a story, followed by the man pounding on Oug's back. They are throwing their heads back, having a good laugh. He is "*talking the piss*' out of a joke that will never be shared with Mom. Oug is ever the critic of her, by the time they return home. There has been an argument, based on something that happened. He is verbally beating her down because of something that he thinks she should have done differently. He tells her to "*pipe down!*" She holds any emotion back, being cautious, because his temper is unpredictable.

~

Grandma Fogt shoots into our house like a bullet. She soon bares down hard on us all. While lecturing Mom, she doles out constant criticism of Oug and she '*rocks our world*!' We dare not talk back to Grandma. If we get *too big for our britches*, she will '*cram a bar of soap in our mouth*' or '*thrash us with a twig*' to put us in place. She is always in motion, at the pace of a humming bird! As soon as she arrives, she begins cleaning. Mattresses are stripped and bedclothes are washed and furniture is rearranged to put our house in proper order. Her hands are never empty, she keeps busy with whatever needs washed, bleached, moved, wiped or folded. The house soon reeks of vinegar, chlorine bleach and soap. Her energy is boundless. Next, she sits me down with my head between her knees, to keep me still, while she pulls my head back and yanks the comb through my tangled hair until tears come to my eyes. Her face is twisted in a blend of revulsion and exasperation as she writes a schedule for all of us. She charges me to read a chapter a week or maybe it is a chapter a day. You know, good and well, Grandma has us scheduled and busy washing dishes and cleaning the house. She is strongly focused against Oug and steady controlling of Mom. Yet, I actually like how she manages a house and a family. She lovingly puts her hand on my cheek and I am comforted by it. I remember her cheeks, when she kisses us as being very soft and pleasant, with old skin pressing against new, but wrinkled like a rotted apple! Even at eleven I know Grandma has some charm. Her manners are as perfect as her housekeeping. I admire her style. We listen from the next room as she tells Mom, *"You MUST commence to get these children doing some chores!* We are worried at first, but after a few visits we know that when Grandma leaves everything goes right back to our normal. Soon the house is a mess again and we are no longer required to wash dishes and clean the house unless we choose to do it for pay! The only changes that really matter are any that can't be undone when she leaves.

In the 'good ole days,' Mom dries the clothes outside in warm weather on a clothes line. In winter laundry is dried inside over the register on a clothes rack. Summer finds her out in the back yard hanging out clothes with a rope clothes line hung between the box elder tree on the north and the walnut tree on the south, propped up with a long pole. I ask for a piece of extra clothesline rope to make a jump rope. She has the clothes pins in her mouth and a few more are in her basket below, a fading yellow rose pattern sheet set, two pillowcases and a few pairs of her underwear. I bring out a kitchen knife and she cuts a length long enough for me to play jump rope. After hanging the clothes, she is humming to herself as she comes into the kitchen. She wears a kind of lounging house dress called a duster at home. She has a few and she wears them in all seasons. The duster is similar to a nightgown, gathered at the yoke and zipped or buttoned up the front.

Ruthie Bell stops by with some neighborhood gossip. *"They try to hush it up, but they are deep in debt and spending money 'hand over fist.'* She goes on, *"I know it and everyone knows it! I kid you not,"* she says, *"time brings these things to light and people will find out!"* As I brush Mom's hair, Ruthie Bell leaves and Mom tells me never to gossip. Only a lower class of people discuss other people like that.

She says, "*Important people talk about ideas.*"Sitting deep in the chair, she draws her knees up to her chin, and asks me to brush her hair, as she gazes at me in a way that I wish I could bottle and store like fine wine. While I brush her hair, I ask her to tell me about that night when I was born. She says, "*I've told you that already, and more than once,*"but she tells me again anyhow! This is all for my own romance, of course!

I put a few bobby pins in her hair and she turns down the lights for "*40 winks.*"She keeps her thin hair in perpetual pin curls with a hair net - every day. She only uses a very few bobby pins because they are strewn all around; on the buffet, in the bathroom and on the end tables.

It's November, 1954, and I am eleven years old. The raw chilly air signals the upcoming holidays. The temperatures have dropped and frost settles on the lawn. Ice began to form and the strong gusts of wind brings down a few limbs from the trees, as streams of slush trickle into the streets. The late fall days in Ohio fill with cold raw air that holds a nippiness and the feeling that Christmas is coming soon.

A bell jingles on the door of Al's Old South Bar. As my dad and I barge in out of the cold, I am mortified to go inside a bar. The seating space is very small. There are three small tables on one wall, and there is a counter at the bar with six stools across. It is late morning and the place is not very crowded. There are all men inside, some are old and fat. They all line up along the bar with their backs to us as they hunch over the counter, sitting on stools that are too small. The inside is dim, but warm. I can smell the delicious smells of doughnuts and hot coffee over the stale bar smells of smoke and beer from the night before. My dad leads me to one of the only empty stools. He tells me to sit on the one by the wall and he scoots onto the next one. Al, the owner, comes over. He is portly and red-faced with grey hair and he is nearly bald. He rubs his hands on his apron and looks at us, waiting for my father to order something. My dad is wearing a tan jacket and a felt hat with the brim pulled down, like James Cagney wears as a gangster. He smells of cigarette smoke. I can smell him over the other smells of coffee and doughnuts. I'm feeling out of place, but happy to be out with him. "*Coffee with cream*" my dad says, "*and give us a couple of those donuts!*" Al grins at me and says "*So is this your daughter, Red?*" "*Yep, this is my oldest girl, and she can have a cup of coffee to go along with her doughnut. She's getting old enough*

81

for coffee." Turning to me he says, "*Don't you think so, Kathleen?*" The coffee is too hot and I don't like the taste, so I add a lot of milk. This morning I happily drink the coffee and eat the doughnut because of how warm and grown up I feel, being in there with my dad and all these noisy men! This is a warm memory because it is one of very few times I can remember of us going out anywhere just him and me alone.

Fall turns into winter and Christmas is soon coming to Ohio. Our Christmas is simple and small most years, but no less exciting for kids like us! A few days before Christmas Daddy cuts a pine tree in the country and Mommy pounds two crossed boards to the bottom of the tree as a base to keep it upright. We place the tinsel and some glass balls. We have a string of the fancy new electric tree lights called 'bubble lights.' The lights have plastic tubes bubbling with colored fluids that 'bubble' once their liquid reaches a certain temperature. We cut some construction paper strips to make the garland.

The five brown craft paper wrapped packages under the tree on Christmas Eve are from Grandma Fogt. Sometimes she wraps presents in colorful newspaper comic pages tied with twine. Mommy cuts last year's Christmas cards with her pinking shears to make this year's name tags.

My parents don't give us much for Christmas because money is always a problem. As Christmas looms, Mom grows increasingly desperate. Not that a lack of money isn't a familiar condition in our house all year long. We never do believe in Santa, but we still have the HOPE of children on Christmas Eve. On Christmas Eve Mom reads the bible story of Christmas from Luke 2:1-20. When Christmas morning comes, we will get a gift from my only Grandma. Every year that gift costs exactly $3.00 because Grandma gives Mom the money to get whatever she can find at that price. These packages are usually winter scarves, socks and underwear for all. My favorite underwear is the 'days of the week' panties! "*Don't look the gift horse in the mouth*" Oug says. "HELLS BELLS, *your stockings are filled with oranges, English walnuts, horehound and, 'hard tack' candy, who couldn't be happy with that?*"

But there is a very special magical Christmas box that we receive every year during my childhood. These boxes always create the MAGIC of Christmas for us. Amazingly the box comes from someone we have never met! The box is delivered by mail from '*Aunt Mildred.*'

She is married to Oug's older half-brother, Leo. I don't know Aunt Mildred and I doubt that Daddy knew her well either. Long story, short version: Since being born in 1943, I never know any of his relatives. Leo is a lawyer and Mildred is an elementary teacher. They live in Canton, Ohio which is far from us. They have no kids of their own but she works with children, she knows perfect gifts for kids our age.

Our all-time best gift from Aunt Mildred is a croquet set. A few other gifts that I remember are Mr. Potato Head, Lincoln Logs, Dominoes, and a gyroscopic top. So, every Christmas these packages are our very best gifts and we can't wait for the box from 'Aunt Mildred McMillen' to arrive in the mail. The box is marked, DO NOT OPEN UNTIL DECEMBER 25th! When the box arrives, we are so excited we think we can't leave it alone. We began pilfering and peeking, up until Christmas morning when we are allowed to open! We make a hole in the back of the box and play croquet in the living room, long before Christmas morning!

Mom believes in the old-fashioned etiquette of a written thank-you note. Every year she gives me a piece of stationary and a 3-cent stamp to write my thank you notes to Grandma and Aunt Mildred. I'd rather do anything other than write these thank you notes but I am never given an option! I struggle with what to write, but before the school holiday is over, these notes have to be in the mailbox. Now, I can't help but think that our childish thank-you notes must have been what kept her sending those special boxes!

When we go back to school after the holidays, the teachers will often go around the class letting each kid tell what they got for Christmas gifts. Many classmates have a dozen or more great gifts. We only have a few. I often have to list gifts that my siblings received. I could lie and make up more things, but I don't. I do exaggerate a little though!

~

I am about 11 years old when the whole family's laundry becomes my job. I do all of the family laundry every Saturday morning. I don't really like doing it, but I do know how to do it and I like getting paid 35 cents for the job.

We have a wringer washer and Mommy heats the water to pour into the wash tub. I wash everything in the same water. Whites first, light colors, followed by dark colors and the rugs last.

I use Fels-Naphtha soap and I put a light bluing in the rinse water for the white clothes to come out blue-white. I can never get the wringers to a position where I don't get the water on the back-porch floor, but it doesn't actually matter because there are gaping holes there in the floor.

I trot the basket of wet clothes to the back yard and hang them to dry. When I have the family laundry on the clothesline, I take the 35 cents that I earned and I go roller skating. Skating is my favorite thing to do and it's set for every Saturday in the gym at the YWCA. I usually get the laundry done, in the nick of time, to be there at one o'clock for the first round. Very occasionally, if I run late, Oug will drive me there. In this era a man has to protect his mysteries. He often has other business, and after dropping me off, he will go to the places where he has some business of his own. This particular day he is going to drive me to skating and he impatiently waits in the drive-way for me to finish my chores. He has his arm on the window and he is holding a cup of coffee in one hand and a cigarette in the other. He is ready to leave when I come crashing out the door, knowing that he won't wait long, "*Get your arse in the car if you want a ride down-town,*" he barks. I braid my hair as he drives, because he has already told me many times that he "*isn't a taxi driver.*" He tells us he has to go out daily, "*to blow the stink off!*" As I learn to skate, I am in awe of the rink employees who skate forward and backward spinning among us. I am happy to stay upright while skating with 'smarty pants' boys and 'fast' girls on Saturday afternoons.

That year I save up enough 'chore money' to buy my own Chicago brand shoe skates and a red metal skate box. Just as I buy all of this, Carol's mother buys her the same skates and the same skate box and I'm annoyed because she doesn't ever have to do any chores!

~

When I get back Mom lays down the newspaper and gives me her full attention. She tells me that the other kids have been screaming at each other and at her, and fighting between themselves. She wants me to "*talk to everyone about getting along better!*" She says, "*They will listen when you say things, instead o' me tellin'em!*" She says that I am a 'natural born leader' and, "*they will follow you and do whatever you tell 'em to do!*" I'm yanked by her comment! Now, I'm being asked to deal with Mom's mothering chores. I don't care much about it, I am just a kid. She wants me to help, so I do. Last time I checked I'm not their mother but I often shoulder some responsibilities that should not be a child's work. From as far back as I can remember, there has been an '*adult me*' inside of the '*child me*.' This probably explains a lot. "*C'mon*," she chides. "*At least, you can give it a try!*" When I come back to her after the chat, she slowly begins getting up from the old sofa in the living room where she has been napping while covering herself with the newspaper. I tell her I have talked with everyone, and that seems to make her happy. I am never sure she is right about the leadership part, because no

one listens to me and we keep right on fighting among ourselves as before.

My step-grandpa, Asa Fogt, makes a good living with very little investment as a coal broker in Sydney, Ohio. It is called '*Fogt Fuel and Supply Company*' in the 1940s, 1950s and 1960s in Sidney. He only needs a small office, a phone and a bank account. He buys enough coal for a wholesale shipment of plateau coal from ramp operators. He makes a good living by reselling the coal to retail consumers at a markup of 15 to 25 cents per ton for home heating. Every summer I have a '*Grandma week*' at my only grandma's house in Sydney, Ohio.

About the same time each summer she arranges for me to come to her home for a week with my cousins. Our days at Grandma's house are regimented and she keeps us busy. I learn a lot while there, about other places and being among real families. She has a bedroom for us with grey painted furniture. There are floral decals on the front of each dresser drawer. Her home is large and roomy with lots of nooks and crannies for adventures. She makes us feel special and loved in an ordinary home life. She buys us things and takes us places. When we go to their church, she ties my offering money into the corner of a cotton handkerchief for Sunday School. We have great fun there with Grandma and my two cousins. Staying with Grandma and Step-Grandpa Asa Fogt is one of the finer memories of my youth.

After the week, my aunt brings me back home. Right away I run upstairs to put my ear on the upstairs register to hear what Oug is telling my aunt. He relies on eye movements to convey and interpret important nonverbal cues. I hear him telling her that my eyes show him how nervous I am since returning home. He says, "She has a fast blink that he sees as an involuntary rapid eye movement." It is nervousness, he claims, that is caused by Grandma! As he speaks, my aunt is making her way out the door. I am thinking, *WHAT? I had a great week at Grandma's house.*

~

Most Americans in the 1950s believe that communists are at work in their country. Responding to this fear, Congress passes the Communist Control Act in August 1954. The act declares that, "The Communist Party of the United States, though a legally organized political party, is, in fact, an instrumentality of a conspiracy to overthrow the Government of the United States." The act goes on to charge that the party's "role as the agency of a hostile foreign power renders its existence a clear and continuing danger to the security of the United States." **(History.com/ this day in history/August 14, 1954)** By the mid-to-late 1960s, however, the Red Scare has run its course and a more liberal Supreme Court begins to chip away at the immense tangle of anticommunist legislation that had been passed during the 1940s and 1950s. Today, the Communist Party of the United States continues to exist and regularly runs candidates for local, state and national elections. **(History.com/ Communist Control Act.)**

~

Polio is a viral sniper, rampant in the summers of the early 1950's. The disease is brutally unpredictable in choosing victims. No one is safe, everyone knows someone who has contacted Polio. Children aren't allowed to swim or play in public places. Drinking from fountains is particularly forbidden. Polio is the disease that always shuts down the old Van Wert swimming pool in the August *'Dog Days* of summer'. When we hear of a case of polio, we begin imagining the symptoms: fatigue, fever and a stiff neck. Polio is a lot worse than AIDS and other viral diseases, because polio is so common everywhere. A polio vaccine is developed by Jonas Salk in 1955. Everyone who grew up before the Salk vaccine knows someone who is fat and sassy one day and in an iron lung fighting for his/her life the next day. The chance you could be next are real. My mother set up doctor appointments for us to get the Salk vaccine. I tried to get out of it, telling her that *"I'd rather have Polio than the vaccine!"* But she didn't buy into that! Immunity is easier and cheaper in 1961 when Dr. Savin introduces the oral vaccine. By 1979 the United States is declared Polio Free. Today there are very few cases of Polio worldwide.

~

Oug decides to teach me to fly when I am a young teen and too young to get a pilot's license. He has me follow him around the plane, we're checking the struts and ailerons. He explains some basics such as lift and tailwind. I step into the slim body 2-seater Porterfield plane for an afternoon lesson. I stick to the warm plastic seat as he belts me in and closes the door. The airport attendant, Woody, at Wetzel Airport, spins the propeller by hand while Oug cranks the engine. The prop swings and the propeller blades disappear in a blur of whirling wood. The grass runway on Woody's farm whips against the tires as we motor down the runway. The frame of the plane vibrates and the noise gets louder and we speed up. Oug pulls back on the throttle as we surge forward; we're still picking up speed and finally lift off. When the bumping stops, we are airborne. He pulls higher into the sky then banks it around to circle the farm below. I press my face to the window and look down at the trees as the ground gets farther away, but the wing blocks my view so I lean forward to see the sky. Once we are in the air, he hands me the controls. I turn to the right and the plane tips slightly. I can feel a change in the direction. I revise the motion easing the plane back. The memory of it makes me shiver. After a few jerks, I can bank, climb it higher or dive it lower by adjusting the aileron. Before long, the smell of gasoline and exhaust inside the compartment, combined with the noise and vibrations, sets off my motion sickness. He buys me Dramamine and we try a few more times but my nausea continues and he gives up on me. I can fly but I never learn to take off or land. (This feels a bit like driving a boat that I don't know how to dock.)

"Humans like explanations – God is a good explanation for unexplainable things."

\- Lorna Landvik - Author

CHAPTER FIVE

Religion

In the 1950s soaring birth rates, economic good times and the focus on normalcy and family converged to create the religion and major Catholic-Protestant tensions of the decade. On a typical Sunday morning in the period from 1955-58, almost half of all Americans were attending church – the highest percentage in U.S. History. **(https://news.usc.edu/25835/The-1950s-Powerful-Years-for-Religion/)**

In 1950s most kids learned the 10 commandments at school or church. Most went to church as a family and worshiped together. Our family is anything but traditional! When I think of my childhood church, it is the walk to Church that I remember the most. The church is on the corner of Washington Street and Sycamore Street in Van Wert. We can easily walk there as children, but we don't want to go. I think Church is boring and I ask, "Why do we have to go to church?" All this aside, I learn all of the Creeds and Commandments and go to church at least half of the time. Around age ten, I am baptized in Lutheran Church. That Sunday afternoon we meet with the pastor and promise to relinquish our life from evil and give our lives to God. I'm not very aware of most of the promises made that day. I sing in the youth choir and the junior choir there. Mom says I look like an angel in my choir robe. I attend Sunday school and church there; I go to two years of catechism in Jr. High and I am confirmed there. And I get married there. But I never want to go to Church!!

On Easter she makes a very nice Easter dress for me, but she has not made one for herself. She is wearing an old gray out-of-season dress that her Aunt Helen had given her, under her faded navy-blue raincoat. As we stand singing, "*He has risen,*" together she puts her hand on my shoulder and gives me a smile that says she is glad that I have come with her!

Mom says she joined St. Mark's Lutheran Church because '*Mick*' had gone there with some boys, when they were in high School. The dad that I know, called Oug, hasn't gone to Church there since I've known him! He has no interest in it. Church for him is '*like a wool suit,*' because it is a big irritant that makes him squirm. On Sunday mornings I have a few tricks of my own to avoid going. When Mom calls upstairs to say, "We're leaving now!" I will call down to say, "I cannot find my shoe, I will be along in a minute!" If I can get her to leave without me, I will look half-heartedly for the shoe, or I sprawl out onto the bed. This same trick works for school days! When she is gone, I know Oug will undermine her in any way he can. He will never make me go!

When she comes back home, we have a mess. We're in pajamas with cereal bowls in the kitchen. He sits stone-faced smoking cigarettes. I get him an ashtray so he won't put his cigarette ashes in his pant cuff. If she complains or even lets her anger show, he antagonizes her further, telling her, "*A good Christian should be joyful! You shouldn't go at all, because, Church only makes you mad!*' Of course it is him who makes her mad, but he loves to do these things to upset her. This time we benefited, or so we thought. He tells us that she couldn't make us go because religion is supposed to be free choice! He says we don't have to go. As our mother, I do believe she is right to try. But even though she makes quite an attempt to keep us in Church and Sunday school, we often don't go.

When I miss Sunday school and go back after a few weeks of backsliding, the Sunday school teacher will say, "*We have missed you!*" Being called out like that is so embarrassing for me that I don't want to go back at all.

I am more aware of Grandma Fogt's wishes that I should commence going to Church and be baptized. She has always been there, lording it over me and still loving me, pushing me around and yet protecting me. I desperately want to please her, but I so seldom do. She gives me a white leather New Testament bible with my name imprinted on the front in gold letters. It has very thin parchment pages with the words of Jesus printed in red.

As much as I don't want to go to Sunday school, I love to go to Church Camp at Camp Luther Haven on Lake Erie near Sandusky, Ohio. I went for several years, from ages 9 to 12 years, with the pastor and his wife along with a core group of young people from my Sunday School class. I love all this woodsy outdoor stuff at Church camp. Being away from home at Camp Luther Haven with these church people is very heady stuff for a girl like me. I am in a cabin with five girls and myself. We eat every meal in a huge dining hall. We do crafts, sing and study the bible in the mornings. Afternoons we go to the beach on Lake Erie or hike in the woods. I wear a plaid skort pinned at the waist with the 'too big' shoes I had gotten from my cousin. I bring the white New Testament Bible that is a baptismal gift from Grandma Fogt to the rustic Chapel candle light services in the evenings. Some of the girls have bibles 'fluffy and fat' as though someone has been reading them. I am opening the pages there for the very first time! It is only then that I discover the OLD Testament is completely missing, and it has always been. Grandma has given me only a New Testament Bible!

As much as I don't like going to the Lutheran Church, I am a regular at Catechism classes at the Catholic Church. I have a lot of friends there and I go there often on Thursday evenings. Mom is worried that I will join the Catholic Church. She tells me that Catholics will never come to a Lutheran Church. Apparently Lutheran and Catholic don't mix! They speak and sing in Latin. I can't even figure out the words. We behave badly and harass the nuns and I only go for the social activities after the class. I have no intention of joining!

"In life you'll meet a lot of jerks. If they hurt you, keep from reacting to their cruelty. Because there is nothing worse than bitterness and vengeance"

- Marjane Satrapi -Author

Chapter Six

The Bad People

I'm 'tickled pink' when I get a diary. I am about eleven years old when I learn to express my hurts, feelings, hopes and dreams in the book to understand things better. On the pages I am not lost in a household of children fighting over our mother's attention. I get a release from dealing with adult problems. Writing saves me! One day 'The Bug' gets into my diary and begins reading my secrets aloud, to tease and embarrass me. I turn on him *'like a cat with its tail in the wringer!'* I scramble and push his arm and cause him to drop the diary. He stands up and punches me. He uses the knuckle of his middle finger raised slightly, called a *'noogie'*. It feels like it completely separates my muscle from the bone. This time I hit back. *"Why'd ya' push my arm?"* he yells back and I conk him in the noggin, shouting, *"Because you are reading my diary!"* He lies on the floor listening to the 'Green Hornet' on the radio, as if nothing has happened!

About this same time, I have a little black address book. I name the book MY BAD PEOPLE BOOK. I list everyone in the book who crosses me or does me harm. Oug is my main antagonist and he is listed more often than anyone else. I have written that he is *'dead inside,'* because he is so hard-hearted.

Although I don't have a real voice, I am going into an angry period of my life. Before Oug went completely off the rails, I had thought that a marriage and a family is about housekeeping and baskets of ironing, mending clothes and darning socks! Probably every girl wants 'Atticus Finch' for a father, but I end up with someone more like Jed Clampett, only angrier. Oug shouts in my face again and he gives me a look that I don't know how to cross. I can walk in pissed off, and if I don't say anything, go quietly to my room because I know not to press him. If he blows a gasket, I dare not to move or speak. I try being agreeable and quiet because I have to. Oug has his own ways to be in control that are hard for me to reconcile. No one dares to lash out at him!

I am in the summer after fourth grade when this incident with 'The Bug,' along with my ongoing disgust with Oug causes me to decide to move out! As the fighting between Oug and me grows harsher, I am feeling a shift and I can't sit in his presence anymore. I am so over living with his domination! My anger stays hard and frozen and I don't give 'one whit' about him. I plan to scrape by, be on my own and live in the old cellar. It is summer and the basement is dry, but none the less, dark and dirty from the coal. I load up a blanket, an apple, my diary and my bad-people book and head for the basement. These are all things that I think I will need to survive there. I make a bed for myself on a pallet and I announce to the whole family that I am moving out! It is NOT a hunger strike; I am moving to the basement! The old bug shows up lickety-split to tell me, "You won't be able to do this!" As I sit in the dark, damp basement of our house trying to put my anger into words, I express myself best by releasing everything into my diary. I get out the Bad People's Book and list 'Bug' right under Oug's name. 'Bug' goes on telling me again, "You won't be able to manage alone!" and "Don't fall into the trap of thinking you've got the hardest lot." I think, "what does he know?" I shoo him off like a fly, because of course, I can do this! He leaves it like this; "Everyone is crazy except me and thee, and sometimes I think thee is a little off!" My younger siblings are intrigued, and they keep coming down to the basement to see all of this. I decide this isn't working and I need to move even farther away.

I draw and leave a map for Mom showing a dotted line between home and salt bins at the Water Works Park, about a block away, where I plan to live. Here I will be free at last! Until dusk comes and I am hungry! I wonder what they are having for supper. I wish Mom will find my note and bring me a little food, but she never does. Worse for the wear, tears begin to fall fast and easily now. I decide to force a smile and go back home sheepishly; feeling a bit like Dorothy when she realizes she has been wearing her red slippers all the while. ... Sadly, I am not able to live at the park yet!

I haven't forgotten Mom's words when I ask her, "*Why don't we ever get to stand up against Oug?*" Mom answers me, as if she has been waiting for this question for a while. She gives me this advice; "*Standing up to him will be a waste of your time and energy; he will never change. You will have to create your own results.*" Following up with more insight she tells me, "*While you are fighting with him about treating you unfair, you could be focusing on your own future.*" Her words are bigger than my understanding at the time, but truer words are never spoken. After that I begin moving forward in my mind.

Another example of the school of hard knocks that I always remember is when Oug tells us that if we ever play with matches, we'd wish we hadn't. Stevie also has been told not to play with matches, and when he did get into the matches, his punishment is to have to light every match and fully burn each stick match to the end in a box of 1,000 matches. He has to sit at the kitchen table and light a match off of the last match in the box until all are burned down to his fingertips. The boy is about five years old and has to burn matches until almost midnight that night. He is tired and sleepy and he falls asleep, letting the matches burn his fingertips.

We are all so sorry for him that we can't watch, but we are wishing this torture to end. It is a lesson that none of us ever have forgotten; yet we were afraid to speak out! This is a case of a child being a victim of torture and cruel inhuman treatment. The punishment is not appropriate to his age and thus a form of child abuse. Mom wants to stop Oug at times to protect us but she fears challenging him. She seems to believe it is a man's place to set the discipline. Perhaps Oug's over reaction is due to the house fire at his house in the 1930's, or maybe the burns that Mom lives with. Regardless of why he did it, it is unacceptable parenting and I cannot condone it.

~

Oug is never careless with guns and he teaches us to be the same. He does not care if we wash our faces or learn to read, or even if we take up smoking, but he cares that we know how to handle a gun. A 22-caliber rifle sits fully loaded and within reach in our stair well for all of the years that I live there. We are told never to play around with it or to point it at anyone. He reinforces this by telling us that if we ever do, he will "*Tear off our arms and beat us to death with them!*" or other times he threatens to "*knock our teeth down our throat!*"

Those threats must have staved off any gun carelessness; we all grew up with our limbs and teeth intact.

I learn to iron cotton dresses with a heavy dry iron and a sprinkling bottle. I learn to sew and mend on her treadle sewing machine by peddling the foot mechanism. Mom teaches me to darn socks by weaving the hole closed with embroidery floss over a gourd. I learn to wallpaper by working the bottom end while she works the top section. Before I am a teen, I do laundry and cleaning regularly. If I know anyone is going to come inside our house, I will clean everything. I put things away, all the glass sparkles, furniture shines, rugs are shaken and carpets are vacuumed. Mom is impressed. "*It looks so nice when you do it*," she comments.

~

Of course, Oug is in charge the summer when we roof the house. "*Who the hell ELSE will be in charge?*" he asks, even though there has never been a question about that! We all have to do whatever he says.

He holds an unlit cigarette dangling from the corner of his mouth as he uses his hand to gesture the exact spot where I should put the nail in each shingle. Not too high, not so low. He says, "*If the nail shows from under the row above, the roof will leak*", that part is important. He places the next shingle, to show us how it is to be done. He watches us a minute before flipping his cigarette off the porch roof. I am afraid of height and I don't want to do roofing but I fear even more disobeying him, so I carefully follow 'Bug Boy' up to the steep north roof to get started. As we work, I wish I was younger so I could work on the flatter porch roof with the three younger kids!

He leaves soon after, and we are up on the second-floor roof alone. Most of the neighbor kids aren't allowed to climb on their own roofs. They ask us, "*What in tarnation are y'all doing up there?*" Fancying up the story with each telling, we show them how to place shingles and we tell them it's fun. Before long we get a lot of the neighbor kids up there. They pitch in to help us, a bit like the story by Mark Twain of Tom Sawyer and the white washed fence where he convinces his friends that it's not tedious work but an enjoyable privilege.

After World War II ends, the American dream is to settle in, raise the family and make an honest living. Many Americans are eager to have children because they are confident that the future holds nothing but peace and prosperity. Baby Boomer refers to the generation born between the end of WWII into the mid-1960s, when 77 million babies are born in the USA. Baby boomers make up about 40% of America's population. Because of these large numbers, the Baby Boomers are an economically and politically influential population. I am 'almost' in the baby boomer generation, but technically I am a war baby, born during, but not after WW II. Between 1945 and 1960, the gross national product more than doubled, kicking off 'the Golden Age of American Capitalism. (www.aristeon.net/golden-age-american-capitalism.html)

This era is a huge growth in economic development in America. These are the years of my childhood. But they are very lean years for my family, producing very little income for us!

Sometime in the mid '50's, Oug 'sets about' to fix some of the things that have fallen into disrepair. He can fix anything! He knows about all electrical, carpentry and mechanical repairs. We playfully called Oug, 'the original innovator.' Oug and 'Bug' put in a bath tub and we get running water in the bathroom and the kitchen. He even adds a hot water heater. Next, we move up to an electric refrigerator and a gas stove. All are added at different times, of course.

President Dwight Eisenhower signs the Feral-Aid Highway Act of 1956. The bill creates a 41,000-mile "National System of Interstate and Defense Highways." According to Eisenhower, it will eliminate unsafe roads, inefficient routes, traffic jams and all of the other things that get in the way of speedy, safe transcontinental travel. Eisenhower's Interstate I-75 is the route travelers take from Ohio to Tennessee to arrive in only six hours.

Many people consider this highway system a greater American accomplishment than the Apollo Program or the creation of the Internet. I won't argue the convenience but the travelers' going from Tennessee to Ohio breeze along down the interstate highway now at break neck speeds. These travelers miss the colorful and spectacular Tennessee country quilts and the weathered houses and barns. These places are still there, in the scenic towns and roads of the Cumberland valley, being missed now by most interstate travelers.

Rates of unemployment and inflation in the Eisenhower era are low, and wages are higher. Much of the Eisenhauer "Golden Age of Capitalism" in the 1950s comes from the increases in government spending: The construction of interstate highways and schools, the distribution of veterans' benefits and most of all the increase in military spending on goods like airplanes and new technologies. All of this contributes to the decade's economic growth. Middle-class people who have more money to spend than ever before are buying a variety of the new consumer goods that also help to expand the national economy in the mid 1950's. American spending on household goods increased by 240 percent as electrical appliance manufacturers cranked out new innovations and enhanced current appliances such as refrigerators, vacuum cleaners, electric ovens, televisions and radios which became affordable for the average family. As household incomes rise, during the 1950s, and mass production increases, electrical appliances become affordable to Van Wert homes.

I really want to have a record player and a hair dryer most of all. Mom got the natural gas stove, but she still wants a few more lamps in the rooms and all of that needs more power. A house built in the early 1900s or before, like ours, has a fuse box with two 30-amp fuses. They will easily power a home from earlier times, without a television, a refrigerator, or any small appliances. In most rooms of our house there is only one wall outlet and we are often *blowing a fuse.* We don't have a television quite yet, but because we traded the ice box for an electric refrigerator, we are getting '*too modern*' to function properly under these electrical conditions.

As usual, Oug knows what needs done, and he sets 'The Bug' and me to fishing Romex wiring through the walls from one room to another to create more outlets. Now we have more appliances and electricity expenses. When a light has been left on upstairs and Oug wants it turned off, he says the electric meter is leaking his money away! He asks us, "*Do you think I'm made of money?*" The depression is almost over, the new wartime economy is flourishing in many other places, but we never do catch up.

In about 1956 for the cost of some exterior paint from the Montgomery Ward store and some minimal patching and sanding, we transform the ivory house, that is more common in the neighborhood, to a shockingly bright egg yolk yellow with chocolate brown shingled gables. Mom and the young 'uns paint the lower portions, while Oug and the older kids paint the gables. I am 13 years old and I am '*in between*' the younger and the older. Our only instructions are to start at the top and work down and to work in the shade, out of the sun's glare. Within a few days we have a new BRIGHT YELLOW look that will never meet any architectural community standards today!

~

There are times when I can peer through the present and I see some layers left over from the past. I have an image from being eleven years old. Mom attempts to explain the facts of a girl's life to me. She is embarrassed to go into very much detail about menstruation and no details are given about sex. That kind of stuff is usually a mother and daughter moment in most homes but since Mom is uncomfortable talking to me about my body, we never discuss any of that again. That part is OK with me. I shrug it off because I already know most of this information from my friends. After *'the talk'* about two more years pass and we still haven't bought any sanitary products for me to be prepared. She has had a hysterectomy so she doesn't use them. I am the oldest girl and I haven't needed it.

As the years pass, I am beginning to get a little anxious when friends start their woman hood. I wonder when this will happen to me. I am 13 years old when I get my first period. I am at home in the bathroom on my lunch break from school, when I discover it! I call out several times to Mom to *"Come in here!"* I need to ask what I should do next but she won't come. Finally, Oug shows up at the door. *"She is eating lunch, what the Sam Hell do you want?"*

Looking for a way to cut through this, I try again to get Mom, but he insists. I don't want to go through telling him instead of Mom! Sensing no escape, I show him the blood stain and I say, *"Tell Mom I'm bleeding!"* *"Ye Gods, kid, you don't need your mother! Go over to the grocery and get yourself some sanitary napkins!"*

That, more than anything, shows me how difficult things have gotten. I do go to the store, but I am mortified. I fold in embarrassment again when paying for the sanitary napkins and I see a boy from school in line. I only have one item and he is right behind me! *Oh my, I don't think I can do this!*

There is another incident in the bathroom around the same time. I am standing in front of the mirror and pulling my hair back into a pony tail when Oug appears at the door. Staring straight at me he says, *"You have an ear like a SAIL!"* *"You should cover that ear with your hair!"* These words stay put with me forever. I have never pulled my hair into a pony tail since. Things like this seem to happen when he is around. There is no rational explanation, he has a *'way'* with words. The best I can do now is to record all this in my story and remember.

"There are moments when you pick the time, and
there are moments when the time picks you."
　　　– Senator Ted Kennedy

~

There are moments in life that change folks. Mine came in 1956. I am starting seventh grade when I make a new friend. I am invited to spend the night at her house on a school night. When morning comes, she is dressing for school. Her mom makes us a nice breakfast and curls her hair. I see that she has 3 closets and all three are full of beautiful clothes, hair accessories and shoes. I hadn't planned to stay and I don't have anything packed for wearing to school that morning. After she dresses, her mom is going to drive us to school and she takes me home to get dressed. I would have been mortified to invite them inside. They wait in the drive way while I run in and look for something clean to wear. I search the cardboard wardrobe that I share with two sisters but nothing at all is hanging there. I finally pick up something from the floor to wear. I throw it on and I dash out the door. I've got to fix this!

Another night, we pick up this same girl at her house. We both get into Oug's Cadillac. He takes us for a ride on a back country road. We both watch in amazement as he accelerates and the speedometer continues picking up speed. First sixty, then seventy then eighty, ninety until he takes it up to ONE-HUNDRED mph. He calls this 'burying the peg.' What he means is the speedometer is off the dial. Trying to impress people is an important part of his personality! But we are 'freaking out!' When she tells her mother about all of this, she is never allowed to get into a car with him again!

"Hard work spotlights the character of people. Some turn up their sleeves and some turn up their noses. Some don't turn up at all!"

- Sam Ewing -American Baseball player

CHAPTER SEVEN

We Both Go To Work

The very next Saturday after my talk with Mom, about focusing on my own future, I walk the eight blocks from our home to the White Hall Inn. I want to get a steady job so I can have the things that my classmates are getting from their parents. I know they hire kids like me, as young as thirteen. Yet, my eyes get wide and my jaw firms up when I am hired immediately. After I get that job, I look into a mirror and I never see my child-face again! I harden into a more mature personality because working gives me some new freedoms that I could only have imagined before. I am excited because I will no longer be stuck! This job will give me options. I like having a place to go outside of the house and I love having my own cash!

White Hall Inn is the John H. Humphreys home. Built 1895-97, it becomes Whitehall Inn in 1930s. Duncan Hines is a famous pioneer of restaurant ratings for travelers, visiting the Inn once. He recommends it in his book, *"Adventures in Good Eating."*

~WHITEHALL INN 1956 ~ Van Wert Historical society

The White Hall Inn is a special place to eat; they host Sunday dinners for the town's most elite families, Rotary club meetings, dinner every evening and special occasions like bridal showers, etc. Working there is an immediate game changer for me! I need to have white support shoes and a white uniform for the job. As soon as I earn enough money, I buy my own work shoes and uniforms. From the git-go I gladly 'suit up and show up.' The rush I get of earning my own money is exhilarating!

With the sheer force of my will, I realize that the job is not what I am or am not given, but what I make of it. I am at the center of my own universe. These are new moments, and new opportunities for me! I see crisp linen table cloths and folded napkins, stemmed glasses and water goblets. I save my money and I begin plotting some immense changes. I want these nice table settings, too! I want to take a step up to an ordinary life lived large. I want to know the joy of living like the folks who dine at White Hall Inn.

Evelyn is the Inn manager; she is very stern and precise. She manages the White Hall Inn restaurant with an iron fist and she requires perfection. She is a hard task master and I have an experience gap. We all jump to attention when we hear her high heels tottering across the wood floors, as she comes down the hallway between her in-suite apartment and the restaurant. As young girls, we get some good training there. We are taught to use proper place setting, serving and social protocol. We've mastered setting a proper table and using the correct silverware. I still serve from the left and clear from the right, and set the table ' *just so.* ' Most kids resent Evelyn, because she is often '*foaming at the mouth*' over something small, but she provides the discipline that I need. Even when Evelyn smiles, I feel her taking my inventory. I can feel the force of her curiosity. It's not arrogant curiosity, she only wants to know more about who I am. Of course, it is very unsettling for me when I feel her trying to expose my turbulent family life.

I spend more time away from home while working or out with friends. Lima, Ohio is under one hour away and that first summer I take a commercial bus trip on Saturday to shop. I buy new school clothes and shoes in Lima's upscale downtown department stores. Most people will agree that no matter what we do we want to do it well. We want to feel important. Between my parent's work ethic and Evelyn's training this helps me to learn a lot about who I am, and what I can do in the world. Once someone asks me, "*Have you ever noticed that you work harder and longer than everyone around you?*" I do work harder; I try to leave a place better than I found it. I carry my own load and I do more than my share, because work gives me opportunities. They definitely get their money's worth for our work and the wages we receive! I am paid 45 cents an hour and we split the tips with the kitchen help. I work at White Hall Inn from 1956 to 1958. The Inn closes in 1964...it is demolished in 1967.

We kids sneak the rusks and banana salad all the time, but if we were to eat something, Evelyn whips out the door from the back dining room to the back porch and she is off into the kitchen raising hell. One day when the potato rusk dinner rolls were cooling, I have one stuffed in my mouth. I think she is going to fire me! I would have missed the 45 cents an hour. We work all week and our checks are between $8.00 and $12.00 for the week. We even haul over there on our school lunch hour every Mondays to serve the Kiwanis club. Those serving trays for Rotary and Kiwanis Club dinners are heavy for us young girls. We definitely earn our money! After two years of working there I am still paid 45 cents an hour, standard wages in 1958.

~

Oug works 3:30 to Midnight as a janitor at Continental Can Company. He sleeps mornings and will not allow any noise in the house until he gets out of bed around noon. Oug wants Mom to get an outside job – but she feels that she should be at home with her children. Throughout my childhood, this argument doesn't stop. He says, "*She could work, instead of sitting around all day!"* Her argument is that she is a mother first, before all else. She will get a job outside the house when her youngest child starts school. That day comes the same fall; Wagtail starts school and Mom goes off to work. This happens within a few short months of the year that I got my first job. Things are a-changin' around our house!

She comes down the stairs in her work outfit, a new-looking white blouse tucked into a black and white houndstooth wrap skirt. She has red patent leather shoes and a neck scarf to tie it all together. She waves and smiles pleasantly, saying, *"I'll see you tonight!"* Going to work looks good on her!

~

Mom has never made any friends with other women. Now she is walking about ten blocks to work from 8a.m. to 5p.m. in the payroll dept. at the Overall Factory at Main and Market Streets in Van Wert. None of us drive and the car is "his." Having no use of the car equals no mobility and no freedom. This is one sign of his excessive control. We soon find that he can't allow her the freedom of being out of his sight and he can't allow her to know people that he doesn't know. Stopping on Main Street after work for coffee and a chat with female coworkers is the kind of thing he won't tolerate! Her new freedom causes him major suspicion and angst. He's losing a little of his control! I can either pretend that I don't hear, or I can act like it doesn't matter; either way the arguments go on nonstop.

We also find out that her having a salary creates some new and unexpected problems at home, too. He thinks she should buy groceries and pay utility bills and allow nothing for herself. Precisely, he thinks her money should be handed over to him. They get into a fight over the cost of sugar! It has always been our policy to take the groceries home and pay the grocery bill on his payday. He becomes aggressive now if she charges food at the grocery, as she previously has done.

His face works into an ugly twist as he details how his money is 'his' and he wants hers, too. When he gets into her purse and takes her money, she drops her head in defeat. If she tries any defense, he will bully her and wear her down with his male chauvinistic tactics toward her...and all women. She still isn't likely to outright defend her rights against him bullying and talking her down. I pay them 'no

102

more notice!' In the1950s people in a bad marriage seem to turn the other cheek and let it go on. I gave up on them.

In a more passive way, with her new income, she buys some much-needed new furniture and an automatic washer. In our dining room now, there is a new modern style, blonde wood buffet and a matching blonde table with six matching chairs, replacing the older Duncan Fife table. The new furniture in the dining room is still a place where things get piled up. Mom isn't entertaining anyone and she isn't serving food there either. Next, she buys a beige frieze sectional sofa and mid-century modern light wood tables. Even with new furniture the housekeeping is still lacking and dirt is collecting everywhere!

~

I am thirteen and in Junior high with budding breasts and hips, periods and pimples and I'm worrying that I might gain weight and never fit in. Junior high classes are new and different, too. We change rooms for classes like Choir, Home Economics, Gym and Library. Bells ring to let me know when to shuffle to the next class. Mrs. Kennedy teaches algebra and I'm not understanding anything about it! Home Ec., as it's called, is only for girls. We are learning sewing and cooking and baking. We make a hand-stitched sampler and at school we use an electric sewing machine in sewing class.

The boys in our class meet us after school hoping for a fresh baked cookie or chocolate brownie. I find that the boys are a little more interesting and civilized than they were in grade school. I take more interest in caring for my face and hair. My beautiful cousin tells me I should brush my wavy dish water blonde hair 100 strokes each day to make it smooth and shiny, so I do. I buy some Jergen's body lotion, and I smear my face every night with Ponds Cold cream. You go, Girl, wash your face!

I make friends with a girl at school and she nicknames me 'Kathy' Until now I'd never been called any name other than Kathleen. Kathy sounds nice, but my parents want me to be called Kathleen, so I don't mention the nickname around home at first. As it becomes more widely used, I think I should tell Mom about my changed name. This breaks her heart; with furrowed brow she tells me, *"Kathy is a kind of nice name, but isn't Kathleen a better name?"* But she never wins this one.

~

When Christmas bells ring in 1956 the holidays are a little more prosperous than they have been in years past. Mom's job brings in extra income and she loves Christmas! She has put money into a Christmas Savings Club at the bank. A Christmas Club is a type of savings account in which people make routine deposits throughout the year. The accumulated savings are withdrawn before the holiday season to provide funds for holiday shopping. The ever-critical Oug points out that she isn't getting any interest from the Christmas Club. But her interest is in buying real gifts for everyone. She can buy extra fun things like dolls, match box cars, playdoh, hula hoops and even clothes. A new era of different music replaces the old conservative swing music and the big band and ballroom dances of the 1940s era. The newer jitterbug, stroll and twist style of dance of our new rock and roll music begins with Bill Haley's *Rock Around the Clock*. That song changes the face of music in 1955. Dick Clark calls it "*the national anthem of rock music.*"

Elvis Presley appears on "The Ed Sullivan Show" for the first time on September 9, 1956, attracting 60 million viewers. "The Ed Sullivan Show" earns the best ratings on TV. In those two years the show becomes the most-watched TV broadcast of the 1950s decade.

~

Oug has an inflated sense of his own importance that manifests itself in his excessive need for our admiration and attention. We all deal with his ego at one time or another. With Mom being gone all day this leaves him to fend for himself and he looks around for a 'a new target' for his taunting aggression. As the oldest daughter, he chooses me! He tries getting in my face and talking me down one minute, then follows with something softer and nicer the next minute, in order to get his way. This is something he does to Mom. He acts completely innocent, about his 'cat and mouse game,' as if he cannot understand my disgust with him and his taunting. I soon find that when I snub him that causes me even more trouble. There seems to be no way to work this out with him. We haven't spoken at all since he screamed at me last week.

Mom is oblivious to his verbal attacks on me, because she is at work. He has always been difficult, but he can't stand that I am growing up to be such an independent female. I try to avoid him by keeping him at arm's length, with as few words as possible. He's furious when I try to clip him out of my daily life. Next, I choose to travel a different path with Oug. Like a fork in the road, I cross over without even a bit of respect. I am cold and indifferent toward him, and he is the same to me. Still, he gets worse when I shun him in the house by not looking in his direction. I avoid speaking and acknowledging him in passing. My disrespect for him makes him behave even worse!

When I won't cooperate, he searches and gets a neighborhood teen, Patsy, who is the same age as me. Patsy has problems with abuse at home so she sides with him that he has a perfect right to act in this male dominate, perverse way. He isn't doing diddly squat around the house, but he jabs at me by telling her, "*Don't you think my daughter should cook and do things for me?*"

I feel empowered when I make it apparent to him that his '*taunts*' aren't going to work with me. I nail him with a look to back off! When I don't give him the attention he craves, our relationship continues spiraling downward until I can't be around him at all. He continues trying to force me to cave in! He wants me to '*wait on him,*' '*bend to his wishes*' or anything to show that I appreciate him in the way that he needs. I never do accept any of this, my adrenaline sets in and we lock horns. We are in a war with each other.

As kids we express ourselves openly. I am as harsh with him as I dare to be, but I am still afraid of Oug's temper. I am reduced to keeping a heavy distance. I avoid him, but I don't dare to challenge him head on! A cold war is on between us! I can stop talking to Oug, but I am never able to tell him how he hurt us all, so I keep the anger inside. I often wonder, "*What the HELL is going on?*" I sit up for a long time looking for a solution that I can't name. Surely there is hope for a better life!

Mom is more passive, she won't often deny him the attention he needs, like I do; she knows better ways to work him. She will say th' she has been '*delt the cards and she has to play the hand!*' But she ' tinues doing the same thing, and she gets the same results.

As a teen, I have fire and strength but I don't know 'one s about a narcissistic personality disorder. My understandin'd much later when I learn that with narcissism, Oug is cor has no empathy. He is ALL for himself, and angry wit' who is against him–like I am! Only people who live 'glow' can be accepted by him. I'll be straight abr have moved outside of the glow of him! Neithr because someone outside has stollen his affection and we are both reduced to a distance.

It is Saturday evening and Oug is shirtless in the bathroom. He shaves with cold water and soap in the sink. His hair is drenched with Royal Red Rose hair oil. He is getting ready for a night out! He often leaves on Saturday evenings, being very mysterious with us all. He lives in a different world from the rest of us; he has a life we know nothing about. He is disgustingly full of himself. When he heads out for the evening, he says, *"See you subsequently!"* to anyone still listening. We all pretend not to notice him! Long ago we have given up on him. He makes a life for himself that doesn't include a wife and screaming kids as he often reminds us. He steps out onto the porch and we see him flip his Zippo and he lights up. He inhales deeply and in a New York minute he is sailing down Walnut Street in "*his*" Cadillac Convertible with the top down. He is smoking hard and fast! The blazing hot summer air blows through the car to cool him as he drives out of sight on most Saturday evenings. He has a way of turning women's heads; I don't see why he can't work his charm on Mom! But she accepts his ways of thinking when he tells her, *"Everybody needs a little salt in their shaker, just for keeping the sediment out!"* As his life changes, Mom thinks she has no alternative but to take his mid-life crisis in stride. Mom stays home with us while he goes out on the town. His urgent business is to '*see and be seen!*' Oug likes the Van Wert night life at the bars on Main Street, and at clubs like the Moose Lodge on Saturday nights. Oug says it "*takes the rag off the bush,*" when he has a car problem and he can't find anyone to help him! But we have been living years without a phone in our house, and none of us know where he goes. We don't ask, we all have long ago accepted that he has some private business out there! Mom esn't question a thing! She tries to hide the resentment because too, is afraid to express the anger that she is feeling. So, none of ke him accountable! That is probably what he wants!

Bu all the time he spends outside of the house, this makes The wh wonder what else we don't know about him. Around 1956 can thirteen and The Bug is fifteen, he has an idea of how we alwa what's going on! We become good detectives! His car is works vhen he is at home, and he has the only car key. Oug sleeps. sleeps mornings. We find the car keys while he e key into some bee's wax to make a mold. Then

106

we mix some epoxy glue with sawdust and pour it in the mold. When it hardens, we pull away the wax and we have a key! I keep watch from the porch, while 'Bug' searches the car. When we find a package of pictures of him with a woman, hidden under a side door panel in the back seat, we think, "*Well, if that don't beat it all!*"

We take the pictures of him with a woman from the car. We '*bust him*' because we think she should be told. When he is at work that night, our tongues are as sharp as a switchblade when we tell her straight up, "*MOM, HE IS HAVING AN AFFAIR!*" She holds her gaze on me until we show her the pictures. She looks at him and his lady friend together. She cries when the obvious is before her eyes. She probably already knew, and now she cries because we know! I am thrown off when she says, "W*hatever he does, he does,*' as she takes this all in, '*with a grain of salt!*' I think this one should have taken the whole shaker!

When it all comes out, Oug is furious! "*What in tarnation is going on?*" he asks. Oug has often told us, "*Never lie if the truth serves you better.*" So, he admits the whole thing, except he doesn't name the woman in the pictures. No emotion is left in Mom.

I thought he might hate what he has done, but, as a classic narcissist, he is comfortable enough with himself to continue this for five or more years. It isn't a surprise to me that after that they quit functioning together as a couple. Fixing any of this isn't possible. The details of his affairs come to me unexpectedly years later.

~

Living with Oug is like living in a minefield. As I continue through the teen years, I never talk back or slam doors, I do not dare! I know how far I can go and I stop there! It never occurs to me to aggravate him on purpose. I often do stomp off as I resist being short changed. Just below the anger there is a hurt – that hurt is sucking the life outta me. I am tough to please with an ongoing campaign of demanding more from my parents. I am outspoken and quick to put my foot down when I get less – which is most of the time! My '*don't tread on me*' attitude gets me NOWHERE! But my feet are set in concrete, not likely to move! By now, Oug and I hardly know what to say to each other. I walk on eggshells near him and I refuse to look at him. Disagreeing with him is like standing in a heavy wind. I imagine his face hardening and I wait for the jab that I imagine he is preparing. If he tries to talk, I pretend not to hear. The caring families I see on television and in novels seem more normal. No one has to point out that our home life is not normal. No one has to tell me about that; because I am witnessing it with my own eyes. Oug is unrelenting and hostile as I fight for self-respect, along with the difficult process of being a growing teen. I've known that something isn't right, but I can never put my finger on it. He would be labeled as abusive in today's world.

~

I am 15 years old in the spring of 1958, when I began to wonder what better opportunities are available for me. I leave White Hall Inn for the higher wages of 65 cents an hour and for more hours that are available at GC Murphy's Five and Ten cent store. All retail stores are closed on Sunday and open 9 a.m. to 5 p.m. weekdays, except closed on Wednesday afternoons. This store is doing a brisk business on Main Street, just down the street from the Rexall Drugstore, and right across from the Van Wert Court house.

~

I start high school in the fall of 1958 as a nervous freshman, constantly on guard as I try to squeak by at school. The student body of Van Wert High School is pretty typical for a small-town American high school. There are a couple of fairly well-defined groups sharing certain characteristics and they tend to hang out together. There is a group made up largely of the children of the town's doctors, law-yers, accountants, politicians and such. These kids tend to affect a conservative, clean-cut, buttoned-down appearance; they drive shiny new vehicles and wear clothes purchased from establishments whose names didn't end in Mart. My clothes from Murphy's Five and Ten will stand out in stark contrast to the designer names sported by our more affluent classmates. They're at ease with each other as they erupt in laughter with each other.

Boys at school seem to have turned into more reasonable humans. I even like a few of them! My real life is only at work or school. I worry that I might do or say the wrong thing, but I am always happi-er at school than at home. Most of all I want to appear normal among friends. I find a place for myself among this lesser affluent group who are none the less popular, active and pretty girls. I think that being a part of this group makes me look COOL, as if I can acquire some of their allure for myself. I'm such a fake as a young teen. I go in and out of the house conjuring up a fantasy life to hide behind. I tuck away parts of myself to stay unnoticed in classes. I can't attend a school dance without a formal dress. A popular senior girl I met in a study hall sells me a homemade formal for my first high school dance. The stories I tell myself can go either way, to move me up or to hold me down.

From my group of friends, I acquire a fairly good sense of normal living. With the popularity of a group, I can fade into a crowd! What it comes down to is this: the more fun I have with friends has made it even harder to come back to the reality of my home life. Families don't have to be perfect, but fear and manipulation is unconventional. Oug' s self-focused rules are all different from the other fathers and his authority is absolute. He does as he pleases, meanwhile I try to pass as a normal kid despite him.

I am fourteen years old the fall before my sophomore year of high school when I meet Doug DeCamp at a friend's house. We are immediately attracted to each other but we don't go to the same school. We are both casually floating on the same cloud when I see him very occasionally at Dolly's Restaurant after school. We don't date for a while because I have another boyfriend during the school year. My other guy is a straight A-Lister at school because he plays on the high school basketball team. Being on the basketball team makes him *so* popular and I think I can '*glow in his light*' by association when we meet at our lockers between classes. I hold onto him through the basketball season but we never date outside of school.

I keep trying to find my place in school by joining Y-teens and acting in the senior class play. I am a reporter for the school newspaper and planning school spirit activities with the pep club. I am in Girl's Athletic Club all four years. GAA is a Girl's Athletic Association of Intermural games where girls play half-court basketball without any audience. Girls don't have any other high school team sports in this era. No one gives a care about girls in sports. We don't know the rejection but we do know everyone reveres male athletes.

My grades are average because I don't totally focus on my school work. I don't have a desk or a quiet workspace at home. Sometimes I study with Carol at her house or go to the library to use encyclopedias. No one asks if I have done my homework and often I haven't. I've been known to cram for a quiz in the hall outside the classroom!

I work at the Five and Dime store until my junior year when I get into the (DCT) Diversative Cooperative Training Program where

I enroll in the Dental Assisting program. This program is in the last two years of high school for students who are focused on vocational training. DCT is a class with a job that I am paid for and my school days go like this: I attend classes in the mornings and work in the dental office for Dr. Fred Fugazzi, DDS, during weekday afternoons. Diversified Cooperative Training at Van Wert High School is for the working-class kids like me, who for one reason or another didn't have a post-secondary education in our immediate future. I ditch college prep classes for vocational training because I believe this training is a great deal for me. But I can't have it both ways and I end up paying the price for that decision later. I am sixteen when I start paying for my own dental expenses. In addition, Wagtail has an over-bite and I also set up a payment plan for braces and a retainer for her.

Most people around high school age develop some kind of plan that becomes a driving force in their life. Not that they always do these things, but plans are forming about college, work or whatever is next. I am that girl who doesn't even know where to start!

Our DCT instructor takes our class to a convention at the Ohio State University. After visiting the campus, I see a college campus for the first time. I dare to dream of going to college there. In the DCT program, I don't take college prep classes, but I casually decide that I will go away to college at Ohio State anyhow. I believe I can do this because Mom has always encouraged college, saying, *"If you want to go for higher education, I will find a way."* So, I believe her on that, but I have no idea of costs or how this will be possible. In this phase, I plan that I will get a college education but I never ask for any help from the guidance office, since I think they work with the affluent group who are all preparing to transition straight into college after graduation. I never guess they could help me with any questions I might have about financial aid or classes that I might need to take. I assume that the guidance office only caters to people who might have parental assistance and money set aside for college.

"I'm just a small-town girl with a big town dream."
- Song by Dusty Springfield

CHAPTER EIGHT

Happy Days - I Meet My Man

The heat of the summer is diminished in early September 1958 when Doug DeCamp comes to my door unannounced and unexpected. I haven't seen him around town all summer. He can't call me before coming because neither of us have phones in our homes. He's 'styling' with a flat top haircut. I am home alone and I'm not planning to go out. I am giving myself a *'Toni'* Home Permanent when he shows up! I greet him with *"Long time, no see!"* I follow with, *"What's up?"* He is going to the Van Wert County fair. He asks me, *"Do you want to go to the fair with me?"* My heart is thumping! I am totally up for that! He looks genuinely happy when I say, *"I sure do; give me a minute to wash this stinky stuff outta my hair!"* I clean up and I run up the stairs to jump into a new 2-piece, matching red sweater set, with a red felt full circle skirt. I am fifteen and I have recently purchased this for my sophomore year of school. The radio in my room is playing *"All I Have To Do is Dream,"* by the Everly Brothers, as I tease and rat up my long hair with a rat tail comb. My hair still carries the smell of permanent hair curling solution and my bangs are shellacked into place with Aqua Net hair spray. The summer humidity begins to wilt that hairstyle! O well, what can ya' do? He smells like Old Spice cologne with just a hint of cigarette smoke. We are off to the Van Wert County Fair for our first date. He is quiet and dependable. Right away I like his good manners and his quiet and reserved style. He has a delightful chuckle that soon works its way into a full-sized belly laugh. The sound of his hardy laugh is my all-time favorite!

We make small talk as we thread our way through the crowds at the fairgrounds that evening. We are both so smitten that I want to freeze the night forever! When he takes my hand, he thinks awhile about what he'd like to say. It throws me off when he gives me the side eye, but he doesn't speak up! Heat passes between us so warm that it warms my hands! I know he wants to kiss me but he doesn't. He must have felt the same heat, because it is not long before he completely gives up spending his leisure time with the boys from Convoy. He is hanging around my house with some serious interest! By November he gives me his class ring! I wrap the back of his ring with yarn to make it fit my finger. Everything between us is new and exciting!

Dating is the perfect distraction from my family life. Before any date I clean and organize things in the house. I put in some heavy elbow grease to make it really clean, but even then, the household furnishings are old and barely presentable.

Doug has to share his father's green 1956 Buick with his two older brothers. Anytime he can use the car he drives the seven miles from Convoy to Van Wert. Most couples that are 'going steady' dress alike with matching shirts. Within weeks we buy several matching shirts and sweaters for going out together, so that everyone around can see that we are going steady!

He is the sweetest, funniest and most attentive guy I have ever known. I can be intense and serious, but he can lighten me up with a chuckle. He is reserved and quiet, but I love being around him. We dress up fancy and go to Fort Wayne for dinner at nice restaurants. I love those date nights because NONE of the local boys at my school are taking their dates to the city! Without any responsibilities we are on the same page and we click and mesh together perfectly. He encourages and respects me, often putting my needs above his own.

He lights up a Lucky Strike cigarette while staring into a cloud of smoke. That surprises me, not a bit and it's not a deal breaker because lotsa kids smoke. I don't smoke because it is an expensive habit that I can't afford. My mother tells me not to smoke. Period! I leave cigarettes alone. No one knows in the 1950s and before, that smoking can be hazardous to anyone's health. We do know that it is addictive and if a person starts smoking it will be hard to quit. After a while I beg him to stop smoking. I soon learn that 'you can lead a horse to water, but you can't make him drink.' He doesn't stop smoking, but we have no idea of the far-reaching benefits of that choice, until much later.

In the late 1950s we cruise downtown in Van Wert, Ohio, '*to see and be seen*' on Main Street. Cruisin' is big fun! The streets of downtown Van Wert ring out with the sound of car radios playing, "*Rock around the Clock*" by Bill Haley and the Comets and "*Love Letters in the Sand*" by Pat Boone and "*Young Love*" by Sonny James. One night he has his dad's car and we cruise on Main Street East up to Cherry Street and we loop back west down past the Brumback Library all evening. When Doug goes home, his slack-jawed dad is wondering, "*Son, where did you go last night?*" He asks because Doug has put 210 miles on the speedometer and we never left Van Wert! The warm summer nights are endless fun in '*these days*!' These times are later labeled '*Happy Days*!' and indeed they are! As he drives, I am sitting close, almost on his lap. We are jumping in and out of the cars, and running around to jump back in; we're calling this a 'Chinese fire drill.' The drug store has a soda fountain and long counters with little stools that we love to spin. We girls comb and flip our long hair as we smile and flirt with the boys and drink our 25 cent milkshakes. Another favorite is driving through the Root Beer Stand where a hot dog is 25 cents and a large Mug of Root Beer is 10 cents. The carhops deliver the food to our car windows on a tray. Dolly's Restaurant on Main Street is the place in our town for teens to hang out in the 1950s and 1960s. Dolly's has good 20 cent hamburgers and French fries. They have Cocoa Cola in the green bottles with paper straws. The jukebox plays all the latest music of the day. Whenever we go into Dolly's we play our favorite song "*My True Love*" by Jack Scott on their jukebox!

My parents are not big on store-bought things. This is a part of their somewhat deliberate effort to opt out of the consumer culture. This is symbolized by their anti-television stance, our homemade clothes and hand me down toys. We don't have a TV blaring the "*Leave it to Beaver*" show in our house until 1957 when Oug brings home a used 13- inch table model long after most of the neighbors. We are very happy to get that small television. We like the sitcom families on the 1950s radio and TV shows like The Ozzie and Harriet Show. We turn the TV on after school and all of us kids gather around for the Mickey Mouse Club. We also tune in American Bandstand, an American music dance program with Dick Clark, which is Philadelphia teens dancing to the latest teen songs.

~

High School football games are as good as it gets in Van Wert. The Van Wert Cougars have a record setting run, being undefeated in the five years from 1957 to 1961. Some of the players go on to become famous coaches. Doug and I are always 'hand in hand' at the Van Wert high school football Games. We don't miss any of the school dances after the games either; these dances are called 'Sock Hops' because we dance in stocking feet. It's an informal dance event also called a record hop or just a hop. The hops are held after Friday night games in the gyms at both of our high schools. We are dancing to, "*Doing That Hand Jive*" on TV!

~

As is the custom of the times, I follow in my mother's footsteps and I accept that we are unequal. He is stronger physically and financially dominant. I am the submissive, passive and dependent female. These are the roles that we know and accept. when we are young and in love. Sexism isn't a '*thing*' to anyone in 1950s and nothing like that ever matters. I have been groomed to do only average things. My mother lives vicariously through our budding romance. She can hardly contain her own bubbly excitement! I meet his parents. As I get to know this family, I realize we are as different as night and day. His dad is an engineer in management where he wears a white shirt and tie. Oug is a janitor, a union man. He works with his hands and is paid by the hour. His dad compliments and respects his mother. His people are reserved and nicer to each other. They call each other '*honey*' and '*dear.*' Where I come from, we just '*fight it out!*' We live by *'Bite or be bitten!'* Conversely, his family arrives early – and they wait impatiently. My family will be late to our own funerals – we're rolling in on two wheels at the last minute. We're thinking up an excuse for being late as we drive!

His family life is a source of fascination for me. After having four sons his parents love having girls around. All the DeCamp boys have girlfriends; we quickly become the daughters they never had! Sometimes they buy me things which is unusual to me, as my parents never do. When I come for dinner, we eat in the dining room because I am a guest in their home. I gravitate toward the light when I wake up every day, knowing good things are happening!

~

Throughout my high school years, I confidently begin looking forward to a future of entertaining and having nice things when I have a house of my own. My mind races with thoughts of what to do with my life and I'm dreaming of a thousand subtle life changes. I hold onto the hope that my world will be different, with the path I am choosing. With energy and commitment, I have a few solid ideas and an action plan. The John Earl Department Store is so expensive that I can't afford to look at my reflection in the windows! It's a store, as fancy as they come, around Van Wert. There are cool canisters that fly around the store on wires taking change back and forth from the office to the sales registers. I linger along the aisles in the high-ceilinged main floor to inhale cologne spritzes. I take in the chatter of the shoppers. An elevator operator takes me to the second floor. I savor the scenes at the big Department Stores in Lima and I particularly love John Earl's in Van Wert.

A hope chest is a piece of furniture traditionally used by unmarried young women to collect items, such as clothing and household linen, in anticipation of married life. The term "hope chest" or "cedar chest" is used in the Midwest or south of the United States. The collection is a common coming-of-age rite until approximately the 1950s; it is typically a step on the road to marriage between courting a man and engagement. **(https://en.wikipedia.org/wiki/Hope_chest)**

He buys me a cedar chest for Christmas as a hope chest. When I get paid at Murphy's five and dime Store, I head to the John Earl Store where I can layaway goods and make weekly payments. I keep working and filling my hope chest throughout high school.

My childhood of conflict leaves me with a truck load of disfunctions that I need to dig out from under. I set some goals for fancy living and I follow through by collecting a stock of things for a lifestyle of '*sit down*' candle light dinners. I buy table cloths, a bed & bath set, white with a violet flower pattern. I make payments for weeks until each set is paid and I can bring them home. When that is paid in full, I begin stacking in plush towels, matching sheet sets and fancy linens for my hope chest. I do the same with a set of copper-bottomed Revere Ware pans. My plan for my world will be different, with the path I have taken. After a lifetime, most of this is worn out and gone, but I've used these same pans for sixty years and they are still good!

During my second year of high school, I buy a walnut dresser and a bed with a walnut book case headboard for myself. I buy a new mattress to replace the old iron bed with cotton mattress that has been in the house since we moved there. This is the nicest furniture in the house! At times I wake up in the night just for the joy of seeing it! When I buy it, I make it clear that I will take it when I leave home. But that doesn't go without conflict when I take it away, because Mom has to buy a new bed for my sisters. I take it with me anyway!

I have only one wall plug in the bedroom that I share with my sisters. I have to unplug the lamp to listen to the WGN Radio station and again to play my 45rpm stack record player. I have quite a good collection of the seven-inch single records; I can stack about six discs on the pedestal at one time. I buy them at Pollacks record store where I can play them in a sound booth before deciding which one to buy. They cost a dollar for two songs, one song on each side by the same artist.

Meanwhile in my hot stagnant upstairs bedroom, the late afternoon sun shows through the screens and I sit anxiously on my bed. I am fiddling with homework, but I am giving the homework a low priority, as I am running to the front window with every car door that I hear closing outside!

Boys are Oug's favorite, though he denies it! The boys are definitely held to different standards. Bug boy goes out driving in Oug's car when he is sixteen, but I'm not allowed. Because I am a girl, I am confined at home and I've never seen Mom in the driver's seat. In Oug's view females have no rights. We are groomed to get married and have children at a younger age and to be totally dependent on our men. Boys need a car for dating. This, once again, makes me feel belligerent and cheated by him. Later on, The Bug buys a "beater" that he purchases for cash with savings from after-school and summer jobs. I never do have a car of my own and I am never allowed to borrow Oug's car. I don't get a driver's license right away, because, what do I need a driver's license for? So, after school and work, I walk home and I usually stay there.

Doug and I write letters to each other almost daily, mailing them via US mail the fifteen miles between Convoy and Van Wert. His letters to me are full of passion, love and silliness. I open his letter and I see that he has written that I am as "*Cute as a speckled puppy under a red wagon*". I am not sure where he got that, but I think it's cute!

We get together at least once on most weekends. When he arrives, I open the front door and take him by both forearms. We swing around as he makes his way into the house. When we have a date, I clean the house before he comes, but most nights when we go out, we come back home to laundry dumped on the couch and the dishes are in the sink. Mom just doesn't get it! This embarrassed me on a first date, but once he is a steady boyfriend, he gets used to it! We move the pile of laundry over so that we can sit down.

Several times I have parties at home, with kids from school. I clean all day to get the house ready when I plan a party. I sweep, dust and mop to the music of Frankie Avalon singing "*Venus*," or "*Tom Dooley*" by the Kingston Trio and "*Mack the Knife*" by Bobby Darren. I move the chairs around the outside edge of the room so we can dance in our bobby socks, in the dining room. I buy some Pepsi and potato chips for snacks and arrange everything on the buffet. I stack some 45rpm records on my small hi-fi record player and dress in my pink poodle skirt for dancing. We love anything by Elvis Presley like "*Don't be Cruel*," or "*Hound Dog*" and "*Blue Suede Shoes.*"

Occasionally I walk uptown carrying my small transistor portable radio for music. I listen to songs like "*Itsy Bitsy Teeny-Weeny Yellow Polka Dot Bikini.*" I go into Derry's Drug Store to get a marshmallow coke and a Seventeen magazine. But I mostly go to see who might be cruising' on Main Street. Every kid wants a transistor radio in the 1950s. But 'Rock and Roll' on transistor radios and hula hoops are a passing fad!

In the warm Ohio summers, we go to the Van Wert Drive-in on the Lincoln Highway west of Van Wert. We see Bing Crosby, Tuesday Weld and Fabian in "*High Time.*" The drive-in costs $1.00 per carload. Movies start at sundown. We, as well as all our friends, usually bring in extra people inside the trunk of the driver's car. A speaker is hooked on the window for sound. Families will park in the front near the concession stand, couples like the darker area in the rear.

During the winter months we go to Schine's Theatre at Main Street at Market Street in Van Wert. Doug usually has about $2.00 in his pocket, that his dad gives him for the evening. On Sunday evenings he pays 35 cents each for us to see Sandra Dee in *"Gidget."* The next week we see, *"Some Like It Hot"* with Marilyn Monroe. My favorite '50s movie is *"Pillow Talk"* with Doris Day.

One evening Doug comes over with his eleven-year-old brother. 'Wagtail' is eight when I dress and fix her hair for her *'first date.'* They look so cute! They are so excited because, as a special treat, we are bringing them to get a root beer with us, at the B&K Root Beer stand on West Main Street in Van Wert. *"Little Deuce Coupe"* by the Beach Boys is playing as the carhops are delivering Coney dogs with frosty mug root beers served alongside. As the four of us savor the moment, we hear, *"Stranger in Paradise," "Mr. Sand Man, Bring Me Your Dream"* ... but Elvis Presley is *'The King'* with *"Heart Break Hotel."*

There are endless shenanigans at our house! When Doug and I are in the living room at home, Wagtail or one of the twins will get under the end tables and stay quiet to spy on us. They want to hear what we are talking about. Kids will do what kids do. Since there isn't much privacy around my house, sometimes we park in other more private places. One snowy night we *'park'* on a country road for privacy. We listen to romantic songs like *"Moon River,"* and *"Volare"* and *"Chanson d 'Amour"* on the car radio. We have a chat and a few kisses. But we got the car stuck in the snow. Doug walks to a farmhouse nearby to get help. He tells the guy we were forced off the road by a passing car. That guy comes out and helps us get out of the snowbank. What we don't know is that the wife works with Doug's mother. The following morning, she tells his mother the whole story! This is a small town and we can't hide anything, anywhere. Another night, an even more scary thing happened. We parked along Union Quary. From the rear passenger side window, we see a man peering into the glass watching us. He is RIGHT THERE! Doug spins out spewing mud. When we get home there is muddy hand prints on the passenger door handle! YIKES! We never go back there.

~

I feel passionate about having a solid future, but I am still reckless with the details. Later on, I learn that there won't be any money from Oug's check for any college tuition. I just didn't know Mom doesn't have access to any money. I hide behind my strong will to do everything on my own without asking anyone for help. I am a junior in High School and I think I will go away to college at Ohio State. Mom tries to get Oug to let her mortgage the house for my education, but she has no power or money of her own and Oug says a huge NO to mortgaging the house or spending any money for my college. There is no college in or around Van Wert and I didn't have a car or any real money. I find out quickly that there sure is a big difference between setting a goal and making it happen!

I still want to go get some job training and I learn of a shorter dental assistant training program in Chicago. Next, Doug drives Mom and me up to see the place and explore the costs, etc. When we get back home, we find that there is no money for that either! I do wonder why she hasn't explored any of that with him BEFORE we made the trip to visit the dental college!

~

Susita and I are cutting each other's hair. We have no beauty school training; we cut, if we don't like it, we cut some more! Sure, it grows back, but there's nothing quite like an epic hair disaster. We do try to take our hair cutting more seriously. I cut a layer of short hair around the crown in back. Dr. Fugazzi often asks me, "*What happened here?*" Or, I will sometimes look in the mirror and I see my hair is too short in front and I think, "*What have I done?*" Susita loves cutting and fixing hair, so much more than I do, and she is quite good at it. A few years later she goes to beauty school and makes a career out of it!

Wagtail is nine during the March 1959 launch of Barbie. The doll world has never been the same. Barbie is born as a full-blown hottie in a swimsuit. She has passed through 6 decades in perfect lock step with the times. In 1965 flying to the moon as an astronaut, ethnic types battle racism in the 1980's, she ran for president in 1992, Olympic Barbie, front line worker and more. Proving to 60 years of women that adapting, proceeded by hard work, is necessary for survival. You rock, Barbie!

~

In March 1959, no money is available for me to attend college, but Oug plans for our first international trip! With our family of seven that's a carload! International travel is quite unconventional for anyone at the time and this is certainly out of the ordinary for our family. Oug, being a discerning kind of guy, plans every detail of the trip before we leave. He takes Spanish lessons and studies at home with language records. He is disgusted when I take French I and II in high school instead of Spanish, but Spanish is not being offered at our school. He can speak well enough to arrange stays in the local Spanish speaking hotels and to order food in restaurants. We each bring two sets of clothes in a cardboard dress box. This concise packing is because we need the trunk space for sleeping. We drive Oug's 1954 Cadillac Eldorado from Van Wert, Ohio to Mexico City almost nonstop. He configures the car so that we can all go through a hole where the convertible top folds down to sleep stretched out in the huge deep Cadillac trunk. Mom tries to squelch her own self-doubt, but she never learns to drive very well. She puts the fear into us all on a narrow mountain road in Mexico, when she swerves too near the edge.

We have a driving schedule that includes the four of us who are old enough to drive, taking two hours driving shifts. The driving is 24 hours per day with each shift being two hours of driving and two hours of navigating by map reading and observing from the passenger seat. Oug is adamant that we don't slow down or stop moving to exchange drivers. The navigator slides over while the driver goes under to exchange seats while going down the road at full speed. When the driver is off duty, he passes over the back seat and into the trunk to just relax or sleep. No one drives alone without a navigator. Someone in the back seat moves to the passenger side of the front seat to navigate. Our driving trip is across the United States, entering Mexico at Laredo. Driving inside Mexico to Monterrey, San Luis Potosi, and Queretaro to Mexico City. From Mexico City, Oug, Bug and I take a bus trip to Acapulco. A few of the highlights of Mexico City are the Mosaics on the buildings downtown on the Avenue of the Americas, Chapultepec Park and Xochimilcan Gardens and we love running through the out-door markets at the Cathedral of Guadeloupe. As is our usual style, we run freely in the streets of Mexico City, going to the outdoor market most days. We quickly learn to say "*cuánto Cos-*

tus?" to find out how many pesos we will need. This trip is about 2550 miles each way (5,100 miles total.) We are only gone for two weeks.

~Siblings on Mexico Trip~

After we return home, I buy a long, light-blue, layered formal for my senior prom. Doug and I dance the night away at my last Van Wert High School prom. Later on, I cut up the skirt of my dress to make a baby bassinette skirt. I graduate Van Wert High school and turn 18 the same month. My graduation is held outside in the stadium. We walk across the grass, pick up the diploma from the principal and it's over. Mom comes along to watch, but Oug doesn't attend. There is no announcement, no gifts and no party.

The dental office where I work moves into a medical building that is about 2 ½ miles from my home. After I graduate Van Wert High School, I have the DCT Training completed and I can continue working at Dr. Fugazzi's office.

~

The endless struggle with Oug is again in the fore front. As soon as I turn 18 years old in May of my senior year of high school, Oug tells me that "*With each new privilege comes a responsibility!*" With my graduation, I am now supposed to pay rent for room and board, if I want the privilege of staying there. He says, "*If you're old enough to draw a paycheck, you're old enough to pay rent.*" This is my final push from the nest. Whatever childhood I'd had, or never had, is over. Knowing that there will be no further help with anything, I make plans to leave as soon as possible. If I am going to pay somebody some rent, it won't be him! I'm frustrated and powerless because I really didn't have a place to go. I don't have the will to stay put here, but I don't have a car or earn enough money to rent an apartment. I despise living at home and paying rent, I'm saving some money and we have almost everything to fill a home. Doug and I share the idea of getting out of these small towns. My hope chest is over flowing, and we're plotting our escape by making exciting plans to move to the '*city!*'

Since I don't have a car, I take a taxi back and forth to work every work day for the next year. When the taxi passes the high school mornings in the next fall, I am sad to see that I am no longer a part of the school fun–I miss the high school lifestyle. I know now that I was raised in a small town into a family with mundane expectations for the future. I want to do more, but I haven't been raised to expect or encouraged to dream of anything more. I pay the rent at home and I work at the dental office for another year.

After high school Doug finds a job in Fort Wayne at Lincoln Life Insurance Company. He works in the mail room, delivering mail around the office. He buys a red 1956 Ford Convertible; he goes to college at Purdue in Fort Wayne and he commutes from home. He isn't required to pay rent and his dad pays his tuition.

"Everything is going to be alright.
Maybe not today, but eventually."

– Roy T. Bennett -Author

CHAPTER NINE

Married with Children

Six months after my high school graduation, we get engaged at Christmas. He gives me a diamond ring with four prongs in a white gold setting. I stare in amazement at my new diamond ring. Oh my! How shiny and sparkly it is! This new diamond has become a symbol of our new shiny life together. Sadly, he has to drop out of college for a semester to pay for my ring. Mom excitedly lives vicariously through this engagement and she is SO happy for us! She announces our engagement in the Van Wert Times Bulletin with a professional engagement photograph. The announcement says that a wedding date has not been set.

I am nineteen years old and we had been together for 4 years and engaged for 4 months. In early spring 1962 I am pregnant. This throws me into the future with little preparation. I'm feeling bad for myself! With this huge leap into adulthood, I feel a heavy responsibility. I trust him and I have never stopped trusting him but I am a bundle of nerves, frayed on both ends! We are on a wheel going 90 mph with no idea of where this is going! I need someone to tell me it's going to be ok even if it looks like it won't. Doug says, *"Don't worry, everything is going to be all right,"* but I am so worried, I cry and he looks at me crying and gives me a smile of love and hope with an air of good cheer that really helps. He follows up with, *"If this is the worst thing that happens, it's going be a good life!"* After that, I feel lighter – My stride is a little jauntier. I gain some confidence that allows me to feel that a good outcome is possible. Oug always tells us that, *"Life can be beautiful, if you will just allow it to be!"* With blind trust, we ditch college ideas and forge a path to get married. We tell no one! We announce a wedding date and plan for our wedding without asking anyone for any help. Although it isn't a huge affair, it is very nice.

On June 15th just one year after I graduate from high school, we are getting married. I take a deep breath and I walk slowly but surely up the center aisle. Mrs. Edith Dannaker is playing *"Here Comes the Bride"* on the Church organ and Pastor Utz performs the matrimonial service. Our wedding is a candle light service on a bright sunny late afternoon at St. Mark's Lutheran Church. My sisters are bridesmaids wearing light blue dresses with cumber bunds. Mom sews their brides-maid dresses and she makes a dress for herself. Oug doesn't own a suit and he doesn't want to wear one, but I want him to dress in a suit for the wedding. *"Don't that take the cake?"* he says, but he borrows a navy-blue business suit from my uncle Gene, and he adds a bright yellow shirt and ascot tie to jazz up the outfit!! Doug's parents dress appropriately. Doug's best man is his brother, Terry. He is wearing the suit he wore for his own wedding about 8 months before. His brother, Gary can't attend, as he is serving in the military.

June 15th 1962 – St. Mark's Lutheran Church - Van Wert, Ohio

White gowns signify purity. I buy a white gown with a blue satin under lining to signify my impurity to myself. I am wearing a diamond pendant that Doug has given me for a wedding gift. He is wearing a rented white formal jacket with black pants. He chooses a blue sash to match the blue in my dress. The reception is in the church basement Fellowship room with about 50 guests present. A few friends attend, but it is mostly our immediate families with aunts, uncles and cousins.

We have a traditional wedding cake, mixed nuts and butter mints on small paper plates. The servers are my high school friends and some ladies from the church who volunteer in the kitchen. We do not have any drinking or dancing at our reception. In these times, only Catholics drink and dance at weddings at Van Wert.

After Doug shoves the cake in my mouth, and all over my face for the camera, we begin opening our gifts around the cake table. As our family and friends sit on folding chairs watching us, I feel sure they are simply awestruck as we hold up each gift: A hand mixer, tablecloth, crocheted potholders and dishtowel to show them. We even get a plastic flower arrangement. After about one hour of this, the reception is over and all go their separate ways.

We head to a hotel around Fort Wayne for the first night of our honeymoon. We drive to Miami Beach, Florida in his Red 1966 Ford Convertible. Not long after we get on the road, the door handle on the passenger side fails! The door won't stay closed. He drives while I hold the door handle closed all of the way to Florida. When we arrive at the fancy waterfront hotel on Miami Beach, they have valet parking. We have to decline the valet and self-park, so that they won't find the door problem. We enjoy a week vacation at Miami Beach and drive back to Ohio. On the return trip, I am still holding the door shut!

~

When we get back, I quit my job at the dentist office in Van Wert for our move to Fort Wayne. I have a brand-new husband, a collection of furniture, linens and an absolute understanding that it is time for me to get outta Van Wert! In July, 1962, we move into our own place and I think some time and distance will be good! I suppose I wanted to be as far away from home as possible. Doug continues working in the mailroom at Lincoln Life Insurance Company His job is simply delivering mail around the office, a job more suitable for a single kid.

Praise God, we have all of the things we need for furnishing our apartment because of all that I have laid away for the past few years. I do love playing house, furnishing the apartment, making things pretty and we do have lots of pretty things.

I have read that: "*People marry to get what they miss in their childhood.*" Or "*To have someone to witness their lives.*" We began this 'witnessing' in an upstairs apartment in Fort Wayne, Indiana. All we crave is a happy life with enough to eat and a warm place to sleep. Living in an upstairs apartment is the only place we can afford.

We are still quiet about the pregnancy. We don't mention that until two months after the wedding when his mother notices I am popping buttons and she figures it out! Now that she mentions it, in pre-marital counseling Pastor Utz has told us to get a job, get married, buy a house and then have children. That's his idea! Of course, we don't tell him we have already jumbled the order! He tells us how a premature pregnancy and marital breakups are the predictable and the almost inevitable consequences of an early marriage and they're further complicated by a stormy childhood like mine!

In spite of his predictions our marriage begins as exciting, fast and furious as a torrential rainstorm and as hot as an erupting volcano. I assume that being a wife will be a goal that I have achieved, and the rest will be blissful. A marriage is a gamble that we can't possibly imagine. I am quickly on my own, an adult at nineteen. I am married to a twenty-year-old boy. He is the head of our household and I am officially Mrs. Douglas DeCamp. I take his first and last name just that way. I sign my own name '*Mrs. Douglas DeCamp*' until a feminist informs me that I am me and he is he. Whoa! I can be Kathy, Kathleen or whatever first name I choose to use but I stay with the last name. There are no hyphenated family names yet.

I make an easy adjustment from being tormented by Oug to being cared for by Doug. His love is as soft as a new baby! I quickly accept this happier life. Knowing that we are responsible for ourselves quickly divides childhood from adulthood. We have so much trust, but we don't know what we are getting into. Amazingly the many changes in our lives begin feeling tight and uncomfortable right away. We adore each other, but there is no correlation between that love and rewards that go with it. Money problems turn out to be quite an adventure! I create a budget and list each bill and there is no room for any extras. The worry that his paycheck won't cover the bills gnaws at my stomach. At the grocery I go through a mental math deciding if we can buy ice cream.

As a child raised by depression-era parents, I have never been extravagant, reckless with money or a self-indulgent spender. I have to compulsively budget, calculate and tightly hold onto our only paycheck. We have to give up a lot of stuff. Our marriage begins as a blending of talents and an interesting sharing of our experiences. I want to cook grown-up meals and do the best I can with the money we have. As it turns out I have all these fancy table linens, glassware and dishes, but I know nothing about cooking! Oug says I am an 'arsonist' in the kitchen! Luckily, Doug can cook and we balance each other out. I don't want him to know that I can't even boil water. So, I hide my Betty Crocker cookbook on a kitchen chair that I can push under the table when he comes into the room!

Even more important than the cooking, I need to work awhile longer. I had planned to work in the summer and fall of 1962 but no one will hire me. By early fall I am visibly pregnant. I have interviews at several places in downtown Fort Wayne, for office and retail jobs that I am easily qualified for, but at five months along, they see my 'baby bump' and will not hire me. I keep pushing but I can't even be hired as a store clerk, because" *A woman's place is in the home.*" All arguments crumble for me because they can legally say that to women in these days before women's rights became laws. Married women are dead in the eyes of the law. No property rights, no voice legally and we are paid a fraction of men's wages. I am tired of being rejected and I am disappointed that I have to stay home that fall. Though money is short, we think we have this! We deal with money problems by not allowing ourselves to want much, because a mail boy salary doesn't cut it! In these times, men are paid more because they "*have a family to support*" but the mail room job Doug has is not a head of household kind of job. He is a "*Mail Boy*" and he gets a boy's pay. I am regarded as "*Just a housewife*" because I am staying at home. This oddly vague term says everything about the era and not so much about who I am as a woman before the equal rights amendment. We accept all of this until the women's movement.

I have to pinch some more pennies as I keep pushing on, so I take up sewing. Mom gives me some of her flannel sewing scraps and I spend some beautiful fall days sewing at her house using her sewing machine. I sew yellow and green flannel baby gowns and blankets, when we really need the extra money from a second paying job. We are overwhelmed by enormous responsibilities and stress with no extra money. I push through because that is the only option that I have. We do a lot of coupling together at home, because we don't have money for anything else.

We have each other and we have a home but I am sick every day, frumpy and pregnant. Many pregnant women have morning sickness, especially during the first trimester. But I have ongoing nausea and vomiting throughout my pregnancy and not only in the morning! My confidence is at an all-time low. I wonder if he might be disappointed in me, because I really am a '*hot mess.*' My unwashed hair is pulled back in a pony tail. I look and feel like hell, but he keeps smiling whenever he sees me. We have a strong deep love and I don't know what to make of it. I expect that all the financial stress might change him and maybe he will get depressed. I finally get used to him being a patient and nice person. I know I'm too young and I have no business being a mother. I can easily say it's better to wait for more money and maturity before raising children, but in those years, young couples often have families soon after marriage.

~

The draft hangs over every young man in the early 1960s. Conscription is the mandatory enlistment of people in a national service, for performing military service. In the 1960s, once a man reaches eighteen years of age, he receives a letter from the Selective Service System stating that he is eligible for the draft. At age eighteen, Doug is classified as 1-A as a young single male. Deferments are permitted for full-time college students but he's part-time. There are also deferments for married men and further deferment for each dependent child. The ongoing Vietnam war is raging at the same time as the Cuban invasion, called the Bay of Pigs. This causes many young men who are A-1 Classified to be drafted. Oh, we don't need that! That possibility is getting too close to us! But Doug's recent marriage and having a child lowers his selective service classification and consequently he is never drafted for active military service. The draft is abolished in 1972.

~

We relax a little as our thoughts turn to the child who will change our lives forever. I don't know if it will be a boy or girl until birth. I know that a baby is about to change the rest of my life. When two becomes three, I can't imagine that!

That first Christmas we use Doug's Christmas bonus for a few small gifts and a modern Christmas tree made of silver tinsel with a light wheel. When assembled it looks like something that a person might whip together out of aluminum foil. The aluminum Christmas tree is introduced in 1958. More than a million of the trees were welcomed into American homes until they fell out of favor in the mid-1960s. Every year we take it down and put the fluffy silver arms into paper sleeves, to protect it in the box, and every year more tinsel falls off until the tree is too frumpy to use.

Just a week before the baby is born, we use his Christmas bonus to buy three dozen cloth diapers, and a few babies under shirts, etc. We wash and reuse these same diapers, shirts and blankets through both babies.

Doctors in the 1960s don't let women have natural childbirth. We're hit with anesthesia and we aren't awakened till it is over. Baby Gregory is born in December, 1962. The Doctor charges $200. This is about one month's wages, for the delivery. Doug's insurance won't cover that, as the pregnancy is a preexisting condition. So, we owe money to the doctor and the hospital as we evolve from "*us*" to "*our family.*"

New Year's Eve, 1963, is my first, since being a married woman. Fort Wayne erupts at midnight with people calling out Happy New Year, blowing whistles, horns, popping wine bottles and ringing in 1963 with fireworks and sirens. But I spend this first New Year's Eve in Fort Wayne Lutheran Hospital. Doug comes into the hospital to visit. He is carrying a real regulation football that is as big as the baby himself. He drops off this gift for his '*little sportsman*' son before returning to Convoy for an evening of playing cards with his family.

~

We have only one car and Doug has to work 10 hours each day and Saturday mornings in the mail room at Lincoln Life Insurance Company. He has heavy course work at Purdue/ Fort Wayne three evenings a week. When he is home, he has studies, reports and papers to prepare. He has to be early to bed for very early mornings at his job. He lives in a world of work and college, and I spend my days at home with our new baby. In these times no men ever cook, vacuum or change diapers. I have a bucket of cloth diapers soaking to rinse and ready to hang on a line in the attic. I hang them up there to dry between trips to the laundry mat, so they don't lie wet but I still have to take them to a coin laundry to wash them clean sometimes when I can get away. I sterilize bottles in hot water on the stove to make the formula from canned Carnation milk and Karo syrup. The baby is colicky most evenings. We are unprepared for his frequent, prolonged and intense crying and I don't have a clue what causes it or what we can do. This occurs for no apparent reason and no amount of consoling seems to bring any relief. I try to keep him as quiet as possible evenings so Doug can get his lessons done. We have no family and friends in Fort Wayne. This stressful life isn't what we imagined, but it is the life we have.

I am lonely for adult conversation. I miss my family and I have my sisters staying with us as often as possible. Night after sleepless night we take turns walking around with Gregory on our shoulders, walking and patting his back. None of us know what to do about the endless crying.

~

We are struggling financially and his parents are always very helpful. Doug works full time as a mail boy but it's not enough to pay the bills; we are teetering on poverty. They come to Fort Wayne to visit alternating weekends. Doug's dad continues paying for his college and his mother continues bringing groceries, baby blankets and baby clothes. All of their help is huge for us. Even a flat tire or a tank of gasoline can knock us back! Several times we have to borrow money from them. One day we go to his dad for a loan, only to be told, "*The first 100 years are the hardest!*" We don't get any money that day and we have to buy a retread tire. But I can say, they saved us more than once! I work the summer months at a store, while 12-year-old Wagtail cares for my baby. We have only one car. I ride a city bus to work. Wagtail rides the baby around the neighborhood in the basket of her bike.

~

I set off going down the path of marriage with optimism even though half of all children in America will experience the fracture of their family. Ignoring the marriage wrecks that I've already seen in the ditches all around me, for some reason, I envision us being loving companions for life.

It is not unexpected that my own family in Van Wert is falling apart. The timing is kind of weird. I think it's premeditated because we married in June and the Bug married in August. Oug sees this as his chance to get out! He can leave Mom with the girls if he moves out and takes Stevie with him. He will only have to pay child support for two instead of the five kids he would have had, if he had left when we were younger.

I don't know what actually happens on the particular day he announces that he is leaving because I am not there for the buildup. However, I have been aware of the constant threat for years because he is a '*married single*' rounder kind of guy, involved in a five-year relationship with a different woman.

~

My parents are like actors in a play that never ends. She is exhausted by him, yet fiercely clinging to him in hopes that he will stay. The stress of marriage has taken its toll on her, too, but she is not ready to give up. There has never been any doubt about the obstacles she has faced with him. She gave birth to his kids, shared his bed, put up with his moods, washed his '*dad-gumm*ed' underwear, cut his damn hair, and put up with reptiles, airplanes, guns in the house and even his philandering. Her plan is "*to have and to hold, until death do you part.*" She drones on about him, her love of him and our family. Being a family means everything to her, but it's nothing to him. A narcissist can only focus on themselves and things that the narcissist needs. Because he believes he's right he has no remorse for the sadness that sucks all of the air out of her, when he tells her, "*I'M OUTTA HERE!*" Mom is completely struck down by his words and hurting deep down in her bones. She's so devastated when he chooses a divorce that she can barely cope. The end result is that he leaves her in utter confusion.

As mismatched as my parents are, it twitches in my mind that they each probably started out with their own idea of life and each of them must have had a set of dreams. She wanting to settle down, raise a family with a husband who works to make an honest living. Her interest is, and will ever be, of mothering a family of children. Mom might want our family life to be different, but she is unable to cause changes for herself. She is fragile now and she has every right to be angry when he leaves her for another woman. She did what she thought a wife should do, yet the problems with him are never-ending. I ask her, "*Do you love him when he stands in the way of your heart's deepest desire, to raise children?*" and "*Do you still love him when he absolutely ruins your joy?*" I reckon she has done the best she can, all things considered. I believe that nothing can save her, but she remains clueless that she simply married the wrong man. She explains to me, "*Whatever he did, he did. What could I have done differently?*"

I answer her as honestly as I can. "*Because you were so bullied by him you were not powerful enough to hold your own. He runs everything!*" He has her torn down so far that she is broken. She never does seem to understand that he has checked out of their marriage of years. At times like this I want to '*pop her head off*' like a broken Barbie doll!

I conclude that our family is a burden he never chose. For certain not as many kids! He never wanted a "*pack of brats,*" as he often calls us. In the strictest sense this is not true. We know his boundaries and we don't question which lines to cross. He says "Ya'll are a millstone around my neck!" I am grateful that he only hurt us with his words. We are certainly disciplined, but we are never physically abused.

Her living an unhappy life makes me sad, but she wants him to be something that he can never be and that can't be fixed. His leaving is actually a sense of relief to me because he is like a wrecking ball tearing through our family. It only bugs me because she is consumed with grief and depression.

As it turns out, I leave home and so did he, with my thinking that my power struggle with him is finally over! Before long he moves in with the other woman. I don't see him at all for the first few years. I think I might never see him again and that feels okay to me. We have spun out of each other's orbit and begin making our separate lives where our paths seldom cross.

The American Dream in the 1960s is to settle down, raise a family and make an honest living. We never even considered doing anything other than that. I wasn't raised to expect anything more.

Doug and I have one child with both of my sisters in our care when a second child takes a place in our life. The exact cause of morning sickness is unknown, although hormonal changes are thought to play a role. I go through some serious morning sickness again and it lasts all day. I feel the baby turn and kick as I watch for signs of the newest little person. We buy a second crib and make plans to move into a bigger space. We move to a rented house in Meadowbrook in early spring of 1964 and, with that, we upped the rent from $50 to $85 per month, but we are happy to be in a whole house with three bedrooms and a washer/dryer.

~

In February, 1964, Oug comes to our door one evening unannounced. Not just him, but he comes with his new family. What a surprise this is! We have never met them before this. We are both taken back, but it doesn't end there. He notices I am pregnant and he comments that I am wearing a "*hatching jacket again!*" I have been through the fire with Oug, holding my words, and not expressing myself, for too long. I blast him! He stammers, but doesn't apologize, so my words stay put. I take a stand. He won't do this in my house!

Next comes Grandma. A little later on we get a SCORCHING letter from her, about having allowed Oug into our house. She finds his visit to be disrespectful to our mother! When Grandma Mina di-

133

vorced William Resor in 1932, she forbade Mom to ever see her father again and she never does see him. Resor, having never seen her or his own grandchildren, died in 1945. Apparently, Mina wishes the same for us, with our father. Oh my! Will it ever end?

~

Mom continues being angry at the world for several years. For reasons that I never will fully understand, even though she is angry with Oug, she holds him blameless, and instead she is hostile with us! I come to blows with Mom's hostility a few months later, because she is getting support payments from Oug, for both of my sisters. We have Susita and Wagtail at our house, but she keeps the money and refuses to give us any support money to take care of them. True to my nature, I'm not backing down! I go to see her, planning to collect their child support money. We argue and I call her a 'liar' but I lose that battle. She breathes misery! Her jaw is jutted and she holds fast with the money! I think she forgives my words later on, but I know for sure, she never forgets! Even after she dies, I find this incident with me is written in her own *'bad people'* book, which I still have! She settled down a bit when she remarried.

In an earlier era, female friends and relatives help a woman adjust to her new situation. Growing up can be difficult, but most people have the support of parents. At 19 years of age, I become a teenaged mother. Motherhood is hard enough for any mother. It's even harder as a teen without any family support. I learn why it is so important for people to wait to have children until they have more maturity. Some people will do fine, but I'm not ready for it. I don't know much about caring for a baby. I could use some help and advice from my mother and my grandma. But instead of help, Mom says things to me like, *"You've made your bed; now lie in it." "Don't bring your baby for me to babysit!" "I raised my kids and you will raise yours!"*

Looking back maybe she says these things because Oug stopped by our house that evening with 'THAT WOMAN,' or just in the furor of the moment. She might not have held me to it, but I do take her words at face value. Accepting my fate, I do not bring my babies to her for any help! Doug's parents love to help us, and they often do.

In our new neighborhood I'm still needing someone for support when I meet a neighbor who is a little older than I am. She becomes a mentor for me as she prods me to find my adult self. She takes me under her wing, often by her actions over any advice. This sweet lady teaches me how to cook, keep a house, train my kids and to be a good wife. I crave to learn and she leads the way. She becomes *'like'* a mom to me. She coaches me to jumpstart my married life by moving forward in an active way. She encourages me to take a stand whenever I can and I appreciate her views She holds high standards and takes us to church. I am forever grateful for her friendship and all she did for me.

Both of my sisters are in and out of our house for several years, usually spending the summers. Susita is going to beauty school downtown in Fort Wayne. Wagtail is *'out and about,'* a typical teen, but they both help us some with childcare. I have two babies before I am old enough to legally drink alcohol. Our second child, Shelley is a pretty little girl born in May of 1964. She's the perfect baby, with dark hair and brown eyes. She quickly folds close to my heart. She sleeps and eats well and she never cries. She's all around easy to manage – no trouble at all. I put her in her crib or play pen where she lays quiet and contented. Her eyes follow Greg as he plays. We can't believe how easy she is! She is so tiny that she rolls over and she crawls early. She even walks at 10 months. It's fascinating to see such a tiny little girl walking around! She toilet trains her own self when she notices that is what the rest of us are doing. She's a big girl now!

With no seat belts or car seats in those days. Doug builds a contraption out of boards, staples, and padding to fill the floor area of the back seat of our car, creating a safe play area for our kids.

~

The US national economy cannot sustain President Johnson's *'war on poverty.'* His *'Great Society,'* along with his many other social programs, in addition to the cost of the ongoing Vietnam War, causes a rising consumer economy that makes it nearly impossible for us, and others, to live on one paycheck. We're going backwards!

Doug has to sell the red Ford convertible and we get an even older car. We open a Sears Revolving Charge to buy a window air conditioner because the house is hot in the summer. That turns out to be another payment that we can't pay. We just can't catch up! We are in debt, having trouble making payments. We have more than we bargained for with responsibilities. Resentments accumulate.

~

Colorful leaves are tumbling from the trees as I watch them blow down the street in the November wind. On an Indian summer day,

Doug decides to apply for a second full-time job. For a few months he is working two full-time jobs, just trying to get us the things we need, and to get us out of debt. He works 40 hours a week at Lincoln Life Insurance and takes any over time that is offered on Saturdays. He takes on a full night shift at GE Foundry. He's shoveling coal into a blast furnace to make molten iron. That goes on from November to February the next year when he falls on the ice and breaks his leg. He is in a full leg cast and GE won't allow him to work with a cast so he has to quit the second job. He stays on at Lincoln Life mail room where he can work with the leg cast. He is ambling around home evenings trying to take care of two babies with his leg in an itchy ole' cast and on crutches and he is frustrated as hell with all of this!

I have to work to pay for the appliances, furniture and to even keep one car. I look for a job where we can work opposite shifts, so that we share in the childcare and avoid daycare costs. We are both firm that we want to raise our own kids.

In 1965, I begin working nights running a punch press in a plastic factory, making parts and pieces out of Bakelite pills cured in the hot press. It is HOT, boring and DANGEROUS and I'm paid $1.60 per hour. I am rankled by my job, too. I count the minutes until my evening break so I can call home. One day is just like another. I do my best to balance home life with work life. Being with them as they grow and change is important to me, but I am tired. I play with my kids in the mornings and I use all my energy at home, then I go to work from 3:30 till midnight. Through it all, one of us is always home with our kids.

After a year I leave the factory job for a night office job as a contract auditor at North American Van Lines. I work nights, he works days and I waitress at the Holiday Inn restaurant on weekends.

Our kids are paging through the Sears Christmas Wish Book marking toys and sports equipment for their wish list. We don't have big money to spend for Christmas and these are items that we can barely afford. But it's still better than earlier days when I am growing up and we only get candy and fruit and we feel good about that. We buy them several things and they have some good grandparents. (Now, I zoom ahead to my grandkids literally getting so many gifts they get bored with the opening.)

In 1968, we buy our first house in Sunnymede. We pay $300 down for a 900- square foot, three bedroom bungalow that costs $10,000. That same year the average cost for a new house is $26,600.

I have a lot of moxie and spunk, causing people to say I am handy. With this house, I become quite skilled at home repairs from sewing to using tools! I can sew curtains, fix a toilet, hang a picture, paint a room, repair broken tile, replace counter tops, hang a light and almost everything I want to do. I either know how or can figure it out! I credit Oug, the *original innovator* for that!

When they are in nursery school and kindergarten going half-days, I quit working to be home, but I like to be busy and I am never content to observe. I do things like teaching most of the neighbor moms how to sew and we all make play clothes for our kids. I sew fancy Halloween costumes for my kids that win contests at their school. I keep quite busy with the details of who will pick up kids from nursery school and who will bring the food for a potluck. Oh yes, I did finally learn to cook!

Both kids attend a Church Nursery School and I am a nursery school substitute teacher there. For a while I make home and family my career. A big part of a mother's job is to create a learning atmosphere for her kids. I keep them active and entertained with very little money. We attend a church nursery and public library story hours. I teach them colors by sorting laundry. I teach Shelley to make pies. She's on a chair beside me, I organize things and I measure for her, but she puts it all together herself. All of this parenting keeps me busy and satisfied for a while.

Our social lives are from one neighbor's home to another. We are all in this together because none of us have much money for going out. We trade child care and usually entertain at home on front porches and back yard barbeques. Several neighbors are our friends and our kids' friends. We young moms hang out together days while our kids are playing. I am fierce in motherhood, driving to dance, carpooling to sports, hosting birthday parties, and enrolling our kids in tap and ballet classes. I'm collecting for charities in the neighborhood and volunteering at Sunnymede kindergarten. I even become chairwoman of the Church Christmas Bazaar. I want it all and I do it all!

One evening Wagtail and I dress in dark clothes to avoid detection. Silently we go out the back door, crouching behind bushes as we move along. We're avoiding the beams of the full moon, as down the hill we go! Our mission is to have a little harmless fun scaring Greg and his friends who are sleeping in a nearby tent–until our covert actions are detected by a neighbor. He bounds across the lawn to capture us because he thinks we plan to harm the youngsters. He is more than a little bit surprised when he captures the mother of one of the boys. He, not knowing my accomplice, focuses mostly on me. *"MRS. DECAMP! What are you doing here?"* he exclaims! By this time, I'm a bit embarrassed and the fun is over. The boys come out of the tent to find out what all this commotion is about. Our plot has been destroyed after the encounter, and after that, it's back up the hill for Wagtail and me.

"Growing up in a small town gives you two things: A sense of place and a feeling of self-consciousness about one's education and exposure, both of which tend to be limited."

Elaine Lobl Konigsburg - American writer

CHAPTER TEN

I Believe I Can Do This!

Married at nineteen and forgoing my dreams comes with some problems; such as he is getting a degree and I am not. His parents pay for his tuition, mine do not. Heartsick for my ambitions, I fight against him, looking for my own purpose and some kind of direction.

In September, 1968, I am hit '*head on*' with the idea that I can go to college and manage a marriage, kids and a home. That fall I have a 6-year-old and a 5-year-old both starting elementary school. I have the tenacity to forge a plan. While my 'young tribe' is in school I can fix and change my life.

In Van Wert there is no college nearby and I don't have a car. But in Fort Wayne, there is a college nearby, and I do have use of a car. I carve a place in my days for college classes and I register. I am 25 years old when I begin attending college class three days a week in the afternoons. The first semester, I enroll in only Composition class. Now, I can do what I had hoped to do after high school. I think I can work this out and Doug has always encouraged me! Making this decision is one thing; actually doing it is another. I think college can change my life for the better, but I wonder if I can do the work! I throw myself into the school assignments late into the night and wake up early to get kids off to school, attend to activities, cooking and laundry, etc. I am a busy chick!

I soon discover the jaw-dropping level of my underexposure to education because I took the two years of vocational training over any college prep classes in high school. I have to begin college with several under-college level remedial classes. I have virtually no math.

139

This is hard to overcome, but the exhilaration of learning fresh new things makes it worthwhile. I burrow into the college library every chance I get. As I progress, I wade through classes and papers that I enjoy. I learn, grow and succeed! I learn Maslow's theory, "*What is necessary to change a person is to change his awareness of himself.*" As I change myself, I learn that to get something I never had, I have to do something I never did! I am introduced to new ideas and view-points that allow me a fresh new confidence. English Composition is required before any other classes. We call it the '*flunk out class,*' be-cause if you don't get English Composition 101 you WILL flunk out! I grow to love creative writing. I relish a sense of achievement as I write creative essays. I attend with two neighbors. We read and share our writing assignments with the other neighbors in the evenings. We three are the talk of the neighborhood as we write compositions and complete assignments. He goes on to write a smutty novel and she graduates from Nurses Training. I start out in Elementary Educa-tion but later I complete a Bachelor's of Science degree in Business. However, all of this takes a long time before I graduate!

The love of learning changes my life! For example; I have a psy-chology class called, "*What You Are, Is What You Were When,*" by Morris Massey. This presentation helps me to understand what makes me tick and why! The values of any generation are revealed by world events that take place during their youth. These events firmly set a person's world views. As I dig in, I begin to see everything around me very differently. I join study groups to discuss our classes and lectures. A bright spot is when I quit working for 2 yrs. and I get a real start in college. I am interested in Early Childhood education and I am on fire to teach! I declare a major in Elementary Education at Indiana University in Fort Wayne. I feel an exhilaration by being in classes in this exciting place. There is a lot of awareness on a college campus that doesn't come out of those books! The 1960s are the end of innocence and the beginning of turbulence in America. Students actively demonstrate against the unpopular Vietnam War, Women's issues and Civil Rights issues to name a few. Young people cannot accept all that is happening in the world and the times are 'achang-ing.' We see sit-ins and peace demonstrations, anti-pollution demon-strations and race riots on the nightly news. The music is mainly set around Vietnam protest songs. The Vietnam War is going into its ninth year. Protests are everywhere! As a student, I become more conscious of the changing times.

~

We ladies continue our old ways as we buy into all of this male dominance of women and work, until 1966. Betty Friedman forms the National Organization of Women, or N.O.W. and this group challenges these cases in Court and paves the way for 'equal access to jobs and equal pay for equal work' that most women enjoy today. I am quickly lured into seeking gender equality. By seeing the common threads that unites us all, I find awareness, and I develop a raised consciousness of being a woman. I begin seeing other choices I had not previously known about, because of the social and moral code for women at the time. This is the opening act for my own feminist views.

The men are immediately taken back by these challenges. Husbands were saying, "*The women have all gone wild, there's no telling what they'll do next!*" The late 1960s is the height of the hippie movement; I didn't take part in any of that, because I am at home with a husband and young kids when all of these shenanigans go down.

~

August 15, 1969, is the date of the now famous Woodstock Music Festival on a dairy farm near Woodstock, New York. Over 400,000 people attend this three-day music festival. They come in droves to see 34 of the hottest psychedelic music acts of the day. They are sitting on the road 11 miles back from the gate. A few of the better-known acts were Grateful Dead, Jimmi Hendrix, Credence Clearwater Revival, Joe Cocker, Janice Joplin, Joan Baez, Blood, Sweat & Tears and more. There is rain and solid mud everywhere. After the show is over, the cleanup crew found 600 tons of garbage left behind. (https://en.wikipedia.org/wiki/Woodstock)

~

At college I register with my full name. Where middle initial is asked for, I put down KATHY in brackets. Instructors will ask, "Why should I call you 'Kathy' when you show that your first name is Linda?" I explain this and they call me Linda anyhow. The same thing occurs when I fill out medical paperwork. As time goes on, I have acquired many nicknames among family and friends. Names like Katqueen, Kate, Kath. I answer to all of them!

~

I am getting to know and admire other students for the wisdom, theories and life dreams. I grow with the classes and have exhilarating conversations with other students and staff. The economic, social and biographical forces of Students for a Democratic Society are active on all campuses, allowing women like me to leave the home to be who we want to be and do what we want to do.

I learn in Business Management class that you can never judge a system by those who succeed, because those people will likely succeed in any system. You can better judge it by those that it fails. I learn a lot of new scholarly theories in the psychology and sociology classes.

I am exhilarated when I learn about the personality disorder of NARCISSISM and how that works. A narcissistic person has all of the tendencies that I see with Oug. Until now, I had never thought of this as a mental disorder. The notion that he can be functional, persuasive and lucid and yet something like narcissism could still be wrong has never occurred to me. People with narcissism may seem very confident. But in reality, they have a problem with self-esteem. This makes them vulnerable to even the smallest criticism. This condition can cause problems in many areas of a person's life.

Narcissism is caused by some kind of security a person lacks. It is usually caused by a disconnect that happens, in childhood, and it can be treated by a psychiatrist. In Oug's case this is probably because his parents and grandparents died at such a young age, leaving him completely alone in his adolescence. Narcissism manifests as a grandiose sense of self-importance. An example of this is that he exaggerates his talents and achievements to impress people. He requires excessive admiration and expects especially favorable treatment. He takes advantage of others to achieve these things for himself. He lacks empathy and is unwilling to accept the feelings and needs of others. He is preoccupied with holding power over others. The narcissist has delusions of grandeur and persecution. He chooses a partner who is passive and lacking in self-esteem and deficient in their own self in order to be able to mold them to being a 'mirror image' of himself. The narcissist can never be WHOLE without the adoration of a self-denigrating partner. He finds such a partner but he soon devalues and discards them in order to manipulate and stay in control. Mom fits that description because of living with 'burns on her arm and body,' and the way her own mother smothered her thinking. But only through self-denial can a partner survive. The initial attraction begins somewhat normally, but the abuse becomes more intense over time. She denies any dreams and hopes she might have. She gives up EVERYTHING to cling to him. Submission doesn't work, because submission breeds more superiority. The mate is soon met with an aggressive, sometimes violent reaction that gets worse over time. His torment of her, and later on me, is his punishment for all who dare to reject his narcissistic needs. It is no coincidence that she always wonders, "*What else could I have done?*" The healthiest parts of her personality are not enough to fend off the tyranny of his narcissism. My dad is a classroom case exhibiting ALL of the classic narcissistic patterns. As I learn and understand narcissism, I finally understand and accept him as the multi-dimensional guy that he is. After this I quit trying to figure why he does things.

Stevie and his young feminist wife go on a chartered boat trip to the Virgin Islands with Oug and his second wife. During this trip Stevie's wife and Oug tangle quite a few times about his attitude toward women and how he thinks things should be done. When they return home, she says of Oug, "*If he's so smart, why ain't he rich?*" The key here is that Oug perceives himself as smart AND rich!

I don't see Oug much for a few years and I'm OK with that. Our estrangement is not formalized; he is doing his things and I am doing mine. Connecting now is an effort for us both, but when our paths meet, I treat him with respect. I find that being a visitor in Oug's house is very different from living with him. As a visitor we sit down and make conversation. As an adult nothing more is expected or given.

He remarries and moves back into the same house where I grew up. My young kids don't know him well and when we go there to visit at his house on North Walnut Street, they are a bit amazed and even uncomfortable in the surroundings that are their grandfather Oug's house. He is their grandpa, but he never allows anyone to call him Grandpa! So, he is just Oug to us. He never has a relationship or even any interest in his grandchildren. Family has never been 'his thing.' I believe that he never realizes what he missed in a family life.

When we first arrive, I introduce him to my children as their grandpa. He says "*Ye gods! Don't call me Grandpa!*" He's too cool for that! Next, he casually asks about his ex-mother-in-law, "*How's Ole Mina? Is she venomous as ever?*"

143

We enter Oug's house through the front door which goes directly into the dining room. We see a bird cage in the front corner. I see a parrot that he says he doesn't care about; the bird belongs to his new wife, called PK. The only thing in the living room is a pool table. In the kitchen, where we used to have the table and chairs, there is now a large monkey cage where a small grey monkey named Crissy Monkey lives. She is a small spider monkey, weighs about 10 pounds, and looks like a big spider with extra-long legs and tail for hanging upside down. Crissy Monkey screeches because we are strangers in the house. Shelley gets too close to the cage a few times and Crissy Monkey, intrigued with her hair bobbles, reaches her long arms out and gets her by the hair. Oug has to get the monkey's hands off of her. In the bathroom, when I lived there, we had a towel storage buffet. Now a large alligator tank is along the floor between the door and the toilet. Though the alligator is in hibernation, my kids are hesitant to go past *"Albert Leonard"* the alligator, in order to use the bathroom facilities. We fill our time with him talking–and us patiently listening.

He is showing us slides of a recent vacation when one of the children asks me, *"Why don't we ever get to go on vacations?"* He pops up with, *"Because they are DAMN FOOLS, that's why!"* He enjoys delivering that little speech to my kids, but my hackles are up! Oug and I have been locked in conflict, an endless battle of wills for too long. I give him a dark look that is full of blame because I am more than a little offended at this. As a young woman I am willful and strong in spirit but I have been expecting the conflict will sometime come to an end. Until now, I have imagined we might sometime live as a father and daughter in peace. But nothing has changed! Nothing except my ability to avoid any further abuse. As an adult I speak my mind in an authentic way. All I can do with him is to accept him for who he is. I've heard him say that *'God takes care of fools and babies.'* I take care of myself now by leaving him out of the details of my life.

When we get back home, my kids have some new tales to tell their neighborhood friends concerning their visit to Grandpa Oug's animal house. His ways will never work for me!

~

Doug has worked at International Harvester for about six years between layoffs and strikes. He works days and goes to college evenings. He is working an entry level job and going to Purdue in Fort

144

Wayne, studying Computer Science. He takes Computer programming classes off and on when he can. He works in the office union, working a swing shift. We are finally beginning to get into the middle class financially.

In 1970, the United Auto Workers Union has one of the longest strikes in history. The strike is against General Motors and it drags on for sixty-one days. When you belong to a union, the union bosses can tell you what to do. All union members at all other auto maker plants have to walk the picket line in support of General Motors. We have a little extra income now, but it isn't sustaining. It's more like a cushion that will catch us in case we fall. He gets strike pay from the union in the beginning, until they run out of money. After over two months, we're teetering on the brink. I am a second semester sophomore at IU-PU Fort Wayne when the strike forces me to quit college and go back to work. I find an office job at Hardware Wholesalers, near home. I think an office job gives me a little prestige but work turns into some exciting and stimulating times for me. The plan is for me just to help out during this strike but as it turns out, I work there for six years and I don't go back to college for nearly 10 years. My home life *gets in the way* of college at times like this.

"In the 1970s we were fighting to be recognized as equals in the marketplace, in marriage, in education and on the playing field. It was a very exciting, rebellious time."

~ Marlo Thomas

Chapter Eleven

For Better or For Worse

Women freed from the tyranny of limited opportunity is called the Women's Movement. I came to adulthood ahead of the shift. I accept not being hired because some jobs were only being offered to men. Doug and I have been in a traditional marriage from the git-go and I came into a woman's world before the upheaval of society. Feminism in the 1970s changes all of that! Laws of equality are on our side now. We began the fight for women's causes with the 1963 equal pay act. We were not all fighting for it then, but now we are all living it now. Before the movement women's opinions are valued only if they pertain to recipes and cleaning products. My generation takes on the cause that rocks America. Gloria Steinem encourages us to burn our bras, sunbathe topless –be who you are! She gives us power when she says *"We want it all!"* Helen Reddy is singing, *"I am Woman, hear me roar!"* Virginia Slim Cigarette commercials say, *"You've come a long way, Baby!"*

But, have we, really? The movement has an enormous impact on America. The path for women who are liberated becomes a new and different path for me. The new *'me'* is gaining confidence and I em-brace controversial new ideas and actions. I join the world of work, clubs, and girlfriends who *"Want it all!* But, be careful what you wish for! We ladies say, *"We want it all,"* but that also gets us DOING it all, and that is not a place I want to be!

Unlike the family women of the *"silent 1950s"* now we have friends who confide in each other, our ideas and problems and how we handle our marriages, families and work life. We are no longer referred to as '*just housewives*' since the Women's Liberation Movement. We don't always know what we are doing, but I am fierce in the 1970s women's movement. At work and at home, we rally for equal pay for equal work on the job and for more help and cooperation at home. The women's movement; it is the story of a generation of women who are shaking off the old ways in an effort to collectively preserve our own sanity. The ladies and I swap stories at lunch. Most of us are just trying to get some help at home. But, in the workplace our mantra is "*Equal pay for Equal work.*" The power struggle between us at home and at work is very real, involving some shouting matches and violent arguments at home as we demand cooperation.

The radical Women's Lib movement is '*the dawn of a new age*' that causes a lot of problems with a lot of marriages as we reject old standards and take on some new powers. The movement causes his gentleness to melt like sugar. This is the lowest point in our marriage.

~

Generations of oppression are now being challenged in courts around the world. Those struggling with these changes are exhausted by the struggle. I have a lot of feelings about my mother being an oppressed woman. She had a hard life and she paid dearly for being married to my dad. He was a tyrant, by today's standards. She remains content to be referred to as '*just a housewife*' but I want more!

Mom finishes raising her kids in the 1960s and she says "*Age is just an attitude*" now. She is in the empty nest period of life, freer to enjoy camping, hobbies, and baking her famous cookies. She regards her empty nest of 1960s and 1970s as the best years of her life. No longer supporting children, she is finally having fun, in her own way! Van Wert in the 1970s is a small town with no local college, and not even a Center of Fine Arts. Mom likes to make quilts, crochet afghans, make ceramics and do some tole painting. She bakes cut out cookies and later on she is known as, "*The Cookie Gran*" because she always has homemade cookies for visitors. (Her cut out cookie recipe is in the back of this book.) Mom pleases herself by serving others. She says, "*I love serving the men!*" She likes to bring them food and drink. In contrast in this same time period, I and my angry generation are saying, "*You can get your own, I am not a servant!*" The point is that after the shift, we are all free to choose.

When I question the hypocrisy that Mom and Grandma previously accepted, I change all the rules and '*I go Lib on him!*' The divorce rate soars to 50% as women begin recognizing "*the problem that has no name*" holds a feeling of uncertainty. Doug comes from a family of four brothers and I come from a family of fivesiblings, and neither of us knows why we're the only ones who never divorced. We're probably all a little or a lot broken.

I give Doug a lot of credit; a great many marriages didn't sustain the movement but he hangs on with me through the tides of change. He seems to understand, "*When a woman shuts you out, picking the lock won't let you back in!*" Our busy life does get in the way of our relationship as I grasp a raised consciousness of these times. Doug and I are even calm and content at times and I can forget we are in the war for equality.

I try to imagine a different reality for myself. A women's lib guru once said, "*Aging is not a lost youth, but a new stage of opportunity and strength.*" I like that! I have all that I had ever planned and dreamed of having, so why aren't I the happiest and the luckiest woman in the world? I often ask myself, "*What am I doing?*" I am troubled by how I can negotiate the terrain between what I want in life and what relationship I want from my husband. How can I allow my love for him to chip away at the life I want for myself? As I ponder this, I have some strong opinions about my responsibility to myself. I am completely disenchanted with male dominance. I can imagine that Oug's disregard for me and all women has hardened my resolve!

I am very proud of the women's movement, where we have been and what we did. We are all fighting the same battle with the men, at home and at work. All that aside, this is a glorious time for liberated women. Until this time I have never done anything as grand or important. A woman's place is unlimited and untethered, I totally get that. Life is wonderful for women that come in the generations that follow the Women's Liberation Movement. Without knowing what we are doing and without self-scrutiny, we change the very foundation of life in America in the 1970s and for the years that follow.

~

Doug has taken computer programming classes for years. He finally gets a chance to test his competency in computer programing. He passes the tests, working his way into a promotion to management. He leaves the office union and moves into the Computer Center where he works mostly nights and weekends. The data processing department job is more money, more pressure and responsibility.

My family responsibilities are more rigorous than his. I speak up about my home and family concerns, but he lives in his own world of work that he often doesn't share with me. I'm all about women's issues and he is not. For better or worse, we are still in the long haul together. When we need to talk he pulls away. He's hard to read. We have lulls at times and we're active and playful other times. My life is a perpetual treadmill in the 1970s, with work, kids and household chores. Each week I carpool to Swimming, basketball, football, softball, track, sleep-overs and bowling in addition to my own 40-hour work week. I complain that I am over-functioning while he is under-functioning. He has a job and I have a job; I have taken on more than my share. With that I think, *I have it all!* I am giving it all, we women of 1970s want to "*have it all*" but we don't want to DO it all.

Our kids are busy with swim meets and we get them where they need to be. We work swim meets, he coaches softball and baseball teams. I bake for the PTA and car pool to AAU swim meets, golf and school sports. I "*run the carpool route*" week nights after school and I make dinner, clean up and run laundry, fold the dry clothes from the night before and pack lunches for the next day. Even when he is home, he is tired, and not much help. This gets easier but never really gets fixed. We have both met our match in terms of ambition, or call it damage if you prefer. Whichever it is, Oug often told us, "*Sometimes it's better to keep your mouth shut and be thought a fool, than to open your mouth and remove all doubt.*" I adapt this to mean that sometimes letting things go is the best option. The only thing we can do now is '*hang tight*' or take a header out!

We never see each other; I am lonesome for companionship and he clams up. He is quiet and shy and communication has been our weak point from the beginning. Doug keeps his opinions at arm's length to avoid conflict. He'd rather avoid issues than rock the boat. I prefer to put it all out there for arguments to be settled. I don't know what to make of his ways, but we do it his way. Our conversation is infrequent and strained. As we navigate this dangerous path, we are together and yet separate. This is not romantic, but we manage. We are not perfect together but we rarely shout, we're just angry. He is so bottled up I can't understand what he thinks. I suppose he will say he was never angry with me and we loved each other along. But I know anger when I see it.

I am happy to be a part of an era when we achieved so much. I am happy that we as women were so successful, but I feel that we were submerged by the heaviness of our load. The men of the 1970s are still trying to put in less time with household chores, because that's always been women's work. Looking back, it seems that neither of us can escape our individual troubles long enough to appreciate each other's situations. Yet we are somehow able to keep our flame alive.

When we hit age thirty, our generation thinks that we are *over the hill!* At thirty Abbie Hoffman coins the phrase, "*Never trust anybody over 30.*" We have been ruled out because we are over the age limit of youth! We are now a part of the establishment that is not to be trusted. Doug takes on a new style with his 30th birthday. He hangs out with students and coworkers after work and he even goes to a hippie '*happening.*' The music of the day is a heavy metal sound that we called "*acid rock*" because it is the music of the psychedelic drug population.

~

I have been at Hardware Wholesalers for six years, beginning in the warehouse office and ending in Inventory Control. I feel on top of my game when I am elected the first female President of the HWI Employee's board. This is a place for a female employee to shine. If there is a committee, I serve on it, I suppose mostly to escape '*the stink of boredom*' of routine repetitive office work. I am driven with hope for a future with this company. I work full time and I am grateful to have a job in the middle of the early 1970s recession. We are in a national economic crisis caused by a far East oil embargo with stagnation caused by high unemployment and high inflation at the same time. These are financially ugly times in America! Both of our pay checks are needed to survive.

In a move for gender equality at work, a few others and I try to break into the Men's Golf League. The men hold the line! When joining them doesn't work out, we start a Women's Golf League. We begin with lessons, buy clubs and begin playing golf in the HWI Women's Golf League. We play on Thursdays after work. The men in the office say, "*You will have to go home and fix dinner, your husbands will never allow this!*" We dye our golf balls in feminine soft colors and place them on our desks all around the office, to claim our presence in the office 'HWI Ladies Golf League.' All that said, our men do '*allow* us' this window of freedom, and we play in this league for many years.

I struggle getting my elementary kids off to school and heading off to work on time. It is like *herding cats!* I am working 9 to 5 from Monday to Friday. There is no '*flex time!*' This is old school rules! We are paid to '*keep our butts in the chair*' with very specific time requirements. There are rigid boundaries between boss and employee. One morning I look at the clock, and realize I am going to be a couple seconds late for work – I have been late too often! My supervisor has been '*on my case*' about being late; he says it is a bad habit that I need to break. I maintain my composure as his tirade continues. I study his face and wonder if this blustery jerk will hear me come in if I slip in, shoes in my hand, walking in my stocking feet? I try that the next morning and it works very well!

~

The Equal Pay Act of 1963 makes it illegal to pay different wages to men and women if they perform equal work in the same workplace. The Civil rights law of 1964 makes it illegal to discriminate against someone on the basis of race, color, religion, national origin, or sex. Hardware Wholesalers is a good company and they are being mandated by these laws to get more women into token management positions. I am tested for management aptitude and I test well. I cannot get very far without a college degree, but they promise me management jobs that never materialize. I want more! *"What the hell am I doing working here?"* Now seems like the time to stop talking about a dream and start doing. People like me keep moving!

~

On something dangerously near a whim, I leave the corporate environment to become a small business owner. Self-employment seems like a good option and I decide to try retail ownership. I attend a trade show and talk with some sales representatives in the area. I have always loved to sew. I learn of an area sewing business that is being offered for sale. The owners are in the New York City garment district, but the store is local. This is my first attempt at self-employment but I decide to give it a shot! Sewing is a 'hot hobby' business. In 1976 everyone is sewing and I am EXCITED to give this '*seat-of the pants management*' a try.

My friend is a banker and I make up a business plan, get a business loan and I buy the existing business called '*Just Sew Fabrics.*' I am going into the Retail Sewing business of fabrics and trims, sewing machines and sewing classes with no real experience but this is right up my alley! We move the location from State Street in Fort Wayne to Lincoln Park Plaza in New Haven. I keep the three women employees who have been working with the past owners. They are GREAT because they know the bridal fabric business and I don't. We go together to buying shows in New York and Chicago. When I go to New York City with two of my employees, we spend days buying fabric and trims in the garment district. In the evening we see the Broadway production of, "*The Best Little Whore House in Texas.*" This Broadway musical is about a real-life chicken ranch in LaGrange, Texas. Going to a Broadway Theatre is 'big doings' for three ladies from New Haven, Indiana.

Shopkeepers often keep their kids behind the counter. My daughter, now a young teen, works with me weekends in the winter months when we are the busiest. She is a good little helper, but I don't think she likes it like I do. She prefers to work as a car hop at the root beer stand in the summers. Between work, sports and school it takes a sense of balance to keep the family where they need to be at the time they are expected to be there. These years are a juggling act to keep all of the balls in the air. There is an awkwardness between the schedules, as Doug's work is early mornings in the office, but in retail I start later and finish later.

Over the years I sew hundreds of things for a lot of people, from Halloween costumes to a wedding dress. I become president of the 'Lincoln Park Merchants Association.' mostly because I don't like the current president's ideas for the plaza. Working with the other store managers empowers me to think of this for long term. I continue to gain satisfaction and confidence with a raised self-esteem. I am hooked on this fabric store, but I am not making much in profit and probably should be going back to college.

~

During the 1970s, a lady, dressed in a flag dress, enters my store to see if I want to join a group called American Business Women's Association. ABWA is a professional organization for women in all stages of their career and in all professions. ABWA is formed for the advancement of women in business. Our meetings are a blast of fun!

The mission of ABWA is "to bring together businesswomen of diverse occupations and to provide opportunities for them to help themselves and others grow personally and professionally through leadership, education, networking support and national recognition."

Members include everyone from teachers and administrative assistants to CEOs and small-business owners. We bond immediately. I love the friendships and everything about A.B.W.A., we have monthly meetings, and we raise funds for girls' scholarships. We attend regional conventions several weekends each year and we pursue life's questions with like-minded friends. The thoughts we share sink into my consciousness. I meet other local women who own stores, and who preside over local businesses. Women who have goals and ideas! I make a sisterhood of lifelong friends there; I learn a lot and most of all we have lots of fun!

For over 50 years we've stayed in touch. We still share the *"Peaceful easy feeling"* and the joy of these tight and honest relationships. Now, they're all grandparents, like me. We empower each other and we cheer each other on. In these amazing friendships, we swear that we will grow old together. We'll buy old lady sunglasses and tan till our skins turn to leather! We even talk of going to the same nursing homes. We're almost there!

Now, when I come back to town, I call my A-team and they show up for lunch. The older the friendship, the longer the lunches. When we meet, pictures of grandkids are passed around the table like fancy hors-d-oeuvres. We are permanently twined together. We tell each other about our surgeries, our aging parents, jobs we've lost and jobs we've found, diets and lo-Cal foods we've tried. We even discuss the "F" word, which, of course, refers to FALLING!

~

In the late 1970s Doug and I are both working, the kids are in school and with two incomes we finally have a little money. We move up the street a few blocks to a house that is twice the size and twice the price of our first house. It needs an update and I get started. I have been raised in a household where we learn to fix and reuse everything. In our new house Susita and I resurfaced the cupboards in the kitchen, we put in a new sink and butcher board counter top and hang some new light fixtures... we do all of this in one day with five toddler and elementary school children in the house! Next, I upholster an old sofa in black fake leather, called pleather. I wallpaper

153

the family room in black and white stripes and put in red shag carpet. With chrome and glass accents we are styling in 1970s MODERN decor!

The following summer, we put in a 16 foot by 32-foot inground swimming pool from a pool kit that I buy at Hardware Wholesalers. We do it with the help of the neighbors. Our weekends in the summer are pool parties for families and friends. We often lie around the pool using baby oil mixed with iodine to encourage a tan. These summer days around the pool are the best of times for us.

~

Doug goes through a gun phase; he likes target shooting. In a spirit of cooperation, I agree to go with him. I try shooting his Smith & Wesson 380 Body Guard pistol. I have both hands wrapped around the grip. I am still dumb struck and afraid to fire. There are things from my childhood that I can't erase. Guns and me don't bond well.

~

My dad retires in summer of 1977 from Continental Can Company after 27 years of service. His neighbors have heard electric saws buzzing and sometimes hammering as he slowly curves the skeleton of the boat that has taken him and his wife, PK, twelve years to build. He presses the pieces of Honduras Mahogany in clamps to get the arch right; slowly the boat begins to appear. He carefully varnishes the wood and coats the surface with epoxy over the wood. Finally, they have built a 34-foot cabin sailboat with a fixed keel and a 5' draft. It is designed to travel 6 to 7 knots per hour. The main mast will carry 4,500 square feet of sail. Auxiliary power will be provided by a 14-horse power diesel engine. The boat will sleep six and is equipped with a galley, refrigerator and toilet. They plan to get their boat into the water for the very first time this summer. They hire a hauler to travel 674 miles of highway to get the boat in the water, but from there it should be smooth sailing, but they never sailed. They live on the boat six years without ever leaving the dock because as they get older, they are afraid that they can't handle their boat. The boat takes them twelve years to build and they sell it without ever sailing!

~

January, 1977, is the coldest winter in history. Twenty-four below zero days dawn grey and cold that month when I learn that my mother has colon cancer and she is faced with a life altering surgery. I try to prop her up during her recovery, but she wants so much to see her son, Stevie. He has firmly isolated himself from the family and unavailable to all of us due to his shame of a long and serious drug addiction. She suspects something and she begs me to tell her, '*What gives?*" with him. I hate to, but I finally tell her that Stevie is deeply involved in crack cocaine!

~

Just as our kids are older and we have enough money to go out without a sitter, disco music comes along. The Disco music is electronically produced dance music played in clubs where everyone is dancing to the pounding disco beat that dominates the late '70s pop charts. Disco is the cheesiest, most garish era of music. Girls in the clubs are dancing up in disco cages for entertainment. They are wearing hot pants (which are mainly short tight shorts) and go-go boots, where modesty had previously prevailed. Their long hair is feathered in 'wings' on the side, as is the style of the day. Doug and I like the '*Saturday Night Fever*' songs for dancing. Several movies play off the disco sound such as "*Midnight Cowboy*" and "*Saturday Night Fever.*" We go out to clubs in Fort Wayne on most Saturday nights. We stay out late with a group of friends and we have some fun. We're like bar flies, hanging out with local friends and coworkers. We have a great time with our group. We spend Saturday evenings just laughing and having another round of drinks with friends, music and fun! The disco music scene comes and goes quickly, to be replaced by a western style Texas 2-Step featuring songs like "*Looking for love in all the wrong places*" by Johnny Lee. Country and Western music became very popular in the late 1970s and early 1980s. For this fad we both buy fancy cowboy hats and boots to dance. The mechanical bulls gain popularity with the release of the 1980 movie "*Urban Cowboy.*" We love the mechanical bulls that appear in bars based on pseudo–Rhinestone Cowboys from the movie. I come home with an ankle so swollen I can't pull my boot off! We think bull riding is a bunch of fun, so even with sprained ankles and bruises we keep on riding mechanical bulls! We and our New Haven friends usually close the bars on a Saturday night, then we go to breakfast. Breaking Night is urban slang for staying out all night. On Saturdays we often don't go home until the birds are chirping.

Even though New Year's Eve follows Christmas and we don't have extra money at this time of year, it's a tradition that we host the neighborhood party. These parties often get pretty crazy. We play a party game where someone (I won't say who) gets under a blanket. He is asked to throw out something that he doesn't need. He begins with shoes, then socks, shirt, belt, etc. Each time we say "No, no, not that!" He is finally down to his skivvies when all he would have had to have done from the start was to throw off the blanket! Of course, that misunderstanding is the point of the game. One snowy New Year's Eve we are sledding down the hill on the street in front of our house screaming and yelling as we sail by. This is sometime between midnight and 3:00 AM. We think it is 'fun' but the neighbors who haven't been invited do not! These neighbors often watch us from their window. Doug likes to harass them by standing in front of our picture window acting like he is hitting me and beating me up! Meanwhile I play along cowering as if I am afraid. They stay to watch, but they never do call the police! I remember another New Year's Eve when our friend falls asleep sitting at the kitchen table. It is late and she is tired when she falls face first into a punch bowl of eggnog. That scene is hard to forget!

The blizzard of 1978 is called the STORM OF THE CENTURY. The big storm hits Jan. 26th, 1978, when two low pressure systems converge on the Ohio valley to bring us 'the storm of the century.' The wind gusts average 50 to 70 miles per hour. These powerful winds and snow cause major complications. Snow drifts reach 15 to 25 feet and reach the rooftops of houses, causing structural damage. As a result, hundreds and even thousands of homes are without heat and power. For the first time in history Interstates and Toll Roads are closed completely. Some are closed for up to six days. Temperatures rapidly plunge from the 30s to bitter-cold single digits in a few hours. Extremely cold wind chills around minus 50 degrees or lower continue throughout the day, making it especially dangerous to venture outside. Cars are buried and people are stranded in their vehicles. This causes supply chain shortages requiring the Red Cross and armed forces to come to the rescue. With zero visibility all transportation comes to a complete standstill for several days. (Lima News) - January 26, 1978)

I am 34-year-old when the only topic on the news stations is the "Blizzard." Snow covers the windows creating a feeling of isolation. We are a family of four with two teen agers. We can't see or go outside because the snow is too deep. We're eating whatever we have in the house and we're playing a lot of Euchre. We wait inside for five days before a snow plow opens our streets. We zoom out and impulsively buy a snowmobile! This is fun for a while, but once the streets are cleared, we can't drive it on dry streets because a snowmobile only runs on snow. We don't have a trailer and our snowmobile is nearly useless without a trailer.

The bad weather is still seriously affecting foot traffic at the store. Without business I can't pay employees and I have to cover all of the retail hours myself. I am running as fast as I can, just to stay in place. This is a place where family life and work life conflict. I am working most evenings until 9 p.m. and Doug goes in to work early at 7 a.m. We each have our own set of problems at work and at home. Doug has his hands full with financial problems at International Harvester. Layoffs and rumors of closing the plant in Fort Wayne are in the air. The details of his work life remain tightly sealed in his head.

Our teenagers are doing battle with us, pushing back on our authority. They are probably going through some hell with us, too. Doug and my parenting styles aren't the same, mainly because we were raised so differently. Times have changed, too. I reject my own loosely controlled childhood and I come down harder than he does. I think that we have given our teens too much freedom and too little discipline. He hates any conflict and he *lets the loose end drag,* leaving the unpleasant bits of parenting to me. We go through a lot of crises where I find it easier to do things myself rather than nag an unwilling kid or husband. We continue, as best we know how at the time. Some things just happen and not everything can be prevented. Married life is not totally in anyone's control. Over time we endure this *"rite of passage"* working into a modern marriage of at least equality! We reach a point of having more than enough; we want to simplify with less things. We want less work and fewer responsibilities, a smaller house and yard and a slower life. We sell the pool house in Sunnymede, to live nearer the high school so that the driving is less!

"You can't go back and change the beginning, but you can start where you are and change the ending."

– C.S. Lewis

CHAPTER TWELVE

'The Second Half'

My second half starts at 1980 when I am thirty-seven. At this stage the sand in my hourglass of life has sifted down about half way. I call this the *'the second half'* because as I write this, I am seventy-eight years old, an age my tribe considers to be a fossil. My younger self certainly would agree. Respect and awe soon turn into slowing down. In a society that idolizes youth and youth culture, it can be difficult to understand and address the challenges that older adults face. As we age, we feel less visible. I'm no longer the youngest, nor the cutest. No one notices me anymore because I'm an older woman. People who once smiled as they walked by are now passing without a glance leaving us older folks to feel unwanted as outsiders in society. Young people can't imagine what their life might look like when they get older. Being elderly is practically incomprehensible and the needs of older adults are not well understood by a younger population. The experience of feeling invisible can be shocking and painful.

~

Doug and I take in a Marriage Encounter weekend in the early 1980s. Presumably we're here because we have a good marriage and you want a great marriage. Marriage Encounter is a weekend experience for any couple–whether you're running the kids to soccer practice or enjoying your empty nest. It's not a retreat or a seminar, and there's no circle time or sharing—just you, spouse, and a better marriage. (https://agme.org/) We learn some communication and problem-solving skills there and this is a great sharing experience for us. We clear away a lot of our remnants of the 1970s wreckage, as we work through this crash course in communication. Sadly, I accept that he can't give what communication skills he doesn't have.

My second half improves exponentially, over my first half. I feel like *a cocoon turning into a butterfly*! Our kids are older and we have some time together. We both love vacationing and traveling. We have many fun adventures and family vacations. We start a tradition of travel that never stops. Some-times I have a clear picture in my memory of a place. But I've been so many places that I can't sort out where the place is or when I might have been there.

I have a theory of aging that goes like this; whatever a person is like in their younger years, they will become 'MORE SO' as they grow older; eg., if your personality is to see all the worst in every-thing, you could become a 'Debbie downer' in old age. A positive outlook will blossom, etc.

Ronald Reagan, as President, has changed the country with his "*Trickledown Economics*". He reshapes our political economy, the rise in the economy and stock market did not end for many years. Americans as a culture started gambling in the market, thinking magically and winning from 1980 to 2007. Everything is big in the 1980s. The US Economy GREW and people began living LARGE. In the early period of the 1980s around the time Regan is president from 1981 to 1989 when Wall Street's modern Bull market began. The Dow Jones average is about 800 and the average household home mortgage payment is not over 25% of the net income. People in this era regu-larly save an average of 10% of their income and carry relatively little debt. Our homes were bigger and the home prices grew 4-fold before collapsing in 2007. Many Americans became childishly irresponsi-ble, willfully and obliviously fat and happy as American Capitalism triumphed in this thriving economy. Delaying gratification became quaint and unnecessary. Americans, being undisciplined, even gained about a pound a year, so that an adult of a given age is now at least 20 pounds heavier than someone of the same age before then. So, what if Americans are overleveraging and over spending and the prices of stocks and houses are unsustainable? Does it really matter that we became over dependent on debt and fossil fuel? Doug and I never do go full bore into all this wilder, faster and looser side of consumerism. We don't let go of some of our parent's depression era values. Without excessive spending and debt, our 401k is growing.

It is a part of our couple hood mojo that he is the more sensible one with money and investments. He likes to invest and control money.

Greg graduates high school in 1981. As we should, we invite Oug to his graduation party. We serve beer and Oug has a few! Greg and Oug share their first time ever 'one on one' conversation over a glassof beer. Oug doesn't care much for kids, but they are old enough to be beer drinking buddies now!

After the summer Greg leaves home to attend college at Indiana University. The college orientation meeting for the incoming freshmen class is one of 'life's moments' for me! As I sit in an auditorium with mostly older grey-haired women and their balding men. I am thirty-eight years old and I wonder, How could I possibly belong here, among these people? But I did, and I am here!

The following year Shelley graduates high school she goes to Ball State University. We want them both to experience campus life because we never did. There is a lot of learning and personal responsibilities on campus that's not coming from their textbooks. They both have cars and credit cards; we are almost off the hook here! Not so fast though, Doug is paying from his savings for Greg's college and I am paying monthly for Shelley's college. I will be sending my whole paycheck to Ball State each month for the next four years.

When the kids are gone and our nest is empty, we face each other squarely. I am thirty-nine years old and Doug is forty and we are empty nesters. A quietness descends over our once busy household. The phone stops its endless ringing; no young friends are coming to the door. There are no curfews to enforce. Even the dog goes into a three-month period of mourning! Luckily, we all negotiate the changes and resulting adjustments fairly soon.

~

Doug's father, Diamond DeCamp, died in March 1983. Death is a hard cookie to swallow and this is our first such experience. We know we are supposed to be prepared for this normal life passage when a parent dies, or at least be more ready to accept it when it happens. We hold each other in support and share the sorrow. Diamond has influenced both of our lives. He is suddenly gone leaving a hole that can't be filled. We are expected to pick ourselves up, close the wound quickly, and move on but we keep on missing him. Sometimes people even think it should not require much time to get over death, but it's a long process!

Doug is really struggling with the grief; he seems distant and shattered. A parent's death can exaggerate other emotional issues in our life. It often brings up feelings about our own mortality or it can cause us to question the value of other relationships in our lives. At the very least, it may underscore the reality of how quickly time changes. Deep in his work schedule he is not interested in many other things. He needs emotional support but he is uncomfortable asking for it. He drifts away from me and goes into himself. He is guarded, proper and professional, but he deals with grief by stuffing his sadness down deep inside.

Nightly he watches television until eleven o'clock, usually dozing with the newspaper across his lap. After the news is over, zombie like, he folds the paper, gets out of his chair, turns off the TV, even if I am still watching it, and he makes his way to bed. I hear the sound of his keys and coins as he lays them down. I hear the rattle of his belt buckle and the shoes hitting the floor and then the silence. I think back to the days when we could not get enough of each other and now, it's the nothingness of us!

~

The winds of change are blowing in the summer of 1983. Doug's workplace in Fort Wayne is closing. Just a few months after his dad dies, he is being transferred to a Chicago area computer center. With the transfer, we feel fortunate that he can keep his job. I am 40 years old when we move from Fort Wayne, In. to Woodridge, Illinois, a place that is foreign to both of us. This move is the farthest away we've been. Not across town, but four hours away from family and friends. We think we have the imagination and flexibility to make a new start. But we miss our kids who are still in college in Indiana and we miss our families and New Haven friends where 'the beat goes on!'

We buy a cheap condo and we fix it up some, but it is never very satisfying. We make a new life with some of the other people who have transferred at the same time, but none of them can fill the shoes of our old and dear friends in New Haven.

In the fall of 1983 with a renewed energy and commitment, I begin some business classes at College of DuPage in the West Chicago area. I am studying for a business degree now, with an associate degree in Travel and Tourism. I want to work in downtown Chicago at one of the big tour companies. Because I have an office job, I have to take both of my 5-credit hour Economics classes on Saturday mornings. I am sitting in Econ from 8 a.m. until 1 p.m. every Saturday for both fall and winter semesters. Because economics is such a dry and boring subject, that schedule is painful! The rest of the weekend is needed to do homework and to power me through the next work week, where I will do it all again!

We're empty nesters now and since we both enjoy travel, we get started doing a bit of travel around this time. Airfare is cheaper in Chicago. We visit Washington, DC, and do all of the tourist sites. We canoe the Fox river in Illinois for two days camping overnight on an island with our dog. Several times we head out to Western Illinois to Starved Rock State Park for some hiking. And we take up river rafting on the Wolfe River in Wisconsin. To me relaxation means travel – the time away refreshes me. We grow and change when we leave the familiar.

~

Christmas, 1983, is Margaret's first Christmas alone. She doesn't like paying for the fancy restaurants and instead she has a potluck at home on Christmas Eve. The family Christmas is never the same without Diamond. Soon afterwards we change to being with her on the weekend before Christmas, so that we can have Christmas with our own families. When we are back in Indiana, we meet Oug and PK at a restaurant during the holidays. He doesn't invite our kids. Someone gives him a hug on leaving, but his arms remain rigid at his side. He still isn't interested in love and family.

~

We move to the Chicago area for his career. I find work at two jobs that I hate. I work to keep a kid in college. There is low pay and no satisfaction. The go-go of the 1980s finds us both in small cubicles in the city office buildings. Every morning I'm packing my briefcases to head to the office cubicle where I will sit behind a desk for eight hours to do some paperwork. First, I work in customer service; the business is via phone and fax. Their business depends upon the personal touch of customer service and inside sales for the quality and reputation of their service industries. I am the face of the company taking care of customers. There are no computers and no internet in the offices. In the dead of a Chicago winter, we have to use small space heaters under the desks because the *blustery jerk* who owns the place won't allow us to turn on the heat that winter. After freezing every work day, I am making my way outta there!

The next place doesn't turn out much better. I am hired to shadow the manager. I'll be office manager and take over when she retires. Well, don't ya know, there is '*bully*' in that office. She is stabbing me in the back and giving me the '*stink eye*.' Because she wants that job! She hates me as cold as steel in January. She intends on making me miserable enough to leave there.

After our Chicago work days are over, Doug and I often meet at trendy restaurants along Butterfield Road for chats and nibbles. We take our first international vacation to the Bahamas. We are busy and happy. These are good times for us, except for the traffic and the workplaces!

I achieve an associate's degree in Travel and Tourism at the College of DuPage. I want to pursue a career as a travel agent with one of the big tour companies in the city. I am ready to give that a shot! But just as I graduate, we transfer to Springfield, Ohio, once again for his job. It is a sense of relief, leaving the jobs I have had in Chicago, when we head to Springfield. But in Ohio my only Travel and Tourism job option involves loading baggage at the Dayton airport. I am not interested in that and the travel and tourism career never does happen!

I am 42 years old in 1985 when Greg and Julie graduate college and marry the same summer. He has grown up a bit during College - this seems to be the turning point where we can get along better. I sew a nice dress for Mom to wear to their wedding. She is just 5 feet tall and she doesn't wear pants or shorts, no sleeves above the elbow or skirts above the knee. The dress is only 36 inches from top to bottom and she loves it! She calls it her party dress and wears it for most of her grandchildren's weddings.

In 1987 we move to Springfield, Ohio, where, at first, we rent an apartment on the Post Road. In Ohio, Doug is still with the same company and I find a job in Industrial Purchasing at Robertson Can Co. I purchase raw steel and industrial supplies for a factory making battery casings. Still there are no computers in the office and I keep inventory records hand written on index cards.

Doug and I are both working and before long we are both back to attending college classes again. We plan to graduate college together. I drop my elementary education major and change to business administration. In making this change, I lose a lot of my college credits. His company is paying for his schooling, where he attends a full-time adult business program weekends at Antioch College in Yellow Springs, Ohio. I enroll in classes at Wright State in Fairborn, Ohio. I attend standard evening classes after work. I usually take 6 or 9 credit hours while working full time. When I register for classes, Linda is the first name on their registration forms. With the move back to Ohio, I decide to introduce myself as Linda, at school, work and everywhere I go, because that seems easier, but that doesn't solve the problem either. Now, everyone I have met since 1987 calls me Linda. Everyone who knew me before calls me Kathy, Kate, Kath or Kathleen. I give up! I often say, *"Call me whatever you want!"* Stuck with a middle name is a southern custom, but they usually use two names together, like Betty Sue. Being called by my middle name has been challenging and I NEVER will suggest naming a kid one thing, and calling them by another!

While taking classes at Wright State in Dayton I have to deal with college algebra. I work my way through all the math that I have missed in High School to reach a college level in algebra. I pay for my own classes and Shelley's student loans. Doug's employer is paying for his college.

I am from the age of manual typewriters and carbon paper. My first television is black and white and my first commercial plane ride was just a short time ago. I learn to use computers when we buy a $3000, IBM computer which is essentially a word processor. In 1988 we are writing college papers and sharing the computer. I take to that like butter on toast. Before long I am spending hours in front of the screen. He does his work week nights when I am in class. I do my work on weekends when he is in class and we finally '*git-er done.*'

CHAPTER THIRTEEN

The 'Grandies' Take Over

Just when I thought I had everything under control, in January, 1989, our first grandchild, Danielle, is born. She quickly steals my heart and she causes me to spend a great deal of my money. She is the first of six that are yet to come!

Every summer while she is growing up, she comes to stay at our house for a few weeks. We are members of an interactive museum for kids, called COSI. This is one of the largest modern-built science centers in the world. We go there daily for her visits because she is fascinated! Danielle becomes quite proficient on the unicycle, but she loves every COSI exhibit!

~

Doug graduates College in December, 1991 - Douglas L. DeCamp - BA Management - Antioch College, Yellow Springs, Ohio and I graduate in March 1992. - Linda K. DeCamp – BS Business Management – Park College - Parkville, Missouri.

I began college in 1967 when I was 27 years old and married, with two small children. I finally attain the bachelor's degree in Business Management when I am 46. Over those twenty-five years I raise two kids and I attend 5 colleges in Indiana, Illinois and Ohio. I change majors from teaching to business because when my kids grow older my interests are different. I change colleges due to Doug's job transfers. I go to classes mostly part-time but occasionally I go full-time. Things like moves, jobs and family things often get in the way. My own kids graduate college before I do! I am the first in my original family to graduate college. But even though this is a triumphant achievement for me, I decide not to walk in the ceremony, mostly because I'm too far past my youth.

Instead, we hold a formal reception in the banquet room at Holiday Inn in Fairborn, Ohio. This is similar to a wedding reception, but ours is a graduation reception for both of us, with dinner and dancing. Someone at the bar laughs when my mother tells him we are there to celebrate her daughter's college graduation. He laughs because I am older and I should have done this years ago.

~

In 1990 we are both working full time with no kids at home. It's so ridiculous how we still haggle over chores. We finally find a system that works for us. It goes like this; We list every household chore and each of us choose our chores like an NFL draft! He chooses grocery shopping, I pick laundry. He chooses vacuuming, I choose gardening. He goes for car maintenance, and I go for cooking. We go on like that until everything is chosen as either his or mine to do. This works because there is no boss or servant relationship. Neither of us is lording over the other. If he doesn't follow through, I say NOTHING and vice versa. This chore distribution system has worked well for us for the past 30 years.

~

We both love river rafting! We have rafted on the Colorado river, the Wolfe River, the New River; the wilder the river, the better we like it! Each one is more challenging and we love it even more! In the early fall, we decide to raft the MIGHTY Gulley River in West Virginia! We plan to 'Run the River' with Doug's brothers. The Gully River is the king of them all, beyond wild in the fall with several Class five rapids. My anxiety rises as we hear of accidents in the wilderness on these Class five rapids but we proceed to the launch. I push through a heavy layer of fear and go anyhow. I continue in fear as we go through foam, froth and unrelenting eddies in the high and fast water. Several people fall out of our rubber raft but all are saved and brought back into the raft by our guide. A little later another person is seriously injured. I hold tight and stay focused on the unrelenting rapids. This one did me in! When we get back to the launching site, I decide this is enough and I never go river rafting again!

~

Graduating college now isn't enough education for me. I started college for my own self-satisfaction and now I open my eyes to some-

166

thing more. Doug and I take a year-long Small Business Management class before I leave my salary job in Purchasing. We move from Fairborn to Columbus, Ohio, to open a small retail store in the Columbus area. We learn from the SBA class that most small businesses must be a destination type of business.

We study the basics of creating and financing and managing a successful small business. We make a business plan, a mission statement and register the business name with the state.

When we study changing markets, I find that a lot has changed on Main Street, USA, since the 1950s. Growing up in a small town in the 1950s is a nostalgia that sounds nice, but won't work now like it did back then. These are days before major credit cards. Not too long before the millennium, our parents do not have cell phones or email addresses. No one has heard of social media or even the internet. As a teen, I worked at Murphy's Five and Dime store and the small-town Main Street is vibrant. We have a mix of Mom-and-Pop stores with two drug stores, clothing stores, shoe stores, a jewelry store and a bakery, two movie theatres, a department store and several restaurants and banks, all locally owned and operated. We share equally with JC Penny Co. and Montgomery Ward. All are open 9 to 5 daily and closed on Sundays and Wed. afternoons. Everyone in town shops on Main Street into the 1960s because there is no reason for anyone to go out of town for anything. The term 'mom and pop shop' often refers to an independently owned firm, as opposed to a global corporation. Furthermore, traditionally *'Mom-and-Pop stores'* is a name given to American entrepreneurship. These stores are defined as small retail businesses that are family owned and operated. As we study to overcome obstacles in small businesses, we learn that they can only survive now in a niche market with personal service and only by selling a commodity that is unavailable in a big box store.

Along comes Walmart to our small town in the 1980s. They move in on the edge of town and buy up a big parcel of land. They construct a hulking big-box supercenter with a huge parking lot that forces people to get into their cars to go there. They are offering everything that the stores on Main Street are selling but it is conveniently all in one store, and often cheaper. When Walmart comes to town, they put the small stores out of business and create a business vacuum on Main Street and simultaneously expand their services to push the other stores out of business. At these supercenters you can get new tires, new glasses, and even a teeth cleaning. This weakens the community's civic "*backbone*" and kills Main Street. All around town things are closing: The hardware store with its tiny drawers stretched to the ceiling holding bulk type widgets; local restaurants, lawyers taking down their small-town shingles. The place is dying! In the absence of a strong leadership among local business owners and community leaders in town, people find themselves buying every-thing at Wal-Mart because there's nowhere else to shop!

I have ventured into the eternal optimism of entrepreneurship, not once but twice. We complete the SBA Small business course be-fore we give small business entrepreneurship the second try. I think I can sell used kid's things cheaper than the big stores. I will pay cash to sellers for good quality, but outgrown goods, I'll operate like a pawn shop for young moms. Self-employment is a seat-of-the-pants type of problem solving that gets my creative juices going.

Knowing all of this, I decide to open UPTOWN KIDS Children's resale shop in the fall of 1992. I consider myself to be a professional bargain hunter. From youth on, I have an addiction to shopping con-signment and thrift stores. I am the evidence needed to show that you can take the girl out of poverty, but you can't take the poverty out of the girl. Buying from garage sales is the least expensive but most time-consuming method of getting opening inventory.

I 'troll for treasures' to set up an opening inventory of nearly new fall kids' clothes, toys, nursery furniture and baby equipment. I scrounge at thrift stores and garage sales that are about 50 miles away from the affluent area where I will locate the store. Browsing in thrift shops and garage sales is fun for me. It is the 'thrill of the hunt' that keeps me going. I collect enough great outfits in every size from newborn to size 16. This takes about 6 months for me to fill a store. I wash, iron and sort and store the clothes by size.

I find a location in a strip mall where Men's, Ladies' and furniture resale stores are already in place. Perfect for my kid's store! I choose this affluent area because the clothes and equipment people bring in are very good quality for resale. On opening day, the shelves are full of very saleable kids' clothes, toys and equipment and my 'trash to treasure' hunt fills the entire store. I have spent around $2,000. for an inventory that is paid in full on opening day. I don't even need a business loan.

The store looks beautiful! Business is brisk from the beginning. I think I can work the store alone for a while, but I find out immediately that I can't manage the volume of work alone. I am quickly buried in work and I need some help. A young girl comes in looking for a job. I hire her on the spot. Immediately, before she can write an employment application, I have her begin sorting and putting clothes away. She stays and works with me for a few years.

From the first day, my customers are Moms coming in from the local area to buy and sell here. I am like a pawn shop of kids' stuff, because I pay them cash if I need their items in my inventory. Buying inventory from customers is hard and they can be annoying when they fight back about a price or the value of their items. I have to persuade them to understand that I can only buy the best things. Sometimes I feel bad if they need the money. However, if I can't use their things, I won't buy them.

Overall, the hardest problem I have to satisfy is to have honest employees available for work when I need them. Finding people who will work for what I can pay, with no benefits being offered, proves to be the challenge that breaks me. I often think, *"I wouldn't work here either, if I didn't own the place."* I do find quite a few employees who will either steal goods or money from me, so I have to stay present in the store every day. I find my whimsey in networking with customers who turn into friends. I learn that I have to really like people, and to tolerate their whiney, misbehaving kids in a kids' shop. I do gain a lot of satisfaction from owning and managing the place. We go on, always being busy for the next six years. Four of my six grandchildren are born during these years and they all love my kids shop!

I love the daily business aspect of the store from 1992 to 1998. Due to problems with the landlord, I mistakenly decide to move the store to a shopping center that requires all merchants to be open every night and all weekend. Very soon I look over my strengths and weaknesses. I can't do it alone and I can't keep quality people. So, it has to end. I decide to close UPTOWN KIDS when my brother needs my help and also because of Doug's retirement. Once I decide, I sell everything out in 2 weeks. When it is all gone, I close my store the Spring of 1998.

The number of Mom-and-Pop stores has been decreasing rapidly in the United States since 1978 when I had my sewing retail business.

In the 1980s I walked door to door with samples of Avon every week. Now, Avon is completely internet based.

Since then, there are even more big box stores. All of them are causing problems for small businesses. When we add mail order buyers to the mix, a small business on Main Street is nearly impossible. As we move into the 2000s we have a Google search, to shop the internet and mail order catalogs. Internet sites often have free shipping and free returns. Now we can have restaurant meals, groceries, electronics and clothes delivered to our door within a short time.

However, it actually does get worse in the year of 2020. While business along historic Main Streets in the USA is not exactly bustling, a few shops are open and there are customers. During the yearlong pandemic their problems become even more extreme. After months of being closed due to the coronavirus pandemic, their rent is still due. With government restrictions and uncertainties there is little hope for the Mom-and-Pop concept of Main Street entrepreneurs. The nostalgic feeling of an old time vibrant Main Street is sadly gone. I shake my head with a wistful smile as we travel around rural mid-west towns. We find the concept of Main Street, USA. has permanently closed.

~

The Red Hat Society is formed with a focus of fun and friendship in 1998. A founder or leader of a local chapter is usually referred to as a Queen. Members aged 50 and over are called *"Red Hatters,"* wearing red hats and purple attire to all of their functions. In 1999 I join a chapter in Columbus, Ohio. Since then, I have belonged to chapters in Ohio, Hawaii, Michigan and Florida. What a great way to meet fun ladies for lunches in new areas when we move!

~

I am fifty-six when I take up rollerblading in the neighborhood. I love the motion, speed, wind, excitement and danger. My grandkids are visiting and we skate to the neighborhood park. My focus is building memories with loved ones. We have a closeness to our grandkids even though we have never lived nearby. They are surprised as I move with grace and ease across the smooth flat sidewalk. I push and glide without lifting my feet, but I still have to slow down and grab a park bench to stop. My grandson is six, young and healthy, when he sees his grams on skates. *"How far can you go?"* he asks. *"I can go as far as you can, I tell him."* It is exhilarated to be his 'skating grandma.'

~

Oug and PK live on their boat in Mobile, Alabama for six years. He is getting beyond the years where they could drive from Alabama to Indiana. I volunteer to fly down and fetch them both back home. I am driving Oug's car and Oug is in the passenger seat. We have been in the car for only a minute, actually still in their neighborhood, when he calls out, "STOP SIGN!" He is gesturing at the familiar octagonal sign ahead, red with white lettering that sits at our first corner. I think *Oh, my God! This is going to be a long trip!* I slow him down with my reply. *"I know! We have those in Ohio, and I know just what to do!"* That ends it for a while and he lets me drive without comment. Things go along easier but eventually we pull in for some gas when PK sees an indigent person with a pack and she goes into a rant. The guy looks to be down on his luck, a rounder, a loser, a traveling man at best, hanging around. *"What is he doing here?"* Followed by, *"I don't want to get out of the car."* Oug said, *"Ye Gods, PK! Everybody has to be someplace; he has decided to be here!"* How very perceptive Oug is!

There are a few other peculiarities during the trip, such as having a car break down and riding on top of the Jerr-Dann and stopping for coffee at a truck stop at midnight when we are only half an hour from their house. Overall, this trip is quite an adventure!

~.

In 1999, after my stepfather dies, Mom is dependent, depressed and doing nothing for herself. Even though she is still very capable, she won't try. She quits quilting, baking and most everything else. Overall, I made a good decision to close the store when I did. By this time, she has trained me well, and those years of training can't be forgotten. She lets me figure things out, so that she doesn't have to! The more I help, the more dependent she becomes. Conversely, if I could have gotten her to fend for herself, that would have been the better way. She figures that if she leaves things, I will come along and take care of everything. Don't ya' know, I do that! I make weekly trips, driving several hours to pay bills or get groceries. I even cook and clean for her, but I might not have done these things for her if I wasn't the oldest daughter of a passive mother. I do, but I shouldn't, because no one is responsible for another's recovery like that.

When I come to her house, we have tea and enjoy our time together; she talks and I listen as we spend many happy hours on her porch. I learn about the parts of her that came before me. She often likes to talk about old times. She tells me about her life; the way things are and the way they used to be when she was a child. These are precious moments together. Overall, I made a good decision to close the store when I did.

Meanwhile, after she is widowed, she begins going 'full on' about her love for Oug again! He comes to see her at least once, and she is thrilled. OMG! In disbelief, I want to take her by the shoulders and shake her silly about that!

"I haven't been everywhere, But it's on my list."
- Susan Sontag, Author

CHAPTER FOURTEEN

A New Millennium

The new millennium begins with a bang in year 2000, caused by anticipation of a unique economic event. I am amused when my dad says, *"Saints preserve us, IF we get through this Y2K BUG thing......!"* Amused because he is speaking as if we possibly won't survive it! You might be wondering why the year numbers ticking up by one is such a big deal when the century changes. The date change, called Y2K BUG, is short for a potentially disastrous computer malfunction. The perceived problem is that, when the 2000 millennium clocks in computers roll over, all the world's computers will reset back to 1900.

For many years in the programs of most computers, it is common to store year values as two digits. For example, someone will punch in 66 instead of 1966. Because the software treated all dates as occurring in the 20th century, it is understood that 66 meant 1966. No one knew what would happen if all these systems flicked from 1999 one second and back to 1900 the next. The cost to clean up the software is over 100 billion dollars for government and business computers. Doug worked on it for his company for several years.

That flaw has to be manually corrected in every computer program in every business and in government. After much build-up in the media about the doom and gloom associated with the coming new year, we are prepared for the worst that the Y2K *"problem"* can dish out. The fear is worldwide power outages with entire cities going dark, even a loss of lives in health care facilities as computers are predicted to go down worldwide.

Like it is with hurricane scares, we seek disaster preparations. Shortages are considered a likelihood due to transportation disruptions. Cases of toilet paper are stacked in businesses and NO ONE wants to be in an airplane at midnight when 1999 rolled to 2000! The world braces themselves as the clock ticks to the midnight hour, When the big moment arrives everyone holds their collective breaths as anticipation builds. There is a nervous energy everywhere as we watch with fear and anticipation. The clocks pass midnight into the new year 2000, first in Sydney, Australia. What we see next is more like the absence of sound! The power is on, fireworks are exploding and everyone is amazed, all is normal. Not much happens around the globe, very few black outs, no global economic catastrophe, no loss of lives and BOOM, it is all over! After Y2K the reality jabs me of our absolute reliance on computers.

~

Oug has always been so bottled up that I have no idea of what he thinks or feels. He dies in June, 2002. I let go of a lot of the frustration between us. I accept him for who he is. His death robs me of things I still need to say, but he is one of a kind and he does leave me with a lot of good stories. I am able to deliver his eulogy. I only choke on my words once or twice. I try to explain his life fully without kicking him in the pants. I can't deny that I wanted to, but I decided to forgive instead, for '*he knows not what he has done.*' (Paraphrased from Luke 23:34 Bible KJV)

Because someone can't always be there, we even renovate Mom's upstairs to make an apartment for a caretaker to live to help mom. We hire her, but before long, Mom fires her! She doesn't want someone in her house telling her what to do. She wants to be the captain of her own ship! My dad is dead, my mother is wasting away. My store is closed. My kids are grown and gone into a life of their own. My brother and Mom's care become my main purpose. All of that keeps my adrenaline flowing. By giving Mom too much help, I enable her to lead a nonproductive life.

~

January 1, 2003, Mom has a heart attack followed by an open-heart surgery. I sit with her for weeks, not knowing if she even realizes that I am there. I am afraid to leave. I rent a room at the hospital. It is as though I think I can keep her alive with my presence. I am only one of her kids and she has five. I take charge and I interview her doctors for answers to unpleasant questions. Family relations are at a steady simmer. She never recovers from the surgery. There is a sadness surrounding me as I watch her struggling for ten weeks only to finally die in the hospital. She dies on March 10.

When she's gone, I'm emotionally wrung out. I often say, *"She leaves me with a hole in my heart where she used to live."* I hope I can leave things from the past in the past, but so far, I haven't. A flood of painful memories comes over me. The pain of my memories drains and exhausts me, and leaves a longing in my heart. Tears fall fast!

Soon after she dies, I meet with a psychiatrist, where I work on my own resilience, my courage, and the pain and muck of my loss. I come in with a lot of grief, anger and resentment. He urges me to take action rather than dwell on sadness. Staring reality in the face I come to work to heal and rebuild until I am whole again, but I'll never be the same as before. I think that putting others first is a virtue and I don't think what I did was wrong.

As we dig into a lot of things, I hear *"You're doing too much,"* for the first time. He tells me to stop being such a people pleaser. Helping others makes me feel good, but selfishly people will take advantage of me. I have always thought of helping Mom as a responsibility, something that I should do. I took care of her and her kids when I was just a kid myself. He points out that as the oldest girl I have taken on the responsibilities of caretaker in the family, while the adults in our family were preoccupied with their own issues. He tells me that growing up with such few resources sets up my siblings and myself as competitors. We compete for everything, including our mother's attention. I'd taken up for Mom at a very young age and I never thought of it as having been '*permitted*' to do her bidding. He notes that I have always cared for others, like my younger siblings. I'm cleaning the house while my friends are out playing. I did a lot of work that should have been hers! I bought clothes for myself and some of my siblings as a young teen. I made monthly payments for braces for my sister when I was only sixteen. One by one I have taken my siblings into my home after I married. I am adrift with wounds from the past and forgiving is the only way I'll get out of this funk.

He tells me, *"You're being a door mat, you deserve to be respected."* He orders me to stop, but rinsing off the past takes time.

My eyes are opened! I'm a text book case! It seems to me that helping is a gift that I can give, but this comes with a certain amount of personal sacrifice. He counsels me that I can change, and I need to take care of myself first, in order to stay stress free and healthy.

He also asks me about Oug. *"Didn't anyone ever ask him why he is so angry?"* I don't think anyone ever did, but I wish they had, because if his narcissism had been treated in therapy, he might have been helped. Since that didn't happen, I have to work through his issues with myself. I begin counseling with a grief support group. I learn it's OK to say NO! I am protecting myself now for not having guilt over anything that I don't choose to do. The fire of my anger becomes the fuel for a new path. It's not my responsibility to take care of anyone else. I need to depart from the path I was on. This is a real game changer for me, but I shift my focus one step at a time to depart from the path I have been on to repair and regenerate. I have to *'let go and let God'* handle these things!

~

Leaving the black cloud of death behind, I feel ready to leave our mundane life in Ohio and recharge our spirits. Doug retires in May, 2003. Both of us feeling lighter and freer by the end of 2003, we move to Kailua-Kona, Hawaii, for an adventure that lasts sixteen-months. We rent a condo on Ali'i Drive facing the Pacific Ocean. This adventure gets us some clarity to break out of our dull existence to be active and playful every day.

We get our blood pumping with a walk along the "Royal Footsteps" of the waterfront stretches along Alii Drive. We touch and feel each moment.

Kailua-Kona is a lively seaside town in the heart of Kona. This is the home of Cruise ships, Mom and Pop waterfront restaurants and plenty of Old Hawaiian culture. Hualhee Palace is where hula dancers wear leis of Plumeria flowers to entertain tourists. Ukulele music is drifting from across the street at the Mokuaikaua Church, where we are a part of the congregation. We visit Kona Coffee plantations and legendary golf courses with dazzling vegetation and ocean views with palms waving in the wind. I am making flower leis out of the tropical flora and fauna that we enjoy all around our ocean front lanai. I watch native Hawaiian fishermen who fish in the ocean with nets. Near Kona there is a blow hole that is a site for tourism. Blowholes are likely to occur in areas where there are lava tubes in rocks along the coast. We go down to watch the waves hit a lava tube and then it spouts back out and shoots up like a geyser. I suck in the energy that comes from the gushing water. If an unsuspected wave comes in you could be pulled down into the rocks before you know what hit ya! There is no place more exciting! I find a new skip in my step. The fullness of living in Hawaii breathes life back into me.

~

Life in America is made up of a progression of at least three different lifestyle segments. These are youthful eras that includes mushy puppy love, college transitions and establishing a career, followed by the work and family years when love is functional with busy jobs and growing kids. The third segment of love, where the couple congeals and accepts each other 'as is' occurs in the slower and easier time of retirement.

The idea of retiring at age sixty-five began in 1935 with the Social Security retirement act. At that time people didn't live as long as they do today. The 1950s brought the expansion of benefits. Today, retirement is a lifestyle change that takes some planning to decide what's next. Move or stay put? People vary greatly in their physical stamina and in their capacity to tolerate change. Even moving to paradise cannot perform magic. Many of these new Floridian retirees find the 24-hour togetherness can turn into a 24-hour hell. In short: Any problems or short comings we have will come along with us wherever we go. Doug will not shed a lifetime of shyness and become a social butterfly.

There is no particular homeplace for us now, because our kids and grandkids are scattered. The winding road of life leads us to Port Charlotte, Florida, in 2006, for retirement. We do well with changes because we have lived in 6 states and 17 different houses before we move to Charlotte County, Florida.

In that winding road of life there has been some potholes and bumps in my road. Neither of us have the will to 'stay put' in any area with snow in the forecast, so we settle in Florida. Doug and I look at cities and towns all over Florida, but Charlotte County is the right place for us because it's a population of 190,000 with several small towns on the Gulf coast and easy for us to navigate. The cities move too fast for us and we have everything we need right here. Interestingly Doug's parents were snowbirds here for many years and his father died here. Now, our daughter lives about an hour away and our son bought a retirement home nearby. This is almost a 'homeplace' for us!

There is a thing called 'Florida Syndrome.' People think that life is going to be great down here. Retirees see beaches, golf, sun and fun

177

with seafood fresh from the water and tropical fruit, tropical flowers and palm trees. Nearly 1,000 people move to Florida daily. This migration comes from all over the United States. We will not die sooner, or live longer, by moving to a retirement community. Once anyone decides to retire, change comes on fast, like hitting the brakes. Retirement is a real adjustment for people who have worked most of their lives, even if much of their work life hasn't been fulfilling.

Retirees think about what their days will be like without many obligations and they plan to live on vacation. But the reality is that vacations are a two-week escape from reality and living on vacation leaves an empty void, sometimes leaving people feeling adrift and ungrounded. I think I will be idle here, doing whatever I want with no schedule. But having no particular schedule leaves a person free floating and restless. Some people adjust and some don't. Extra free time can cause people to drift into an abyss of too much TV or online games or shopping. New friends often can't replace old ones and we miss old friends and family, who keep us balanced. For sure we love the warm winter weather in South Florida. We find out that we need some focus and some rest in equal amounts.

Retirees often imagine that they are coming down to leisure and freedom from the cold, and they plan to live the rest of their lives on their saved income and their Social Security. Because people are living longer, an estimated half of retirees find that they can't afford to live all of these years without working. After a while limited income won't allow them to maintain their current lifestyle. Another reality can also be a serious illness that can rapidly drain the bank account.

~

In 2008, our son and family are living in Australia. We're not finished yet. We have a yen for the unconventional and we want to go someplace distinctly different. We decide to shake up our lives once again to set out on a different course by exploring a new place with a different culture. We arrange a five-month house swap to Australia, where we exchange houses and cars with an Aussie couple; they drive our car in Florida and we drive theirs in East Malvern, Australia. We visit our family; we travel around the local area. That was a very good trip!

~

In 2007, Danielle graduates high school without any college fund. She gets a few scholarships, but not nearly enough. Her parents help her the first year and she goes to Colorado Mesa University in Grand Junction, Colorado. The next year, Danielle moves back home and she attends a commuter college on a tight budget. She is working several full-time jobs just to keep going. I help her monthly by paying for classes out of my savings. In 2008, the stock market crash happens, this is the largest single day drop in history, putting the nation into a deep depression. This financial turmoil impacts many sectors, leading the U.S. into massive unemployment, the auto makers are on the verge of bankruptcy. This mortgage crash is often called the real estate bubble. This causes the federal government to step in and 'bail out' many hurting companies, and the economy fails for several years.

The aftermath of this financial event wipes out big chunks of my retirement savings and I can no longer use my retirement money for her college expenses. I decide to go out of retirement and go back to work at age sixty-four. Work isn't easy to find during the financial crash, but I hear of a job in a nearby real estate office. They're going after some foreclosure businesses and I get hired immediately.

I can't let Danielle down, so I take the job. I work in real estate for twelve more years! In 2012, Danielle graduates from college with a Bachelor's Degree in Graphic Arts. Since graduation she has been successful in several types of businesses. Currently she is a trainer with a leadership role at Angi's List in Denver.

Danielle has a sweet, kind and gentle personality that is loved by all who meet her. She travels to Costa Rica with us for her grandparent's trip. The first morning out, I see her in the center of a group of senior travelers. What could she be saying that is holding so much attention? Before long she has met and won the hearts of most everyone in the tour group, and we became known only as "*Danielle's grandparents.*" Her high school Spanish classes serve her well. I am amazed at her second language Spanish skills as she chats with the locals. She is a clever young lady who knows a lot about many things! I credit her university education for that.

In 2012, we took the entire family on a cruise for our 50th wedding anniversary. On the first day a contest is held to find a '*drink of the week.*' With her mixology skills from college days, and even more by her showmanship, she won the contest and became the 'bartender of the week' onboard the ship. Her drink of the week is featured on the ships menus as *'Danielle's Tropical Mix'* for all to buy. OMG! Danielle is famous again!

~

The social media platforms continue to be very popular with family and friends until Facebook and Twitter became a political force. In my view, social media has caused more harm than good to society: The phenomenon of promoting the "canceling" of people, brands and even shows and movies due to what some consider to be problematic remarks or ideologies. People are often mean, causing anxiety to others. Over the last few years, the social-media trend has gained momentum and become very left- leaning politically in the 2016 and 2020 elections.

My hackles are up and my conservative boundaries are firm! I have lived in a democratic society all of my life –free and happy. I enjoyed using Facebook for a while, but the censorship drives me, and many others, away in 2020. Free societies allow descent among their citizens.

As I have described being amused in the year 2000, when my dad said, *"IF we survive this Y2K Bug*.... That statement jabs me again; another generation later I hear myself saying, *"IF we survive this 2020 Election biz...!"* In the 2020 election the young people bores down on us hard. I find 2020 to be a year of the young for another reason; electorally this is the last stand of the baby-boomers. This 2020 election is the first in which voting is dominated by generations younger than 40, mostly millennials born between 1981 and 1996. We *'oldsters'* were the very backbone of this country for many years. We think that by now, we have learned a thing or two and we should be valued for what we know and what we have to offer as mature, grown adults with life experiences. But what could they think we know, aren't we all invisible to them now? With that thought, I take my place among the silent majority.

I read that in 2020, 52% of young people from 18 to 29 years of age, still reside with their parents for economic refuge. (https://www.pewresearch.org/fact-tank) These youth haven't made their own way in the world, much less have any understanding of how to run a free democracy! Even though the younger of this generation still lives at home, they vote in the election as if they know what they want.

Many Americans are victims of our collective success. There is very little want or hardship here, and our youth have become soft and removed from reality. It is not one bit surprising that these coddled youth want big government programs that will take care of them.

My heart is thumping in contrast; because in 1961, when I am 18 years of age my childhood is over. I receive no further support after high school and I have to pay rent to even be allowed to stay in my own parents' house. Things sure have changed over time!

~

My grandson, Dillon Kohagen, has always been agile and fearless from a toddler driving his Power Wheel Car to skiing on the Black Diamond mountain slopes. He graduates from Clear Creek High School in the mountains of Colorado in 2012. This is the end of one journey and the start of another. He tries college for about 3 semesters. I am very disappointed when he decides not to stay and graduate. Instead, he chooses a career in medical cannabis at the age of 21.

I value higher education and I had a dream for every grandkid to have a bachelor's degree. But I have since changed my mind that education at a public college is a necessity. Dillon shows me how he makes his own way with his '*big personality*' and a strong work ethic. He has established himself as the "*Golden Boy*" in his industry. He manages a big marijuana operation and other companies' owners come to find him with offers of employment! He currently works for a startup company with great pay and he has ownership benefits in the company, which is located in Denver, Colorado. Wherever Dillon goes he will make the best of things. He was lotsa fun when he toured Italy with us on his grandparent's trip.

~

As a young child my granddaughter, Lauren DeCamp, is very high strung and precise. She is about eight when I predict that *she will do great things, but only if she doesn't self-destruct first!* Recently, as an adult she jokingly said," *I still walk a fine line!*"

She spends her teen years living in Melbourne, Australia with her family. Lauren graduates from Secondary Education in 2011 in Australia. When soon after the family moves to the United States, she stays there alone to graduate from law school at Monash University. Monash University is one of Australia's leading universities and ranks among the world's top 100. Recently she studies on her own for a year to take and pass the New York bar exam. Traditionally only ten percent of foreign educated students will pass the first time. Lauren passes in the 90th percentile on the first go around. After this, I believe that I was correct when I predicted she will do great things! Lauren currently works as a contract lawyer for Amazon and lives in New York City. Lauren travels to Paris and Southern France with us for her grandparent trip. She loves the Louve, but when we go there, she loses her ticket and she is able to slip in unnoticed without a ticket!

~

Savannah is shy, but she's mighty. It's 2013 and my granddaughter, Savannah Kohagen, is graduating from Clear Creek High School. This is a mountain school located in Idaho Springs, Colorado. I work with her during her senior year to apply for college scholarship money. We search out local scholarship donors. We write essays and applications that are mostly based on income needs. She becomes the apparent star of Senior Night at Clear Creek High School because she wins so many small scholarships. She gets $1,000 award here and $2000 scholarship there! That night seems endless as they call her name for almost every scholarship. She walks away in a daze! She is given enough money to completely cover her freshman year of college. We are so busy with the applications that she has not taken a minute to consider the enormity of all that has come to her, but I'm not a bit surprised. Now she can go away to college, live in the dorm for the complete college experience. Her choice is Mesa State University in Grand Junction, Colorado.

Savannah goes through college on a shoestring! She works, has loans, scholarships and she works an outside job every semester. She had a mediocre GPA in High School, but in college she fiercely sets some goals. Her vision at Colorado Mesa University is a Bachelor's of Science degree in Marketing. She is selected for membership in the National Society of Leadership and Success based on her academic standing and leadership potential. Savannah tours Italy with us on her grandparent's trip. She especially likes seeing Pompeii, a reserved ancient Roman city, 14 miles southeast of Naples, at the southeastern base of Mount Vesuvius. In 79 CE, a huge eruption from Mount Vesuvius showered volcanic debris over the city of Pompeii, followed the next day by clouds of blisteringly hot gases. Buildings were destroyed, the population is crushed or asphyxiated, and the city is buried beneath a blanket of ash and pumice. For many centuries Pompeii slept beneath its pall of ash, which perfectly preserved the remains. When these were unearthed, in the 1700s, the world is astonished at the discovery of a sophisticated Greco-Roman city frozen in time. Grand public buildings included an impressive forum and an Amphitheatre; lavish villas and all kinds of houses, dating back to the 4th century were uncovered. Inside were preserved remains of people sheltering from the eruption; others lay buried as they fled; bakeries were found with loaves still in the ovens. The buildings and their contents revealed day-to-day life in the ancient world and stirred 18th-century interest in all things classical. www.britannica.com/pompeii

She has been on her job for two years–working hard, making bonuses. Now she is in a management position, training new recruits how it's done!

~

In 2014, Nick DeCamp graduates from Mars High School in Mars, Pennsylvania. After high school he leaves for college at Penn State that first summer. In 2015, Nick tours the Greek Islands with us for his grandparents' trip.

He enjoys his college years and emerges with some excellent grades. He receives some specific supply chain expertise by working with a professor. During his college senior year, he scores several jobs offered by some great companies. Nick chooses Deloitte, a multinational professional services network with offices in over 150 countries and territories around the world. Deloitte is one of the big four accounting organizations and the largest professional services network in the world, measured by revenue and the number of professionals. The company is headquartered in London, England. Deloitte provides industry-leading audit, consulting, tax, and advisory services to many of the world's most admired brands, including 80 percent of the Fortune 500 Companies. (Wikipedia)

Nick is currently assigned to the US Treasury in Washington DC. Nick is a guy who works hard and plays hard! He is a thrill seeker, barreling out of airplanes with parachutes and bouncing into canyons via bungee jumps! As he travels, he enjoys a game of golf at many top-rated courses. But, no matter wherever and whenever Nick plays, most of all he enjoys beating his dad in a game of golf!

~

I continue working at the front office of a real estate company until in 2016, I decide that I should get my professional real estate license. The State exam can be difficult and it is not uncommon for people to fail several times. I shut myself into my home office for about 3 months. I study real estate laws and memorize facts in the study guide. I've done the homework and the rest is fun. The only way to pass the test is to take the test. When I took the state test in March 2016, I passed the first time!

~

In 2017, my granddaughter, Holly, is graduating at Mars High School. She applies to quite a few colleges. During her senior year she is being pressured by parents and grandparents about making her college decision. She tells us all to relax, and she will let us know soon. When it is senior night at the high school basketball game, she is crossing the floor with both parents at her side, when the announcer says, "*Senior, Holly DeCamp will be going to Arizona State in the fall.*" Her parents, are 'slack-jawed' in the middle of the gym floor in front of a full house of parents and fans! Until that very minute, they had NO IDEA of her plans. In all fairness, she told them she would let them know!

For her grandparents trip Holly went to London and Paris with us. There we saw her interaction with an elementary school age French boy. Neither could speak the other's language, but he loved her face and with her eyes and smile she loved him back.

~

It is fall of 2018, I am 75 years old and I'm wearing a boot because I have a broken foot. We are living in a 4-bedroom, three-bath home with a 3-car garage and a good size yard. Doug isn't able to do much in the yard or house anymore, so most of these things are falling on me. That late afternoon finds me in front of the stove cooking dinner. My foot is aching and I am crying and feeling sorry for myself. Meanwhile my husband is splayed out in the recliner sound asleep. This is another of those moments that changes me!

I think I am NOT going to do this anymore! We don't need this much space. We have so many things and we have three cars. I am usually a gal who can create my own results, so I dig in and I quickly '*jack up*' my resolve. I have a real estate license and I'm determined! I begin cleaning closets and the garage. I sell a car and remove some furniture. We advertise a sale of 55 years of our stuff. Tools, ladders, shovels and rakes. We are selling things down to fit into a smaller space with no yard work. We follow by painting rooms, and scheduling some repairs and even a kitchen remodel. This is the end of an era for us. This process takes over 6 months.

By April of the following year, I am ready to market our own house. I file the paperwork and schedule the photographer. We begin a series of open houses and by the third weekend, the house is sold. We begin the search for the condo or villa only to find that everything is selling before we can get an appointment to look. We need to be out in a short time. I know he thinks that I know what I am doing, but I am not so sure! I panic! I get up to search the internet at 4 a.m. because I'm too concerned to sleep. I find a sweet little maintenance free house in a 55+ Community with everything we need. The house is small yet it's adequate for 2 people. I call the agent the next morning and set up an early morning showing. It's perfect! We move into this active adult community. There is an activity director on staff and this place is Disneyland for adults! Here we have a swimming pool, a golf course, a workout room, game rooms, a ballroom, a theatre and a restaurant. In this place things are a bit easier for me. I'm done working after 64 years of work life. I retire from Real Estate and most everything else. I'm finished helping kids with college and I can do as I please. Again, I think I will do nothing! But, how can I lack all focus to make things happen? I need to retire with a meaningful purpose! When purpose is gone life is complicated and difficult. Being without purpose leaves me confused. I'm taking my time to find my place and do what I'm supposed to do. Most of my dreams are in the past. But, what's in my future?

I don't know what to do with myself for a while! I still want to do more and to follow more paths. I want to accomplish more things. Realistically old age is not all about social decay and I can never be idle here or anywhere else. The community is active. My time is finally my own and my life is changing. But I soon get into meeting people and creating friendships. I set up a dining out group that is successful for making new friends.

In 2019, the Covid-19 virus epidemic hits the whole world. Businesses are locked down in epic proportions even though this is a virus that has affected less than 1% of the population. We are instructed by the CDC to stay inside, don't mingle and wear a mask. Heavy handed government control to mask up! Don't gather! Hide in your house! I spend this time writing my story, doing sewing and crafts and reading.

My question is, if masks work, why stay 6' apart? Or if the 6' works, why the mask? If both works, why the lockdown? People are vaccinated and still getting sick! I am completely 'covid fatigued!'

In 1919, the Spanish Flu virus epidemic was followed by the exciting '*Roaring 20s.*' This Covid- 19 flu epidemic will be followed by the '*boring 20s.*' The pandemic will never be fully over and the CDC guidelines have zig-zagged me into a coma. My hope is to be able to travel internationally some more before I die. At this time, I am afraid to put money down on a trip, then, BOOM, another shut down!

Fast forward to 2021 and Holly is graduating Magna Cum Laude from Arizona State. Her GPA is nearly 4.0. She works hard and remains fierce in her love of teaching in a classroom, but during the Covid-19 pandemic, the protocol is for online learning. For now, she plans to teach in Arizona. Her passion is for teaching elementary students. Holly loves children and she will be a GREAT teacher.

"Give the ones you love wings to fly, roots to come back and reasons to stay."

\- The Dalai Lama

CHAPTER FIFTEEN

In Memory of Steve

He has not been to a dentist since 1979 when he had free employee dental insurance. I wish he would have taken better care of himself, and I wonder why he wouldn't. He did not go to any doctors. No doctor has any of his health records. It seems that he will never have time for dying. In the weeks before he died, he had congestive heart failure. His legs and feet are so swollen he cannot walk. In the emergency room at a nearby hospital they began a day of tests and he gets aggravated with the processes. He checks himself out and goes back home. On the following Thursday he goes back, again as an emergency patient. Testing and processing found that his heart is in danger and he is transferred to a larger Heart Hospital. Within hours he dies there alone on Feb 1, 2020. I get the call from an attending nurse. She left a message, because he had put my name and phone number as the emergency contact on the hospital intake paperwork. What a sad way for this to end!

Steve talks to me about his death at different times, saying, *"you will be sad for a couple of weeks, then you will get over it!"* I accept that he is gone, because I have no choice, but he is often on my mind, he is not gone from me in a couple of weeks as he had projected. We spoke on the phone almost daily. Now, I miss his calls. When we love someone, we never stop missing them, no matter how long it has been. We keep loving them, even when they are not there to love any more. Sometimes it does seem like a waste of energy because, there is no absolute logic to it.

I don't think I remember him much when we were growing up in a real sense. I think he is usually nice to me, we get along, mostly because we are just the right distance apart in age. I do remember that he has a way of thumping me with his knuckles, in the center of my back. Those 'noogie's' did really hurt, but I have long ago forgiven him for that.

He always has an excitement for learning or any new project. In this way he is consumed with life. He is always fixing something or tinkering. All manner of things will be lying around his house with wires or parts hanging out, and for God knows how long, or what they are even for!

. He cannot be relied on to take care of himself. Maybe being a Vietnam War Veteran changed him! He has many of the problems that are so typical of persons who served in that war. Maybe he has PTSD from his wartime in Vietnam. Maybe he is damaged by living with Oug as a teen after the divorce of our parents. Maybe he too passive, like Mom, to take care of himself or to bother himself with doing anything he will need to have a good life. Whatever it is, he never lives a normal life

The place my brother, Steve, worked best, in my adult life, is under my skin! Yet, when he needs something, I drop everything and I take up for him. I pray for him for years and often, he gives me cause for some extra prayers. He is a 'Rascal", a "Bungler", an alcoholic, a druggie, a rebel and a 'pain in the Arse', most of the time. He is a partier, skirt chaser and all of that, until the addictions take him down. I think it is the alcohol that finally wrecked him, the same as it did with Oug.

He is always full of it! He just can't get it together. He got his first blow of the white dust in Van Wert, Ohio. He is outside behind a local bar. He said, "Will I get hooked?" "NO," they said. But, for the next twenty-five years, he IS hooked. Crack has a stigma that causes paranoia. He hides it from everyone. Since Steve hides his addiction from our family, he assumes that no one else is affected. He stays away from any family gatherings because he can't face us with "Loser' figuratively written across his forehead. He stays away so that most of us have not seen him for several years. I am very grateful that he does not have a wife and young family at home. Since he avoids any family interaction, I worm my way into his life. I think I can help, even if I don't understand him. I only understand, "It is what it is" and I wonder how I can help. I ask that more for Mom than for myself.

There is a fine line between helping and controlling. When I understand that, I am able to intervene by accepting him unconditionally. I learn that when I accepted him '*as is*' without trying to fix or change him, he responds to me. With his acceptance, I look over his shoulder for years, advising, researching and most of all listening. I smell alcohol and I know he is soused. He tells me that being an addict is more about something he does, rather than someone he is. That description made a lot of sense to me in understanding how he sees himself. He has very little memory of these drug years; he refers it to "*living in the bubble.*"

Over those years of daily cocaine, crack and marijuana use he goes through a great deal of secrecy, mostly to avoid being arrested in a small town. I am never sure if he is really being watched by police, as he thinks, or if he is having drug paranoia. Many times, he expects an arrest will come down soon, yet the drugs never stop. He has no money left to take care of himself. His cocaine use turns into crack use which is way more addictive. Crack takes him down fast! He lives in constant chaos in a crack house. He gets deeper in debt and finally files bankruptcy, yet he crosses a state line daily to convert his cash into cocaine. I tell him to STOP! I promise him that I won't help if he gets arrested.

Our family tries several interventions and we get him to go into a 28-day inhouse addiction program through the VA Hospital. We smother him with help. We clean-up, repair and replace things in his crack house apartment. Beautiful plants are donated. New curtains, bedding and towels replace the rags he had. This will be the home he will return to when he completes the program. We are excited about this new lifestyle! We are excited that he is making a choice to do things higher and better. In rehab he learns that there is a fork in the road and that he needs to choose a different road. But he comes back to the same place with the same 'druggie' friends. There is no new road! Steve thinks anything worth doing is worth over-doing! I keep high hopes, but low expectations.

Within weeks he is worse than he has ever been before! His new plants are dead, his electricity is turned off and he had no money for food. I go to see him every week or two. We sit outside because he doesn't want me to see how he lives and I really don't want to be in there either. He tells me everything he is into. It scares me, but I listen and I don't react because I want to stay close. Sometimes I will buy him food when he is hungry, but I never give him cash. He often tells me that he stays up all night with the cocaine. Yet, he continues to do his job at the Post Office satisfactorily. He is never written up or misses work, until Nov.21, 1994 when he is arrested, while making a cocaine buy in a different state. Officers stop his car with guns drawn. "Out of the car...!" OUT OF THE CAR!" they demand. He is taken into custody but the guy riding with him is not. Steve is trapped! As it turns out the passenger with him is wearing a *'wire'*, his 'friend' is an informant. After a frisking Steve is placed in handcuffs and he finds himself in an out of state downtown City Jail. He is placed in a holding cell with quite a few other people, most are bigger and younger than him, he is so afraid! He can make one phone call. He calls me! He is saying, *"I know you said you are done with all of this, but you have to help me!"* He is terrified and so am I! Steve spends his 50th birthday in a jail cell. He has drug charges in both his home state and the state where he is arrested. He needs lawyers in both states, this compounds the charges and also the legal expenses. They have about 200 pages of criminal discovery as evidence against him. My sister and I copy the discovery and take it to a lawyer in his home town. I get a power of attorney set up so I can manage all of his affairs.

This process works its way through two court systems in both states. For a few months this is ugly! He is given the maximum sentence for his offense. He is the oldest one in a group of 23 people, so they call him the king pin, even though this is his first and only arrest. He is finally released out of state and remanded to 18 months in the Ohio Department of Rehabilitation and Correction. He's the oldest guy there and the young inmates call him 'Pops!' The days there are not too hard, but the sameness of the days is killer! They are up at the same time, having breakfast at the same table. He's wearing the same clothes, seeing the same people, doing the same things day in and day out. Prison is a boring version of living life.

Wagtail and I make a full-blown legal appeal to try to save his job. Putting up a good fight against US Post Office is not an easy thing! The post office charges that his legal battle is a *'public embarrassment to the USPS.'* But he is fired before anything has appeared in any news. Our legal argument is that he is fired ONE day before the arrest is made public, therefore no embarrassment had occurred. Wagtail works in a law library. She looks up some USPS case laws and we create a brief using legal language. We file the legal brief with the US Post Office. We have put together an impressive case that succeeds in a lower court, but we fail at the federal level. There they argued that with the impending prison time ahead he can't come back to work and they are not willing to hold his job. We can't argue that point, therefore we can't save him. He is fired from the letter carrier job that he had for eighteen years. Of course, he has no money for his legal defense. We pay for a lawyer in one state; and Mom pays the other lawyer.

I visit him in the prison every week. I write a letter to him every day that he is there, and I pay his commissary fees monthly. I reassure him each visit. I am his link to the outside. His job is in the prison library. Again, Wagtail and I come to his rescue. We do a book drive by asking for books at garage sales to donate to the prison. We find and donate 600 books to the prison library. He really appreciates all that I do for him, as he should. He takes some college classes in automotive parts and he reads a lot of books while he is there. Best of all he stays out of trouble! He only focuses on getting through this and going home. He believes that he found God, or maybe that God found him, in the prison. After the arrest and 18 months of prison time is served, he decides to leave his hometown and his past lifestyle. He comes home to live three hours away. He's living at our house in Columbus, Ohio. His driver's license is suspended. We charge him nothing and we transport him anywhere he needs to go. He hangs around our home for most of two years. He has a good heart for people and he takes life one day at a time. We enjoy having him around. He seems to have things under control for a while. He volunteers at the local Salvation Army store fixing things, until he finds a job. I create a resume and find him a job that he loves, at a parts store. I buy him clothes, cook for him and do his laundry. We attend many AA and Al-anon meetings together. You can do it, "*Just for today,*" they say! I tell him this is the last time I will get involved, "*I won't help out again!*"

He repays us for his legal fees when he has a job, which I find to be honorable. After about two years pass, he gets his driver's license restored and he buys a car. I think I have done all I can do for him. This is a good time for him to launch. He has a job and he should live in his own place to be whole again. He wants to stay with me longer, but he doesn't need a crutch. His self-esteem will benefit when he has his own home. A man needs that! He and I furnish an apartment nicely decorated but with garage sale furnishings.

He seems to be doing well at first. He makes a few friends, but he keeps going to bars. It is well known that one addiction stopped can turn into a different one. He never gives up the beer but he succeeds in that parts counter job for about 8 years, until he is summarily fired. This time, he files and wins, an age discrimination lawsuit for a year's pay. Before long he finds another job and he seems to be OK again. He even buys a small house but, he is too vague and restless to make the changes needed to take better care of himself or caring for his house. He quits going out and he drinks at home alone. He leads a hard-frustrating life. I am trying to put a time on it, when I stopped worrying about him and start to worry about his lonely lifestyle instead. I imagine that I worry over something about him every night and day, until his last day. Even as we talk on the phone most days, but I never ask him again about the drugs! I hope he will not go back into that, but I never ask. I give him that privacy because I don't plan to go through it with him again. Or maybe if he does, I just won't want to know.

I help him get benefits that he really needs. Right under my nose, he signs away his government pension for a cash payout and he takes the equity out of his house to get cash. Each decision he makes seems to add to his decline. When the addictions and prosecution are over for him, he never marries again. He is tightly snuggled into his life of poverty, loneliness and habits that he can't change. After prison, he never thinks he is 'good enough' to live better. I tell him "You don't HAVE to be a "bottom feeder." He acts like I have insulted him by that, but he is a creature of habit and he has a shame that keeps him from reaching for anything better. I constantly try to get him to help himself in some other ways. I make calls that he should have made, it is embarrassing how many times I gave in to helping him. He listens but doesn't pursue anything. I think there must be a path for him someplace, maybe a path where he has wandered off.

Steve and I are 'as thick as thieves,' I learn a lot about relationships and religion from him. Interesting as it might sound, he counsels me, too. He has a great sense of relationships. He understands the value of communication, though he himself can never stay married. When my life feels too heavy, he will say something to help me and his advice is always good. He says things like "communication is all that you need," "Let them know and let it go", or "Stress is not about the situation, it is about the person." Some people can handle it, some *can't."* All good advice from Steve, considering who he is and where he has been! Most of all I learn to appreciate the strength of his spirit to overcome adversity.

When we retire and move away from Ohio, he stays behind. He and I have not been together for over 15 years, though we talk most days on the phone. With all that I have said, he is my closest confidant among my siblings. He never fights with me, yet he lets me know when he doesn't agree; I am his sister and I am on his side. He never forgets that. He has a good heart, for me and others. We call each other, *"Little Buddy."* I miss that!

Usually, people's brothers become less important over time. Steve decides to stay important to me, to the end. There is a hint of my brother's smile in my own mirror, a tone of voice I can sometimes hear, and most often I want to pick up the phone with something I want to ask or tell him. For that, I can only pretend that he is in another house where I can't call, so I write to him in my journal instead.

I know he would not have done well with this COVID-19 virus. I am glad he didn't have to go through all of that, but this doesn't matter anymore. Sometimes I put my head in my hands, the way people do when something is very difficult, holding there for a minute, before moving on to my life with other challenges. I have to quit worrying about him now, he is dead! It seems that everyone loves someone even after they are gone. I will always miss him!

I decided against coming to his funeral, not because I don't care but because I DO care. I care to talk with him and to be with him and I knew he isn't going to be there! I remember my time with Steve with such good memories that his death now is like a dry leaf crumbling in my hand.

"Softly the leaves
of memory fall,
gently I gather
and treasure them all!"

"I've learned that home isn't a place, it's a feeling "

- Cecelia Ahern - Irish Novelist

CHAPTER SIXTEEN

Conclusions

I left home at nineteen. Since then, I have grown up and I've made my own way. Many of my decisions did come from my own assumptions that somehow things will improve. I have moved to and from seventeen street addresses in seven states, leaving me with little sense of a home base. I am a bit of a nomad, with no real history anyplace. My family is scattered as well. I moved from the house on Walnut Street to find a better life in the suburbs.

Moving all around isn't bad, I don't keep a load of stuff around because I can be more flexible that way. I like new locations because we've developed friendships with a lot of good folks and we have lived in some very nice places. Doug says, *"If we all liked the same thing, everyone would all be wearing a blue shirt!"* I agree! New locations renew me with a fresh new breath of life I have adopted some different world views and I have a drastically changed lifestyle. I have spread my wings to meet many special people and I've seen some fabulous places. All of that said, as I write this, I am seventy-eight and home is just a place where I hang my hat!

I am a work in progress, with many layers. Most definitely the *'first half'* was the hardest. As I look through the rear-view mirror of my life, I think being born in 1943 is the best of times! The depression is over and the US post war economy is flourishing, Social Security is still intact and companies are still giving pensions to workers. I know that because I was born in the back woods on the Cumberland Plateau, in the remnants of the great depression my life is changed for many years to come. Add that to being born in a partially completed house, with no water or electricity, no social interaction and limited experiences, all of this is hard for me to overcome.

Because the first five years of a child's life are critical to their development, I am short changed with no communication skills or relationships with others. I did the best I could back then, and when I knew better, I did better. My childhood is my first life experience and I regret overall the loss of what could have been. I accept that the losses are what makes me who I am. My past is only one piece of my life story. I could grieve what it could have been, but what for?

Some people live with a misconception that they are powerless to let go of the past regrets and disappointments. I can either dwell and be stuck, or let go and be FREE. Of course, I choose to be FREE! As a youngster, I make a dream that I will grow up strong and self-sufficient, and hope that my life will be different. I grew to see the world as a bigger place than the place where I grew up. Now I can see a world full of abundance. My world is free to explore. As I have traveled around the country and all over the world, I have a wider perspective. I am free of my childhood doubts. I leave the past behind and I live in the present. Now all I need is a sunny day, a glass of ice tea with a book to read. Joyfully I can breathe on my own! Oh my God, I was so scared of everything! It's sickening how scared I was, and now I hate that part of myself. My upbringing nurtured me to go from grit to strength. I've come full circle to hating it, when people are too scared to fearlessly live their lives.

Travel has been our '*second half*' focus! We have traveled by car with a tent and we have also traveled by air to fancy hotels and golf resorts and on cruises in Mexico, the Caribbean and Alaska. We have visited most of the United States, Canada, Mexico, Caribbean and much of Western Europe and we have enjoyed every moment of it! My most favorite trip was the Greek Isles.

We spent twelve Thanksgivings with our kids and grandkids at a gulf front timeshare at Casa Y Bel Resort on Sanibel Island. We have had many fun adventures and family vacations, like a Mexican Riviera Cruise to celebrate our 50th wedding anniversary, with our kids and grandkids. We cherish all these memories.

~

I think a lot about The Women's Movement and how our generation changed the lifestyle of women. I think of the things my mother lived with and how she would have benefited in today's world. I like to think that my generation is different from Mom's, only to find that in some ways we are eerily similar. Like others in my generation, I somewhat successfully tried to have it all. In the past century we got a voice in government, the vote, the birth control pill and those washers and dryers. All that gives us choices, freedoms and the ability to strike deals in relationships. Social and legal changes have been so accomplished that young people today can hardly believe life before the lib movement. I often wonder why some women today still feel like we are *'nothing'* without a man. Do they STILL feel that if they can find a man their problems will be solved? Many young women are still confused about what a woman should be and they wonder how is it possible to *'Have it all?'* Why is that? All of these things have been settled for many years. Yet, the younger generation keeps marching, with little focus over what they have or what they want to accomplish. I hear a lot of rehashing of the old debates that have long since been settled. Young feminist complaints exhaust to me! I ignore these young voices! Just make your own life happen!

Today we accept the gifts from the movement, carte blanche. We have more freedoms than any other women in the modern world. We are in the workplace in equal numbers with men. Doors are open, role models are out there, and possibilities are endless for women in America. I still like to have it my way, to do work that is my own, and to have a happy family with both of us around. Even though the range of opportunities for women has expanded enormously over my lifetime, we married ladies have figured out how to make it work, with unity and like mindedness as a couple, because that's the kind of cooperation a marriage is. Today real women negotiate and we try to see each other's position. I want a warm and fun marriage, but doesn't everyone?

At thirteen, I think I am clever enough to change the world! As I grew wiser, I changed myself. I've changed my vision and I like the view! As a young person I needed to have some dreams and hopes that were within my reach. I thought for a minute that my educational opportunities were lost when I married and started a family, I continued with a slim hope that my education wasn't over. In September 1967, married with two children, I work out the details and I start College! I only regret that I didn't give my education a higher priority and graduate sooner.

Now, I've stepped out and I'm no longer living in the footprints of my past. I am a seeker and I keep pushing to keep life fresh. I share what I know and I courageously walk in my own shoes; life is easier that way! I'm candid enough to say what I think. I am liable to do that without much fore thought. I am confident in handling whatever happens to me. My trust is in that!

Higher education has been one of the main focuses of my adult life. I have paid for my own education, our kids' education and helped several grandkids with college. I focus on them, because I want their college education to come easier. Yet, I am skeptical of the liberal indoctrination that has been a part of the education system since the 1980's. College life has a lot of distractions, too many parties, a focus on the 'Greek life', beer and all the rest! Now I know there are better ways for serious students to learn. If I were deciding today, I would choose smaller private schools or home schooling.

I have an associate's degree, a bachelor's degree, several certificates from SBA classes, Real Estate classes, and more. My work life has been 64 years beginning as a waitress at thirteen in Ohio and ending as a realtor in Florida at seventy-seven. Work has been a big part of my life and I have held a total of twenty-two different job titles over these years. I have had a few good jobs and some others that weren't so good. Most jobs were routine and boring. I worked harder and longer than most and often for low wages. The most interesting part has been the journey. I have worked mostly for my "*tribe*," for education, but also vacations, clothes and whatever I thought someone needed. I have owned two small businesses and worked in a wide variety of others. Some of my job titles have been; store clerk, dental assistant, factory press operator, moving contract auditor, store owner, inside sales and purchasing agent, quality control and inventory control specialist and a test proctor.

As I have gone through a lifetime of varied businesses where I've worked, owned or volunteer ed have been as varied as a patchwork quilt. Looking back at this, I can see that I have put my life together with the same disorder, as if I were sewing that patchwork quilt or cooking a dinner using whatever ingredients I can find in the house. But there is a real comfort in that patchwork quilt, because even though I have no particular field of expertise, by now I knew a little bit about a lot of things. Although I have enough money now to buy almost anything I might want. I still carry some of the remnants of growing up on Walnut Street. I still sew and mend clothes to get a little more use. I clip coupons and seldom pass a thrift store or garage sale without stopping for a look around. I start at the lowest price items when I look at a restaurant menu. I keep clutter to a minimum by selling things for pocket change. By now all of this is engrained in who I am.

~

It's never too late to pick up a new focus. We can begin again and again. We are meant to experiences and ideas then to give back. Martin Luther King said, "*Your life ends when you lose your passion.*" As I ponder my purpose in life, I drift for a while, before coming up with the answer that is right in front of me! My purpose now is about giving hope to youth who have limited opportunities, kids like me! My next plan is to be a mentor of youth. I can be the voice of someone who has been through something similar. I can share what I know, so they won't make the same mistakes. Mentoring can be counseling or donations to groups like Boys and Girls Club, schools, the courts or a multitude of other social service organizations. Many young people struggle and could benefit by someone helping them to locate possibilities that exist. Empowering young people through education is my goal. No one knows what they are capable of until they actually do it and I can't want more opportunities for someone than they want for themselves. I am only interested in working with people who are motivated to help themselves. Mentoring is important because the potential of youth is endless. My own potential was endless even then, yet I stumbled along for years looking for a path without much support. I could have benefitted by a mentor offering some guidance toward solutions. I can take a stand but I have to be very careful with who and how I help, because I have a controlling personality with an exactness that is hard on people. I get that from my dad, he was like that! Understanding this about myself, I want to lead but not control people. "*I can't want more for anyone than they want for themselves.*" This is how I can make a difference!

~

In chapter one I said; *I made a dream that I will grow up strong and self-sufficient...*and I have! I also said that; *I hoped that my life will be different from my mother's... and with someone way nicer!* My life has been, just as I had hoped, with someone, very nice! Doug and I share a rich history. Together we have two great children and six wonderful grandchildren. We've shared relatives, cars, closets and toothpaste! We have been together through twenty-two of my jobs, I grew up in an old house but now we've lived in seventeen suburban houses in six states. We have bought and traded-in countless cars, we have met many folks we really like but we've moved away leaving far too many good friends behind. We have attended more funerals than I can count, - we've lived through four wars in over six decades of doing life together. As we move through these years together, I remember being fierce in motherhood, family life and career! There are a lot of plates to spin, kids to raise and work to do and life got pretty frenzied at times.

Together, in the 'second half' we've amassed almost sixty good years of marriage. We have raised our children and spoiled our grandchildren. We have been through the 'richer and poorer' part of the vows we made. By now I know that the lives we share have been a miracle. However, not everything is a simple epiphany! I feel safe in saying that we've beat the odds-on teen-age marriages.

A marriage isn't a quick weekend project like staining the deck, but rather a long-term building project, more like building a Cathedral. I don't always know the precise moment that I figured it out, but I have been married long enough to know that sometimes I fall in love, and sometimes I fall out of love. With a sense of relief, I realize this is really quite simple. Marriage is hard work and it is never finished. If we want to stay married, we have to keep working out the kinks. Whenever the wheels come off, we sit down for a chat. We grit our teeth and keep working on it. Marriage counselors call it 'communication.' Sometimes I am the 'Pain in the ass', other times he is. Sometimes we have each other figured out, other times we don't have a clue. We are usually on the same page and there isn't much more that I need to say about that. NIKE says, "just do it!" If most people work together, and not against one another, 'for better or worse' they usually can make a marriage work. Doug is a," What you see is what you get kind of guy." He is low key and not too hard to please and he is fairly easy to figure out. I am higher strung than he is, and I feel what I feel, but I don't rest easy. Often no one can meet the expectations that I set up; I have a lot of unfinished business going on. At times I don't sleep because I am thinking ahead for what is next, 'like a phone left off the hook!'

A happy ending is never guaranteed, but we survive despite our differences! We shake off some of the romance and slip into comfortable and less emotionally charged stuff like, flannel nightgowns and comfortable shoes. In retirement we find more time to share and

witness each other's lives. That can go either 'good or bad'. We share
sorrows and heartaches as well the love, joy and a subtle peace in our
life together. I am the Queen of late nights and married to the King
of the early mornings. Doug is in his bed early, dreaming his dreams
of fiction books, a game of golf or a stock investment with very little
focus for what's next. Seldom do his interests have anything to do
with me, but he tolerates me well. We spend our time together before he sleeps, watching movies on TV or playing cards, reading or
chatting. After that, he is off to bed and I claim my-late-night self. In
the late hours I might study Genealogy online or I read to understand
or write to reflect. I might read books or write my story, or if I don't
do either, I might sew or do paper crafts. I might even fold clothes at
midnight.

~

Now that both of my parents have died, I shatter my own myth
when I say "*I am freed from chains that I hadn't even known were
holding me.*" Yet I still work to cure myself of wishing things had
been different. I try to leave the past behind and live in the present.
I try not to judge their ways or try to fix them, or even to wonder
why I couldn't get them to be who I wished they were. As they say
in Alcoholics Anonymous, I try, "*Just for today.*" Sometimes I don't
know the true value of a moment, until it becomes a memory. In the
mirror I often recognize my mother's face and wonder, "*How did she
get in there?*" Sometimes I find bits of Oug in myself as if we were cut
from the same cloth, but in no way do I want to fit his '*ways*' into my
life. Some common things that most people are typically afraid of are
Covid-19, Cancer, and random crime in the streets, etc. None of these
scare me like Oug's temper! He is '*20 years dead*' now and he can still
raise my anxiety enough to throw me off kilter!

I used to wonder how he could have that much to say about so
many things! If I had another chance now, I think I might give him a
second listen. I don't have that choice since they both have '*passed*'. I
have said my good-byes, I have handled their affairs and I have coped
with them both in life and in death. These good byes haven't been
easy, but I have found a peace over time. Maya Angelo explains this
best saying,"*I've learned that regardless of your relationship with your
parents, you'll miss them when they're gone from your life.*"

There is a tendency of people to make meaning of their experiences. I believe that life takes on the meaning that I give to it. I

understand the effect my parents had on who I was as a child and who I am now. These are things both good and bad that have changed me. These things are the effects, of some childhood incidents. For example; I like to have a place for everything and everything in its place. I clear out and dispose of things I am not using. I like order and a spotless house because I am uncomfortable in disorder, clutter and chaos. Maybe that comes from growing up in such disarray?

I have been through all of the heart aches of letting Oug define me. I choose my own risks in life. I am not easily influenced; I usually have doubts or reservations. I put ideas under consideration and I take nothing with a grain of salt. Not to be cynical, but I question every fact and idea for supporting data. I take nothing at face value I am and I always have been a skeptic. Often, I '*over question*' but that's no one else's fault. I can be a disruption of the natural order with my skepticism. This doesn't suit some folks, because I often say, "*Who said?*" or "*How do you know?*" or "Where did you get that idea?"

I have lived in a democracy for all of my life – free and happy. I will never be politically liberal nor will I ever "*let the loose end drag!*" Nobody needs to tell me what to believe. I choose for myself and I remain discerning and skeptical. This probably is a result of the way Oug forced us to concede to his every wish. I still have frustrations, but I don't let things build up, as I once did. I might not hold onto a sophisticated position but I am secure enough that I don't care what anyone thinks of my position. I will no longer bend to anyone who antagonizes me to stand with them. I rely on conservative views because they are based on solid historically proven facts. I make my decisions boldly and I stand my ground for what I believe. I do this without apology. The rewards of hard work will always trump government handouts and control.

I accept that not everything in life is within our control and death is inevitable. I have been hardened to life by my own viewpoints. At my age, sometimes I have to disagree and let things go. I'm ignoring the '*new ways*' in order to live in peace. This 'new world' values belong to America's youth, it is theirs to fix or theirs to live with!

~

Budda said, "*No matter how hard the past, you can always begin again.*" There are many angles to view our lives and one person's idea doesn't trump another. Detaching is neither kind or unkind, but it allows us to be separate from other people's choices. Sibling rivalry is over and we are melted into our own lives, far from our childhood. We are all different folks with different world views. My siblings are distant, my children are self-sufficient, my parents are gone, and not much sand is left in my own hourglass of life. My life goes on and I have mostly learned to be ok with all of this loss, but sometimes in the late hours, some memories do sneak out of my eyes and cause tears to roll down my cheeks. Dr. Laura says, "*We have two chances at family life, the family of origin and the family that we create.*" With this information, I started over among the ruins of my younger years to create a separate family built my way!

It's been years since Grandma left us. Even though she interfered too much in our household, I can see a lot of value in all that she tried to do for us kids. She had strong opinions about the way things should be. I know she would have liked for me to read the bible and go to Church regularly, though I didn't until much later. Mom and Grandma disagreed on everything. Maybe that is why mom let us run freely! I am reminded of a plaque in her kitchen that goes like this; "*We get too soon old and too late smart.*" It is a Pennsylvania Dutch saying and I think it applies to me!

To quote Oug one last time, "*Life can be beautiful, if you will just allow it to be!*"

EPILOGUE:

The only way I can tell the story is through my own eyes. All of life is a collection of moments that are not isolated incidents, not separate from the rest of life, but these moments that make me the person that I am. I write my story to taste life twice, first in the living and again in the writing. A life must be made up of contemplation that is followed by action. My contemplative writing records what I have observed.

"When someone passes away without passing on the family life stories, "*it's like a library burning down!* (Maisey Fernandez - September 9, 2017 AARP Magazine)

If this is the story of '*my life*' I will share what I know to become a survival guide, to help someone find their own courage or to inspire someone to overcome some other kind of difficulty. Work has been a big part my life story. It is work that has made all the rest possible.

My story began with piles of notes over many years from many simple and random thoughts that have been written and set aside in these notebooks. There are literally boxes of small slivers of papers that have been stored away for years. Late at night, my mind is subject to jolts and lapses; I find anger as well as patience in myself. When emotions and opinions cross my mind, I can't help but write it down, otherwise they will leave as quickly as they came. I get the storm out of my head where it might be lost forever. My chaotic thoughts can be calmed when I pull it out of my mind and write it in these journals. My typed words are the key that unlocks it all. Every writer works in a fuzzy area between fiction and auto-biographical truth. *No* matter who tells the tale, it remains the story teller's story, leaving the reader to wonder '*exactly*' how the past was.

My story is based on my own perception of family life, as I saw it, based on my place in the family and research that I have done. I have considered social changes that have taken place from past time periods, in relation to the culturally accepted norms of today. My story is a semi-autobiographical mosaic of the human experiences of a child living with Narcissism, love, hate, forgiveness and redemption.

I focus on building memories with grandkids. This is the basis for our grandkid trips. We hope to inspire them to enjoy life with a love of travel to places they will choose. However, the trips have been for our amusement, as well as theirs.

Acknowledgements:

To my husband who encourages me daily.

To my children and grandchildren, I wrote this for you.

To my siblings, I wish things could have been different for us.

To Grandma, who was right most of the time.

To my A-team of true friends who have lasted over 45 years, (You know who you are.) You have encouraged me more than you know.

RECIPES REFERENCED:

The White Hall Inn is known for their famous POTATO RUSKS. The recipe below is what White Hall guests will best remember:

WHITE HALL INN POTATO RUSK AND ICING RECIPE:
1/2 cup sugar,
1/2 cup butter,
1/2 cup mash potatoes,
1/2 cup potato water,
1 cake yeast or 1 pkg. yeast,
2 tablespoons lukewarm water,
2 eggs well beaten (room temp),
1 teaspoon salt,
3 cups flour.

Cream together sugar, butter, potatoes and potato water. Dissolve yeast in lukewarm water. Add to cream mixture. Add eggs, and the salt and flour mix. Batter should be stiff but softer than bread dough. Let rise in cover bowl for 2 hours or put in frig overnight. Turn on to flour board and flatten with hands and cut small circles about 2 inches or a little less. Place in greased pan and let rise 2 hours or more. Bake 15 min. at 425.

Icing: 1 1/2 tablespoons flour, 1/2 cup butter, 3/4 cup confectioners' sugar.

WHITE HALL INN - BANANA NUT SALAD

1 egg
1 c. sugar
2 tbsp. flour
1/4 c. vinegar or lemon juice
3/4 c. water
2 tbsp. butter
8 bananas
1 c. finely chopped nuts – I always use chopped pecans or walnuts
Lettuce

Beat eggs lightly in top of double boiler; stir in sugar and flour. Careful! This can curdle if cooked too hot! Add vinegar or lemon juice and water; cook stirring until thickened. Stir in butter; cool. Peel bananas; slice in half and arrange on lettuce-lined salad plates. Pour a small amount of dressing over bananas, then sprinkle nuts over the dressing. Serve

MY MOM" S RECIPE FOR CHRISTMAS CUT OUT COOKIES:

3 cups sifted flour
*1 "heaping" tsp. baking Powder
1 ¼ cups granulated sugar
*Vanilla
*1pinch of salt
*1 ¼ cup of oleo (shortening)
3 eggs beaten

Bring shorting at room temperature – Mix with vanilla and sugar then put in the 3 eggs and the sifted flour, baking powder and salt together and mix with the sugar, eggs mixture. Cool in refrigerator, roll, cut and bake. We have never known how much vanilla or how long to bake and the oven temperature, but she did! People buy these cookies from her for $6.00/ dozen, which is a high price in 1975

(*I have made several improvements since, and they are even better. I use real BUTTER 1 TBSP of Vanilla, 1/8 tsp salt and 1 TBSP of baking powder
I bake 9 or 10 Min at 325 degrees)

CPSIA information can be obtained
at www.ICGtesting.com
Printed in the USA
JSHW022329100522
25553JS00001B/51